The Mind
J. Krishi

Edited by

Luis S.R. Vas

JAICO PUBLISHING HOUSE

Ahmedabad Bangalore Bhopal Chennai
Delhi Hyderabad Kolkata Lucknow Mumbai

Published by Jaico Publishing House
A-2 Jash Chambers, 7-A Sir Phirozshah Mehta Road
Fort, Mumbai - 400 001
jaicopub@jaicobooks.com
www.jaicobooks.com

© Luis S.R. Vas

THE MIND OF J. KRISHNAMURTI
ISBN 81-7224-213-1

First Jaico Impression: 1989
Fifteenth Jaico Impression (Enlarged Edition): 2003
Twentieth Jaico Impression (Reformatted): 2011

Printed by
Kaveri Printers Pvt. Ltd.
19, Ansari Road, Daryaganj, New Delhi-2

Introduction

"What makes an apparently ordinary human being, unfavoured by either heredity or environment, suddenly achieve greatness?" Here is a question that has occupied the attention of many an eminent mind, and has elicited a variety of answers. A more fascinating question seldom asked is "What makes a great man, tutored from birth in the ways of greatness, relinquish all his claims at the climax of his career to return to ordinary living?"

The present volume is a study of this rare phenomenon as reflected in the life and thoughts of one man who had greatness thrust upon him early on in life and who later achieved a different kind of greatness, only to give it all up: J. Krishnamurti. It is a strange story, now almost forgotten largely due to Krishnamurti's own efforts. And it uncovers a strange mind, still very imperfectly understood.

It should be stressed at the very outset that, by Krishnamurti's own admission, there is nothing 'super natural' about this mind; nothing belongs to it that does not or cannot belong to the mind of every other human being sufficiently aware of his condition. We hope to open that mind to a wider audience.

There are several volumes of Krishnamurti's writings available.

To those acquainted with them and to those who have attended Krishnamurti's talks, this volume may serve as a refresher course. Krishnamurti's thinking is too elusive for those unaccustomed to logical reasoning as well as for those obsessed by it. For the former it is too abstruse. For the latter it is perhaps a pack of contradictions. To understand Krishnamurti it is necessary above all to have an open mind, unfettered by past experiences, ready to learn, ready to unlearn. For, what Krishnamurti does all the time is akin to describing the beauty of colours to a man who insists on keeping his eyes tightly shut.

Krishnamurti's goal, in his talks, in his books, in his living, is aiding self-knowledge, a process as deceptively simple as opening one's eyes. But most of us have forgotten the use of our eyelids. As Aldous Huxley, one of Krishnamurti's more famous admirers, defined it, "Self-knowledge is always an awareness of first-order experiences — of events below the level of words, of mysteries of existence before we have conceptualised them into a specious intelligibility (and paradoxically) it is through words that we are made aware of the subtler form of non-verbal experience" — hence this book.

Those having difficulty in grasping Krishnamurti's own phraseology which oscillates between vague and pithy, may glean more from others' transcriptions of his words. No preparation is necessary to read this material. It is written on the whole in non-technical, clear and simple English. Conversations with Krishnamurti, the most readable and rewarding section, should be able to stimulate even a child's thinking. Here then, is an excellent introduction to Krishnamurti's mind. For those who have not yet read Krishnamurti in the original, a sample talk is provided in 'What is the Religious Mind.'

"Comparisons breed envy, not love", Krishnamurti has said. And comparing Krishnamurti's `teachings' with those of other selected thinkers may be regarded as unwarranted, if not meaningless. I disagree, and hope that the section on comparative studies included here may foster some understanding.

'The Dissolution of the Order of the Star' is a speech of historical interest, one of the most eloquent speeches of the century. Besides, it is a document which reflects that uncompromising integrity that has become Krishnamurti's ever since.

Second Edition

The generally favourable reception accorded to the first edition of *The Mind of J. Krishnamurti,* and some of the criticism, have encouraged me to revise it slightly. A more extensive revision was probably called for, but a writer and even an editor usually hates to tinker with his published work. I have, therefore, confined myself to dropping three chapters and adding new ones. For practical reasons, I could not replace. I could not add to the number of pages. So, some chapters had to go, through no fault of theirs.

The additions are: Henry Miller's J. KRISHNAMURTI — MASTER OF REALITY, Aldous Huxley's THE ART OF SPIRITUAL INSIGHT, and my own reassessment of Krishnamurti — 'HAS KRISHNAMURTI FAILED?' All the three chapters are included at the end, just before the Appendix. I must express my debt to Mr. S. Weeraperuma who very kindly sent me from London, a copy of Henry Miller's chapter on Krishnamurti from the book *Books in My Life.*

Photographs have been added this time and the cover has been changed. For the latter I must thank my friend Diwan, who took infinite pains to make it a work of art.

Interest in Krishnamurti has obviously grown since this book was published though not as a result of its publication! I should like to hear from readers their honest reaction to both Krishnamurti and this book.

– Luis S.R. VAS,

Acknowledgement

Krishnamurti Writings Inc. for permission to reprint chapters 7, 9, 11, 13 and for special permission to reproduce 'Dissolution Of The Order Of The Star' in the Appendix; A.I.R. for What Is The Religious Mind?; The Sunday Standard for chapter 1, which appeared there in a more condensed form; Bharat Jyoti for chapter 19; Chetana for all the other, excepting chapter 22 and 23 and Aphorisms. To all the above our thanks. Aphorisms were collected from various sources over the last ten years. Since there was no intention then to publish them, the sources were not recorded and most have been forgotten. The excerpts being very short, we believe there is no copyright problem involved. In any case we apologise to the copyright holders if any.

Contents

Appendix Section

Part I

Introductory

Chapter   1

J. Krishnamurti: The Man and His Mind
by Luis S.R. Vas

The quest for self-discovery is forever new. From Socrates to Sartre, from Sankara of India to Suzuki of Japan, both the East and the West have produced thinkers who have contributed in varying degrees to the understanding of man's condition here on earth.

In our age, this quest is divided between philosophy, psychology and the social sciences, and many thinkers have stretched their intellect to cover all three disciplines, while others have departed completely from the beaten track, to seek in regions yet unexplored. J. Krishnamurti undoubtedly belongs to the latter category.

As a renowned 'non-Guru', Krishnamurti differs fundamentally from most philosophers in that he has resisted the tendency to weave his insights into a system, though they have much in common with such schools as the existentialist and the Zen.

Jiddu Krishnamurti's career is an extraordinary one by anybody's standards and is of considerable interest to students of human nature and, of course, of Krishnamurti's mind. He was born in 1895, (or thereabouts, for the records are not very reliable) in a large South Indian family of strict, if poor, Brahmins. At the age of 12 he was adopted along with his youngest brother Nityanand by Mrs. Annie Besant who had an uncanny knack for discovering and encouraging talented minds: among her finds can be counted B. Shiva Rao, Sri Prakash, V.K. Krishna Menon and Rukmini Devi.

Krishnamurti was fitted into a role designed to fulfil a curious prophecy of Charles Leadbeater, a demi god of the Theosophical Society, that a Divine World Teacher descends to earth periodically to lead mankind through the right path. Krishnamurti was proclaimed to an astonished Theosophical Society and the world at large as the next World-Teacher in line with Krishna, Buddha and Christ! In due course the Divine spark was to manifest itself in the new Messiah.

Almost immediately after the announcement, scandals broke out in the T.S. A book, AT THE FEET OF THE MASTER, was published by the T.S. under the authorship of 'Alcyone', the 'occult' name of Krishnamurti. It created a sensation and the authorship was heatedly disputed. Now it is widely believed that Leadbeater actually wrote it; Krishnamurti himself remembers nothing of the episode.

Simultaneously rumours were spreading of pederast activities of Leadbeater in the T.S. This was too much for Krishnamurti's father who now decided to reclaim his guardianship over the boys. The case went to Court, but after a series of battles between Annie Besant who defended herself, and Sir C.P. Ramaswami Aiyer, counsel for the plaintiff, the Privy Council took the unprecedented step of allowing the two minors to choose their guardians. Both chose Mrs. Besant.

To avoid further parental interference with the boys' careers Mrs. Besant sent them to England, placing them under the care of Emily Lutyens, wife of the famous architect of Delhi. There and later at Sorbonne the boys studied privately.

An Order of the Star of the East was set up with Krishnamurti as its head to spread the teachings of the World-Teacher. Thus all was set for the coming of the Messiah. Then in 1922 Nityanand, who was ailing, grew worse and the two brothers moved to California in the hope that he would recover. The trip however, did not have the desired effect and Nityanand's death followed in 1925.

This event had a profound effect on Krishnamurti. The shock made him experience a 'total change' in himself. He began to re-examine his thoughts and values, reconsidered his plans for the future and finally decided on a course of action: in 1926 he dissolved the Order of the Star, "a decision all the more remarkable" according to a Times Lit. Supt. reviewer, "in that he had in fact had mystical experiences of great intensity ... but his role as he saw it was... not that of a Messiah of the T.S.", nor "that of a private guru", but that of an independent thinker, and in this capacity he has been writing (FIRST AND LAST FREEDOM, LIFE AHEAD, THIS MATTER OF CULTURE, THE ONLY REVOLUTION, FREEDOM FROM THE KNOWN) and lecturing to whoever will listen in the five continents. He still pays periodical visits to India and lectures in its principal towns.

As one listens to this handsome, silver-haired and intense looking man, one is struck by his genuine concern for the human condition and by the lucid, analytical style in which he dissects man's perennial problems.

His talks have little of the customary manner in which speakers generally address their audiences. They are exercises in self-analysis. In the process of thinking aloud he probes the depths of the human mind and attempts to unravel its intricacies.

The reason for Krishnamurti's unorthodox methods lies in the fact that he does not seek to expound a theory, formulate a concept or prove a thesis: to do this would mean indulging in abstractions and propaganda, to any form of which he is totally opposed. Instead he undertakes the task of developing in his listener a new attitude towards life. "Life", he says, "is movement in relationship." And he sets out to analyse our relationship to whatever surrounds us: the fellow men whom we love, hate or are indifferent to; the universe of science and its omnipresent effects; the world of our profession; the field of our emotions;

our unconscious mind. This analysis paves the way for our understanding of the process of psychological conditioning to which most of us willingly or unwillingly submit.

Little do we realise how even the commonest events of our daily life evoke in us some emotion and control our actions. Thus, for instance an insult hurled at us may generate rage; flattery may create pride; a compliment to a rival may produce envy, and so forth. Now some of these emotions are pleasant and these we crave, the others — the unpleasant ones — we consider undesirable and try to get rid of. So, invariably, we invite situations calculated to bring us pleasant emotions and try to avoid those that evoke unpleasant emotions. The causes of both agreeable and disagreeable feelings are not always easy to find, and once found, once we realise their power over us, they are never easy to dispel. The following episode serves as an illustration:

"One morning an irresistible force propelled MIT Professor Marvin Minsky to one corner of his class room and pinned him there as securely as a butterfly impaled in a museum showcase. It was force of habit — a brand new habit imposed upon him on the spot by a group of playfully experimental students. The boys had him at their mercy, as if he were a robot slave and they the masters at the controls.

"They 'robotomized' Minsky with a psychological ruse much like the methods for teaching rats to run through a maze, or training a dog to fetch a newspaper. Soon after class had begun a few students started manipulating him. Whenever he paced to the right, they whispered softly to each other, rustled papers, dropped pencils, and created other minor distractions. But when he happened to take a few steps to the left, they sat up and obviously paid close attention to the lecture. In short they conditioned Minsky by repeatedly punishing him for moving in one direction and rewarding him for moving in the opposite direction. Within half an hour he stopped pacing altogether and stood like a cigar store Indian near the left hand edge of the blackboard. So subtly had he been habituated that he did not realise an experiment was in progress, and that he was the guinea pig — ironically so, since Minsky is a leading authority on the theory of automations." (Think, November-December 1969)

Habit, then, is a conditioning factor too. It permits us to view everything as a routine, as a repetition of what happened the previous day and is expected to happen the next day, and saves us the trouble of thinking anew, from 'moment to moment'.

Consequently we are only partly conscious of what affects us and react to it automatically, living a life of somnolence, doing what the interplay of emotions and habits will have us do.

In his book, "THE ACT OF CREATION", Arthur Koestler says, "There are two ways of escaping our more or less automatised routines of thinking and behaving. The first, of course, is the plunge into dreaming and dreamlike states.....The other is also an escape from boredom, intellectual predicaments and emotional frustrations — but in the opposite direction. It is signalled by the spontaneous flash of insight which shows a familiar situation in a new light and elicits a new response to it.....it makes us understand what it is to be awake, to be living on several planes at once....."

Koestler's book is, among other things, an attempt to formulate the theoretical foundation of this phenomenon. But it gives no more than an inkling of how this 'escape' can be effected, of how the 'flash of insight' can be made to occur. On the other hand this is precisely what Krishnamurti seeks to do, so as to enable us to live a life free from psychological conditioning by acquiring a 'sensitivity', an 'awareness'.

With life being in a state of constant movement, he argues that we must not regard any of our relationships from a fixed standpoint. "We must be willing to accept change in others and be willing to change ourselves". This willingness must be, not merely an intellectual disposition to change, but a desire to *feel* this change continually.

And how does one get to feel the change? In Krishnamurti's words, "by being what you really are. By trying to see what *is*. You see, sir, (somehow) I have acquired a certain character. Now I must try and see myself as I am and I must make no effort to be anything else....I am not advocating self-indulgence, that a thief remain a thief. I must not submit to my weakness but I should not indulge in the opposite of my weakness either, as a way of getting rid of it...."

Let us imagine that we are at a given moment, envious or bored. These emotions are painful. We do not like them and so we try to avoid them. This creates a conflict between what we are and what we want to be, between envy and non-envy, between boredom and excitement. As a result, we do not really get away from envy and instead grow progressively displeased with ourselves. If, on the other hand, we were to observe this envy in a passive and dispassionate way, with a receptive mind determined to examine the phenomenon without passing judgment, without condemnation, seeking the cause of these emotions with our total attention, but never trying to push it away, then we would find there is no conflict and the envy can be apprehended from an entirely new angle. "Suddenly I will discover that a transformation takes place in myself without any planning on my part, a creative transformation. My sensitivity has come into play." The radically transformed envy has now abandoned its original form and we no longer wish for it to leave us. And what is true for envy is no less true for boredom, hate, anger, fear or for that matter joy; for even joy and other pleasant emotions condition us.

Now impervious to all these emotions, we take to living richly and fully; always intensely conscious of our existence and of our relationships, assuming once again, full control of our lives, which until then seemingly ran on automatic pilot mode, making of us creatures of habit.

Krishnamurti emphasizes that only constant and complete awareness can achieve this result. No amount of discipline and concentration can do it for you. By disciplined effort and concentration you can at best produce a state of self-hypnosis and through it a feeling of well-being and peace which, far from being an escape into the unconditioned state of mind, is merely a flight to a yet more unreal level of self deception.

Although the aim of Krishnamurti's analysis is 'freedom from the known', he covers the gamut of human thought, aspirations and endeavour; he discusses the relation between idea and action, the contradictions of effort, the perils inherent in the uncritical acceptance of tradition and dogma, and a host of other subjects. Nobody can read and listen to him and in the end not know himself better for it.

Chapter   2

Introducing Krishnamurti
by B. Sanjiva Rao

The story of Krishnamurti's life is one of the strangest that one can imagine — men have given up many things for the sake of Truth; money, power and even life itself. The Buddha renounced a throne to become a monk and walk the streets with a beggar's bowl. Krishnamurti set aside deliberately the allegiance, the devotion of a well organised band of a hundred thousand followers for the sake of coming down the steps of the spiritual throne erected for him by Mrs. Besant and becoming an average man for no greater reason than that for him there was no condition or state more blessed than love. I dare not use the word 'renunciation' to describe the action — for it is so palpably absurd and false an expression to use in connection with Krishnamurti.

The world has almost forgotten the legend that was woven around him. Mrs. Besant recognised the extraordinary promise of unusual spiritual gifts in the young lad of 12 — she prophesied that in due course of time he would be a World Teacher and usher in a new era, a new order of things. Within 17 years a huge organization was built up consisting of a remarkable group of men and women drawn from all the important countries of the world. A great stadium was built for him at Sydney to enable him to broadcast his message to the world. All the resources which Mrs. Besant's great organising ability could secure were freely poured into the movement.

Krishnamurti was most carefully educated. He had at his disposal all the facilities which money and social influence could obtain for him. He deliberately set aside all such advantages and chose the strangest of courses. He rejected wealth, he renounced every adventitious aid, he approached life directly instead of through the thoughts of the learned. He read the faces of men and women, loved them, suffered with them and therefore understood them as hardly anyone of our generation had done. Of the many people who loved and helped him, no one rendered greater service than Mrs. Besant. She gave him an indescribable love and a supreme understanding. She was so reverent that she did not seek to interfere with his freedom of movement and action. She allowed him to break up the order that she had founded for his work. She acquieseed in his decision to be free of all organisations, including the Theosophical Society of which she was the President. She allowed him to go out alone in his search for Truth.

Such a life in spite of the halo of glory and sanctity around it has its tragic side. Men and women of the world today have built round themselves enclosing walls which effectively isolate them, the one from the other. There are a few — and surely Krishnamurti is one of them — who have broken their walls and come out of the prison of self-hood. The lives of such liberated men are in a sense more lonely than those of the hermits, the solitaries living in the hills or the deserts. The hearts of men are closed against them. They wait in patience, often weary of their long vigil for the time when the doors of the hearts of men will open to let in the light.

Krishnamurti has read few books. He is a graduate of no University. Yet he draws abundantly from that great book — so inexhaustible in its variety and profundity — the book of life. He has met thousands of people who gladly reveal the most intimate workings of their hearts and minds. They know that he loves them and understands them. He offers no false consolations. He cries with them, for the tragedy of life moves him to the depths. He suffers with them. He would save them if he could. For the world with its mounting sorrow, he has an indescribable compassion. The cry of the beggar, of those who are bereaved, of those whose hearts are desolate, of those who are unloved, throws him into a state of agonising sorrow. He does not make one false gesture. He knows that no one can make another happy, that man is his own saviour, that redemption does not come from outside. So men and women go to him, conscious of his great love, but conscious also of his utter and complete allegiance to Truth.

He knows many men and women of outstanding achievement in Literature, Art and Science. He is very humble. He listens to everyone with such closeness and understanding that he almost appears to put on the cloak of the humble learner. If he uses any of the words or thoughts of some of his highly learned or intellectual friends, he says with a real feeling of humility: "Sir, I have not read this, but have heard this from so and so — you see I hardly read books.'

To one with the supreme capacity to read the book of life directly and who combines with it a matchless gift of loving understanding which unlocks the secrets of all hearts, every situation in life is ever new and of absorbing interest. It is not strange, therefore, that books, however great, however true, have no great use for him. The thoughts of others, however wise, are but screens between him and Reality. He looks at life directly without the glasses of erudition and traditional wisdom — of course he is not the first of the seers of Truth. Others have seen as he does. But to see the Truth directly is ever a new experience and therefore his message bears the stamp of an authentic and original contact with the Real and the Eternal.

What is wrong with us? Krishnamurti says that we have forgotten how to love. We have enclosed ourselves within walls made by ourselves — and so husband and wife, father and child, the labourer and the employer of labour have built walls of separation, of isolation. So there is no communion between man and man. There is no love, no real affection. And where there is no love, there is no beauty. All our values are sensate. Because there is no love, false love and lust have become important. Because there is no richness of inner life, outer wealth and luxury have assumed such vast significance. Because there is no beauty of living, of feeling and thinking, no real beauty even of the body, all the devices to create false beauty have come into existence.

Krishnamurti has already created a flutter in the hearts of those who come and listen to him. There is such wonderful poise, such unutterable love and compassion not without a touch of sadness, there is a beauty and simplicity of Truth and Wisdom that men begin to ask, who is this mysterious figure that moves so quietly amongst us, who seems to bring a certain luminous quality into all the things that he says. He evinces the strange power of reading the inmost secrets of our hearts. Yet we never resent it, as we do not resent the entrance of Light into the dark places of the world. He seeks to help us to understand the confusion and the sorrow in our midst. He almost makes us believe that if we could only love, the world would be saved.

Was Mrs. Besant right, after all, in her intention about Krishnamurti? After having done his best to destroy the legend about himself is Krishnamurti going to fulfil in the most unexpected way the prophecy of Mrs. Besant? He renounced the role of the Teacher and has come to us as a man among men. He is one of us: He is, and says he is, nothing, and yet, to be nothing, is that not the height of spiritual attainment? For when one is nothing, one is all things.

Krishnamurti refuses to accept the role of a teacher. 'I cannot 'teach' another' he says: 'the perception of Truth, of Reality, of what is, is essentially an individual process.' I will report a discussion which took place on the 27th January at Carmichael Road, Bombay. I was one of a large group of nearly 250 people that gathered together on a terrace. The background was perfect, the open sky, the setting sun and the view of the sea — we all sat on the ground except a few who sat on chairs at the edge of the crowd. He sat on a raised seat and asked us to follow what he was saying not verbally, but at our own level — i.e., as he spoke we were expected to watch the processes of our own thinking. To report his words would be a dead process. I will, therefore, give an account of the way in which I tried to carry out his intention. He took up the simple problem of dullness. He asked: "are we aware that we are dull?" One gentleman thought that we were not dull all the time, that sometimes we were bright — there were many answers from the audience. Each answer was a self-revelation. To some it was a verbal discussion; others were puzzled a little bit — we are being asked the strangest of questions. Here is a teacher of great distinction anxious that we should have a perception of God, of Reality , of Truth, starting the discussion with this odd query: 'are we dull; aware that we are dull?' I asked myself: "what is meant by dullness; am I dull?" Judged by the ordinary standards of the word I felt that superficially I would not be justified in calling myself dull. But I felt sure that that was not what Krishnamurti was saying. So I began to examine myself and as he went on repeating in many ways the same persistent query: 'are you aware that you are dull? Did I watch the sunset and the beauty of the sky? Am l alive, sensitive to the beauty of the landscape, do I see the face of my neighbour and see the havoc, wrought by suffering on that face. Some of them laugh, but am I sensitive to the cry of pain which the laughter is intended to cover? When I walk into the crowded streets, how do I react to the beggar, to the refugee who has lost everything, home, property, friends, all that is usually considered worthwhile. I hear the sound of the flute of a passing flute player — how do I react to it? In fact what is my response to the tragedy of the world, to its laughter and tears, to beauty, to ugliness, to squalor? Am I aware of what my wife thinks and feels? What do the boys and girls that I have taught think and feel? Am I aware that they live in a world different from my own, that they have their own values different from my own — am I aware of their many desires, their frustrations? Or am I so wrapped up in my own cares and anxieties, that I am insensitive both to the beauty and the ugliness, the joy and the suffering of the world?" I watch all these thoughts passing through my mind as Krishnamurti goes on repeating "are you aware that you are dull?" and then the question is slightly altered: "why are we dull?" I ask myself that question. Why do I not feel the immense sorrow of the world, how can I spend my life in such inhuman isolation, that I can have peace and joy amidst the holocaust that is going on all the time? What is wrong with me? What has made me so narrow-minded, so small, so childish in my desires, so petty in my pursuits? As I keep on asking myself I discover that at no time did I ask these questions, that never before was I so alert, so eager, so deadly serious about my dullness, my superficiality, my lack of real interest in myself or others and the thought struck me: 'but now, just now, I am not dull!' The very awareness of my dullness, my feeling really sorry to be dull, has made the difference! I am not dull at all, I am concentrated, full of vigour and affection as I keep on following Krishnamurti's advice and observe myself in my daily comings and goings, thoughts and feelings, words and actions, I learn about myself, I discover the man I am; the man I have made of myself by not caring, not looking, not knowing, by not seeing myself against the background of others, in relationship with others. To discover others is important; to discover oneself is crucial; we are limited most when we do not know our limitations.

And suddenly the feeling of 'all-this' hits me like a tidal wave. I am no longer thinking 'all-this' — I am living it. I realize suddenly and powerfully the self-made hell in which I am keeping myself and in the very agony of realization I perceive that I am 'not-all-this', that I am no-kind-of-this; thought loses hold and ceases; the apparent solidity of a whirling mind is no more when it stops rotating and is at peace at last. The peace is also bliss. Anxieties and longings disturb our mind easily, for we are lacking in virtue, which is freedom from disturbing elements.

Krishnamurti is never tired of repeating that without self-knowledge, the fruit of attentive and persistant self-observation 'free of approval and disapproval', man is not complete, not mature, not fully human. His mind and feelings are still on the subhuman level, distorted by false desires, corroded by false pursuits, serving a non-existent entity, a fiction, he remains a creature of false imagination. To know the 'I' as false, to realise from moment to moment that it is only a mental habit, a way of thinking, is the gateway to liberation.

Chapter   3

The Language of Krishnamurti
by Rene Fouere

Before Krishnamurti's teachings can be properly examined, it may be useful to give attention to the language and style of Krishnamurti, for there is always a close relation between the thought and its expression in words.

His English is superb, his style is simple, adapted to psychological investigation, free of all mythical or religious reference. It is even free from all fixed terminology; he avoids standard terms, having a traditional and well established meaning; on the other hand he often infuses a word with an unusual and unexpected significance, and opens within the most common words depths and heights which we would least expect to find. He is a great philosopher, if by the word we mean somebody who makes us see the dark and hidden face of things apparently familiar, who shows us the wonderful and unexpected in the most common happenings.

There is something strange, even bewildering, in the transparent clarity of Krishnamurti's style. It seems sometimes that in a few words, apparently simple and innocent, he manages to condense the entire mystery of the universe and our own mystery too. When spoken by him the words become inexhaustible of meaning, like mirrors facing each other and reflecting endlessly.

Whoever has listened to his lectures can notice at once that Krishnamurti is solely concerned with the inner transformation of his audience and cares little for method and doctrinal elaboration. No wonder therefore that he often takes opposite stands in quick succession. He does not want to build an intellectual system but releases his listeners from the certitudes in which their minds and hearts have fallen asleep. 'People need to be awakened, not instructed'. he said once. This explains the vehemence of his expressions, which often appear to be unduly contemptuous or harsh.

Often it is not easy to know the full depth of Krishnamurti's thought, which may seem sometimes obscured by rhetorical necessities. But the thought is there, important and original, although Krishnamurti says that since truth is impersonal, it cannot be his own.

It is not at all easy to put Krishnamurti into a system, even to repeat cogently what he wants people to learn. For he wants us to 'learn to learn', to take life as the teacher and learn to understand its language of events and facts. For life is the only teacher that will not betray us. If we follow it, it will take us to our goal.

(Translated from the French)

Chapter 4

The Essence of Krishnamurti's Teachings
by Claude Bragdon

No one has affected me more powerfully than Krishnamurti, which is not surprising, for this distinguished Hindu with the face of a god, wearing modish clothes and speaking with an Oxford accent, is a man to be reckoned with, as many have found out besides myself. As a disturber of complacency I have never met his match, though unlike Gurdjieff he makes no deliberate effort to that effect.

Heralded as an avatar by a world-wide organization, Krishnamurti had to find his way out of this intolerable situation alone and unaided. That he did free himself shows strength of character of an extraordinary sort. He dissolved the society formed by Annie Besant to exploit that messiahship which she and Mr. Leadbeater had thrust upon him; he gave back the money she had raised to ensure his economic independence; he returned to its owner the estate in Holland intended for his permanent home; and he stopped the publication of the magazine devoted to his promotion. By such drastic action he gave plausibility to the very claims he was repudiating, for how much more difficult it is to unburden oneself of power and possessions than simply to refuse them.

My first meeting with Krishnamurti occurred at the time when he was just beginning to shake himself free from these various entanglements. It was what one might call casual, though there was this little element of strangeness about it: In going from Lexington Avenue to Fifth, Fiftieth was a street which I habitually avoided because at that time it had been closed to vehicular traffic in the interests of a near-by school, and the games of playing children were interfered with by passing pedestrians, with whom, in turn, the playing children interfered. But on that particular day I had absent-mindedly turned westward on Fiftieth street, and afterwards thinking there might be some reason for it, I continued on, curious to see if this unconscious action would find justification.

It did; for as I reached Fifth Avenue I saw three men approaching from the south, one of whom I immediately recognised as Krishnamurti. I felt justified in introducing myself, for we were linked by many friends. He was kind and cordial, and asked me to come and see him at the Hotel Cotham on the following day. I did so, and it was the beginning of a relation which, whatever it may mean to him, has meant much to me.

Our next meeting was in the same locality as the first one under the shadow of the Cathedral — and it happened in a somewhat similar way: I was waiting for a Fifth Avenue bus, and suddenly woke up to the fact that I had let two buses pass by without boarding them. As I am not ordinarily absent-minded, I surmised that by this lapse of attention some purpose was perhaps being served. And so it proved; for down the street I saw the elegant and slender figure of Krishnamurti coming toward me. He told me that his brother had just died and that he himself was passing through New York incognito. Nothing worth recording passed between us except the fragrance of sympathy and friendship, but it was yet another, in a chain full of golden links.

For there is no doubt about the influence exercised over me by this dark-skinned, bright Ariel. Always, after I have been in his company, I feel spiritually purged, and he seems to stimulate my creative faculty. I began The Eternal Poles immediately after

a meeting with him, and it was to him I dedicated it because —
although I have not his assurance to that effect — I believe The
Eternal Poles to be but an elaboration of certain of Krishnamurti's
fundamental teachings.

Here is my earliest impression of him, the occasion being one of
his first public appearances in New York; I saw a young Hindu
Brahmin, with a face of great beauty, nobility, and — intelligence.
He spoke with the cultivated voice and admirable diction of the
English University-educated man. His manner was modest and
gracious, and he wore his well-fitting clothes with an indefinable
air of elegance. He seemed, however, to be far from happy in
the thing he was engaged in doing, and he appeared to be doing
it not particularly well. His body swayed like a reed in the
wind; his gestures were stereotyped to a single pattern; his voice
fell sometimes to inaudibility, and he depended too much on
his paper memorandum. The total effect nevertheless, was not
one of weakness, but of power imperfectly controlled. He was
ardent and intense, and he radiated that order of psychic energy
for which we have only the poor word "charm". In his answers
to questions, free of the incubus of his memorandum, he became
more master of himself and of his audience, even though some
of the questions he was called upon to answer seemed to inspire
in him a mixture of irritation and despair.

What I felt first of all about Krishnamurti was a number of
CONTRADICTIONS; he seemed, more than anyone I had ever
known, a living paradox. Though physically male and ethically
Hindu, he was of the androgynous type, and as much of the
West as of the East, he was both powerful and fragile; astringent
and sweet. Honey and wormwood had been his daily portion,
for though lapped in luxury, garlanded with adulation, the
Giana's Robe was an intolerable burden — that was easy to see.
Exasperated by unguessed indignities to the essential manhood
in him, seared by outrageous suffering, shot through by ecstasy,
soothed by strange peace, he inspired wonder, pity, and a kind
of sacred terror, even as might have the Ancient Mariner or the
Wandering Jew. Although advertised as a messenger of peace

and goodwill, he appeared at moments more like some dark, avenging angel, and what he preached had so much in common with anarchism and nihilism as to cause one to wonder if he would escape some modern equivalent of the stake or the rack. His flamelike intensity, his unsureness of himself as a person and his sureness of himself as a power, his unbitter cynicism and his unbrutal brusqueness, his manner of toppling over firmly implanted idols with the feather of some casual remark — these things seemed to be the fruitage of some inner travail necessitated by his unique predicament of being called upon to fulfil egregious expectations in pre-determined ways. By reason of this, and in compensation of it, he had been visited by some experience, had suffered some transformation, undergone some apotheosis, the reality of which was always with him as a continuing process. By not seeking to escape this acid bath of suffering, his soul had been made bright.

Every time I saw Krishnamurti, on those infrequent occasions when he visited New York, he appeared to have grown in spiritual stature, and today he is in many ways a far different person from the one I have attempted to describe. Though still a destroyer of agreeable illusions and a disturber of complacency, the old scornful bitterness seems to have leaked away. He appears now the embodiment of a power which need not assert itself in order to be felt; of a wisdom which need not explain itself too much in order to persuade; and of a love which, like the sun, shines equally upon all.

Those who look to Krishnamurti for a new religion or a new philosophy are bound to be disappointed. He does not offer something *more*, but something *less*. He is a subtractor of everything which stands between man and his maker, which is man himself — which is Life Itself. He strips bare, as he himself was stripped bare, in order to arouse action of Liberation. Life is the only god of his salvation, and life, he says, manifests and fulfills itself anew in every action. Canons, creeds, systems, formulas, are all crystallizations of spent actions — the living, willing and thinking of long ago — and should therefore be transcended lest the house confine the spirit. Nor should we build "more statelier mansions" by organizing new spiritual movements, but rather live unhoused under the naked sky of love and truth. "My teaching is neither mystic nor occult," Krishnamurti affirms, "for I hold that both mysticism and occultism are man's limitation upon truth. Life is more important than any beliefs or dogmas, and in order to allow life its full fruition you must liberate it from beliefs, authority, and tradition. But those who are bound by these things will have a difficulty in understanding truth."

The very simplicity of Krishnamurti's teaching confuses over-sophisticated minds. "I was told in India that if I would make my teaching more complicated, I would have more followers," he once said. For this release of life through action ever new he lays down no rules, prescribes no technique, no matter how insistently urged to do so. He would perhaps reason out that life as it unfolds develops its own technique much in the same way that powerful thought precipitates the fitting phrase without aid of grammar or rhetoric. For to the question: "In what way shall I express life through action?" his answer was: "Think and love." Some complain that there is nothing new in his teaching, and according to his own declaration there is not; but who has ever exhausted the possibilities implicit in "Think and love"? The difficulty with such objectors is that they want to be *fed,* not roused into action. Instead of — loaves and fishes he offers only the white flour of love and the sharp hook of truth. "Now bake your own bread, catch your own fish." he seems to say.

He sets great store by honest doubt, the concomitant of straight thinking. "Of what importance is that to which you cling" he asks, "if doubt can destroy it? Of what value are your traditions, your beliefs, and your accumulations, if doubt is capable of sweeping them away? A man who is afraid of doubt will never find the truth. Doubt is a precious ointment; it heals though it burns greatly. If you are afraid of little burns, you will never destroy the impurities you have accumulated throughout your lives. In avoiding life, in fearing life, you shelter yourself in decaying things, and in that shelter there is sorrow, but in inviting doubt you will create that which will be eternal, and bear the stamp of happiness."

Krishnamurti's teaching will seem anarchic and destructive only until we perceive that his blows are aimed at *our fetters:* until we realize that life, unconditioned by personal fears, ambitions, and desires, is not a void but a plenum. We exist for *life;* each one's individual uniqueness, when purified of all egoism, becomes a vehicle through which the Universal can particularize itself, can dramatize itself anew. Every individual life in this way, enriches the sum total; and the point at which this gift is handed over to the life universal is what is called "liberation," for it is then that the ego relinquishes that which it has helped to build up, and a greater life takes over. To talk of so-and-so's "obtaining liberation" is a misnomer; that which is liberated is always life, not the person; indeed, it is at the expense of the personal self that such liberation is achieved, for life alone benefits by the transaction. It is true that the individual uniqueness which persists on both sides of the liberating process finds that instead of belonging to the purely personal consciousness it had really always belonged to the life universal but this discovery is only made at, or after, liberation. The process leading toward liberation must always seem like the killing of the personality — hence its painfulness. The saying that a man must die in order to live is, in this sense, true.

To Questions as to the difference between life before and life after liberation, Krishnamurti answered that there was one simple mark which identifies every manifestation of pure, or universal, life; it acts but does not react. Until we get rid of our egoism, most of our conscious life is made up of reactions. Take love, for example: in most cases this is a reaction set up within us by some person who attracts us; a person who does not happen to set up this reaction we do not love. But after liberation, when pure life is in control, love becomes a life-force going out from ourselves.

Such is the essence of Krishnamurti's teaching as I understand it. In two words it is: "Trust life" — Most of our troubles come from our fear of life, religion itself being a refuge from that fear. But if we trust life instead of fearing it, life will not betray us — only by ourselves can we be betrayed.

Chapter 5

Right Beginning
by Robert Powell

It seems to me that we do not sufficiently appreciate the importance of the right beginning, that is, our initial attitude in anything we undertake. Whether it is the creation of a work of art or an enquiry into what is true and what is false — in either case the outcome stands or fails, depending on the state of mind with which we approach the task at hand.

The problem of right beginning can only be solved when we have understood the relationship between creative being and its expression. As long as there is even one thought, an intention to create — which presupposes a motive — the ensuing expression cannot emanate from the Void, which is the true source of creativity; and thus there cannot be right beginning.

Unfortunately at present most creative effort in the world comes under this category, the artist's motive being "recognition", (consciously or unconsciously) his activity is therefore ultimately the outcome of frustration. This was not always the case in the history of mankind. For example, the great cathedrals of the Middle Ages were built and decorated by anonymous architects and craftsmen. A good many of the inspired writings of the ancient Vedas and Upanishads were anonymously composed.

On the other hand, where there is true creativity, there is no thought given as to its expression, so it may or may not be expressed but that becomes totally unimportant. It is because of this very lack of regard for expression, that it may turn out to be purely spontaneous. The activity then springs from a non-beginning and this can therefore be called "right beginning"; in this case it would be more accurate to speak of a "reflection: than of an "expression" of creativity. To readers of this journal the all important question is naturally, "What is right beginning in the spiritual quest?" Here, unfortunately, most of us rush in where angels fear to tread. For example, when someone claims to be seeking God, is that the right beginning, is that even being serious? If he is seeking God he must first know that God exists, otherwise this search becomes just meaningless. Furthermore, in order to find God he must first know what God is; how otherwise would he recognize God and be certain that what he found, was God?

You see, the trouble is that it is easy enough to invent words, but the words in themselves have no meaning. The truth is, of course, that we do not know God — all we know is the word and with that we are satisfied, in that we find a refuge.

For most of us there rarely is a moment of true beginning, for whatever we do is a continuation of the old, a reaction from thought, which is memory. When we set out to meditate it is because we have heard about it from others, about the necessity to cleanse the mind, how to do it, and so on. But what we do is repetition, not independent enquiry, and it has therefore no value.

There is true meditation only when the mind enquires into itself — not from any compulsion, or idea of social desirability, or according to a certain blue print laid down by others. Thus, the mind itself, whose inherent nature it is to act from a motive, to be guided by collective consciousness, can never initiate meditation. There is therefore meditation only when the mind has come to an end, has died to all it knows, believes and hopes for. It dies only when it has completely given up all its nefarious activities, and this can only be when it sees their futility, their voidness. So what is essential to us is right ending — without which there can be no right beginning.

There is right ending, and so the beginning of meditation, only when what happens proceeds from the Void, when it occurs in spite of yourself, in spite of the mind's machinations. That is why a moment's true meditation is like a miracle; it is truly a moment of illumination for it so clearly throws light on all the false movements of the mind that forever keep us in the dark.

For most people creativity is inextricably associated with expression, as soap is with water. They think that the creative energy only comes about in the process of writing poetry, music, painting, dancing and so on. Yet it is maintained here that there exists a kind of primordial creative energy, which is totally divorced and independent from these activities, although they may flow from it. It is this energy which affects the whole person and not a mere fragment, and it has no connection with capacity and knowledge, although it may use these. On a deeper level, we may say it is Creation, as yet uncontaminated by Thought.

However, not only are creativity and expression one in the public mind, but what matters most is the result, the expression, which may be "beautiful", "useful" or "fashionable", and so in a materialistic world we can put some price on it. Thus we can see that the climate of collective thought has given undue emphasis to the value of expression. And obviously, if we consider expression more important than Being, then we are still caught up in the play of the world; for why should we express the inner at all unless it is to fulfil ourselves in the outer? At the same time, have we perhaps not noticed that as the creative tide in us rises, the urge to fulfil ebbs away? If in this state there is an expression it is completely spontaneous without a single thought to impress.

This then means the introduction of an element of casualness, a certain playfulness, into the creative process, without which, what passes as creativity is not at all of the order of Creation. As soon as the activity becomes "serious business", i.e., the result of "effort" the course of the creative effort becomes suspect. In fact, the words "creative effort", however commonly used without being given a second thought, are really deeply contradictory.

This applies particularly to meditation, for in its pure form meditation represents the creative process *par excellence;* and without the element of playfulness there can be no true meditation. It is because of this condition that the "I" can never meditate, for however superficial, frivolous and scatterbrained in its manifestation, in the core of its being and secret intent it is always deadly serious. Because it is always scheming, calculating, end-gaining, it can never be playful, relaxed and fully alive.

The miracle of meditation as true creativity is that it is experienced as the ending of one thing and the beginning of another. The other is the purest substance of 'play', and moreover a play which has no shadows because it is all-illuminating, being beyond the movement of the opposites. All this and much more is involved when Krishnamurti talks about what it means "to be serious", showing us incidentally that unless we pierce through the words we shall be bogged down in their contradictions.

How many of us can truly say we are serious in Krishnamurti's sense?

The lack of clarity in certain circles regarding the problem of right beginning is no more clearly illustrated than by the confused thought about meditation as "mind discipline". There are those who favour this as a proper path towards enlightenment; and others who oppose it on the grounds that deliberate spiritual training only constitutes the "manipulation of the ego" and not its transcendence. But, if it may be asked, "Who is it that manipulates the ego?" The above quoted statement is therefore still based upon the false notion of duality, for the manipulator and the manipulated are one. Spiritual training — either deliberate or indeliberate — can thus only be meaningless action, and not more relevant in this connection than, *e.g.*, going to the pictures. But before we shed the false notion of spiritual training, we must clearly see it for what it is – just another escapist activity.

"Training" always entails looking into the future, does it not? It implies that in time the desired result may be achieved, by continuous patient effort. We shall be happy, not today but next month, next year, or next life, if we perform the prescribed exercises regularly and assiduously. Now, by thus fixing my goal in the future, by keeping my eyes fixed on the ideal, which does not exist, I avoid looking at the actual, which is what I am here and now.

For if there is completely clear perception of what exists in the present, do I then still need to "train" myself? If I have seen without distortion, that I am ambitious, greedy, envious, do I then still want to get rid of these properties, gradually, that is bit by bit over a period of time? Or, having seen myself as I really am, is there not a purgation all at once?

So it is necessary to have this attention to deal with the here and now; and the looking at the future, at the ideal to be gained in due time; distracts from the perception of what is now. Thus any premeditation to do something, any plan for future action, can never constitute right beginning. Have we not noticed how the most significant events in our lives have always taken place unexpectedly? There is right beginning only in the total absence of any thought of beginning. It is the empty mind, the mind that has completely let go of all ideas about achieving goals, which dies continually to every experience, that is in a state of complete attention to what *is*. Therefore, to such a mind, which is all the time living under the shadow of Death, everything is new, fresh, and so every moment is a true beginning.

Chapter 6

An Approach to Krishnamurti
by Robert Powell

It seems to me that we cannot know the man if we do not understand his teaching. Krishnaji — as some of us affectionately call Krishnamurti — talks about life seen and experienced comprehensively, not according to any particular viewpoint or school of thought, but completely afresh, free from the dead ashes of yesterday. It is therefore, really a misnomer to talk of a "teaching" for this word implies something static: some information, a set of rules, which is to be applied in order to obtain a certain result. His is the very voice of life itself, undivided within itself, flowing eternally.

Most people will only take note of Krishnaji's teaching (for lack of a better word, we shall go on using it) after knowing who he is, what his qualifications are, etc. etc., because they want a guarantee that they are not wasting their time. It is this very urge to be certain, flowing from insecurity, that prevents the state of listening or undivided attention, which is so essential for proper understanding.

In this article, which aims at briefly introducing the reader to the work of Krishnamurti, we shall mainly concentrate on discussing the obstacles that frequently present themselves to newcomers. I hope this may serve some purpose and consider this certainly more useful than any formal explanation of his teaching.

The commonest approach one finds people have to Krishnaji is to look upon him as the Teacher, who through his teaching is going to give them something. It is this very attitude which Krishnaji exposes again and again as false: often as bluntly as in the following words: "I have nothing to offer you". If there were only an elementary understanding of the teaching such an attitude would not exist, for the very essence of what Krishnaji tires to convey to us is the absolute necessity for standing on one's own feet; and until we do this nothing will be of much avail. Physically we are obviously dependent upon one another and nothing is going to change this — but psychologically to depend upon another for one's happiness means that one will always remain a psychological cripple.

It seems to me that the main reason for this futile approach is a failure to understand the right significance of "knowledge". When we go to *guru* we have the mistaken idea that there is somebody who "knows" who can tell us how to live. We do not yet see that *nobody knows,* for the simple reason that in spiritual life, knowledge counts for nothing. No information, no blueprint for living happily and sensibly exists; life cannot be imprisoned within a formula, and that is the beauty of it. The only thing that counts is "being", and being is always fluid and never fixed; it is the Unknown, and can therefore never be reduced to an extrapolation of the known, which is an abstraction, a static picture of the past. The trouble is that we are so mesmerized by words that we think the known and the Unknown are a pair of opposites; we do not realize that what lies beyond these words is not just the usual antithesis, but that they represent dimensions of reality, which are so utterly different, that they cannot reasonably be expressed in symbols which normally refer to the one dimension only.

Another common misapprehension concerning Krishnaji is that his teaching consists of ideas. If they were ideas then his teaching would be a conventional one, consisting of a body of theories, either speculative or doctrinaire. But it is nothing of the sort. Ideas, concepts, are bundles of thought oriented within a certain neat fashion which we call "consistent" or "logical". These concepts can in turn be bundled together in a neat and more or less elegant fashion, in which case we have a "theory" or "philosophy". But concept or philosophy, both are woven in the texture of thought; and can thought ever liberate us?

In our ignorant state we constantly go from thought to thought, and all our misery (psychologically) exists within thought. Thought can be painful or pleasant, depressing or hopeful, which is the play of the opposites, ever changing, ever looking to the future, and thereby building the whole illusory world of the mind, its conscious and subconscious layers — according to whether its constructs are recent or ancient, acceptable or inacceptable to the social climate.

There is no limit to the ingenuity and grandeur of the conceptual constructions the mind builds for its own gratification and security; they appear so plausible as to give an impression of truth — and so we get caught, for we always underestimate the power of the mind to create its own illusions. After all, we have only got to look at dreams to see the dramatic capacity of the human mind. So in this web of unreality, which is of the mind's own making, we are imprisoned.

The mechanism of thought is that it operates by association, *i.e.*, one thought leading to another — and whether this sequence is logical or illogical, that is besides the point. In other words, we are *"being taught"* how to think, rather than encouraged to produce "our original" thought. Because of its determined nature thought can only lead to more thought, but can never reach out to what lies beyond thought; therefore, ideas can never liberate. We may say that suffering *is* thought, and that liberation is freedom from thought, although not its suppression or the escape from it. Or, in different words: when suffering, we are the tools of thought; when free from suffering, thoughts are the tools of Reality, and such thoughts are in the service of Love rather than in the service of the thinker.

So if for lack of a better word we talk, in slip-shod manner, of Krishnaji's "ideas", we must be aware that they are not "ideas" in the true sense of the word, but psychological facts presented to us in a way which is most likely to awaken us to their truth. Therefore, it is not a matter of agreeing or disagreeing with them — as we do in the case of opinions and theories — but merely to see or not to see their variety, and it is only the truth in them that will set us free. The best way to see their truth is to look at these facts, as they actually manifest themselves from moment to moment in the mechanisms of our own thinking; and not to project them outwardly, either onto others or onto society as a whole. When we know ourselves we shall know the world, but not the other way round.

Contrary to popular opinion, for seeing the truth of what Krishnaji talks about, no effort or favourable spiritual pre-disposition (if there be such a thing) is necessary. Here, we are all on equal ground, regardless of our intellectual or professional attainments, regardless also of our social positions or the colour of our skins. The curious thing, the wonder of it all, is that only one thing is necessary, although this is absolutely essential, for our benefiting from the Talks. And that is that we *listen* — such as we have never listened before, with all our heart and soul.

There is this peculiar quality which the word of truth has, when spoken by an embodiment of truth, such that the very listening to it has a liberating effect. It is the immediate impact of the word and the man that matters, and this is not to be obtained by making notes and taking them home for study, as though it were a college lecture. Also, listening in the required manner presupposes a state of pure listening in which there is no "listener", with his knowledge about the speaker and the spoken. Thus, in such listening there must be no prior knowledge of the speaker as the embodiment of truth — for this very knowledge would influence us, e.g., by accepting him as our authority or by serving as a reaction against him, and thus prevent the state of listening. Many are lured to attend Krishnaji's talks on account of his reputation as an extraordinary man, the supreme teacher, etc. This so easily gives rise to an attitude of exaggerated reverence, the worshipping of the teacher, which goes at the expense of, and actually runs counter to, the teaching. After all, the "man", however extraordinary, is not of great importance to us, only his teaching is; as Krishnaji himself once remarked "the teacher is not important, throw him overboard".

Another, all-too-common view of Krishnaji's teaching is that it deals with "problems". At the Saanen Talks in 1962 a lady assured me that she must under no circumstances miss the next Talk for she felt certain that on that occasion her own particular problem would be dealt with. Certainly, Krishnaji deals with human problems, and a great variety of them such as envy, fear, hatred, love and so on; but does he solve them?

That we have problems in our lives is an undeniable fact, and that we cannot just leave and ignore them, is only too obvious. Yet, at the same time it can be observed that no sooner have we solved one problem than another crops up — and so we are never free from problems. In other words, to continue "solving' individual problems one after another —which also means, of course, to be in a state of continual conflict — does not have any better result than to ignore them. In the former case, it is like a festering sore, but nicely bandaged, which all the time undermines our health and saps our energy. In the latter case, it is like the symptomatic treatment of a disease; no sooner have we got rid of one symptom than another becomes evident. We have not cured the disease at all but only varied its manifestations.

It is for this reason that Krishnaji throws back the problems at us without solving them; he refuses to be a glorified Dorothea Dix. He is not interested in the problems as such, but only uses them to get at the underlying state of malaise which has thrown them up. Thus it may be said that problems are only incidental in Krishnaji's teaching, since in spiritual life the solution of a problem is merely an escape from it. So, although Krishnaji appears to discuss just about everything under the sun, he is really talking all the time about the same thing; each time in a different way perhaps, but always pointing to that intangible something beyond the words, which is the only thing that matters in the world.

Also, in a paper that discusses the difficulties which confront the person anxious to understand Krishnaji, something may be usefully said about his medium of expression, the words he is using.

The extraordinary thing about words is that, when applied to spiritual things they distort and often create, on superficial examination, the very opposite impression of what was intended before the idea was verbalized. So we hear, for example, people talk only too often about Krishnaji's 'technique' of setting the mind at peace. Thus a description of certain aspects of his teaching has apparently created the impression of a technique, a practice to be followed, which is, indeed, the very opposite of what was endeavoured to be conveyed, and this notwithstanding Krishnaji's exceedingly clear and outspoken remarks on this point. The spiritual way of life lies so much outside our ken, and its 'otherness' is so total in relation to our normal way of functioning on the level of the intellect, that only a thoroughgoing examination of what is involved reveals the truth that there cannot be a technique, a path.

To the person who is wont to the intellectual, analytical approach, here lies one of the greatest stumbling blocks. Being used to juggling concepts, he expects Krishnaji to supply him with a neat package of nicely labelled ideas and theories upon which he can get to work. But just because Krishnaji knows our fixation on words, he uses no technical jargon whatsoever; in this respect also Krishnaji is unique amongst the world's great religious teachers. And further, the simple ordinary words he uses are not necessarily employed in their accepted everyday meaning, but rather in their significance to be understood from the whole context. Herein lies, of course, the danger of misinterpretation for the person who is foolish enough to pick up only a fragment here and there of the Talk. Many an intellectual has come away from Krishnaji's meeting with one or two isolated sentences firmly fixed in his mind — or jotted down in his notebook — and promptly proceeds to build a whole philosophy upon this false basis. And, of course, these idle thought structures are always closely interwoven with the prejudices and preconceived ideas of the person concerned!

Then again, with Krishnaji words are never fixed but always pliable and fluid, he may use the same words at different times in totally opposite senses. Although the teaching itself has never changed since his enlightenment — and had it changed it could not have been true, for only philosophies and theories change, but the Truth which is timeless, just *is* — the expression of the teaching has changed considerably and words such as "emotion" and "experience" have acquired an altogether different meaning. For example, in the early years when his expression was very concise and many things were implied but unspoken, Krishnaji used to say that if you wished liberation you should seek experience. These days when he is more explicit and easier to follow, he says that no amount of experience will lead to liberation.

On a strictly verbal level these two sentences *taken out of their contexts* obviously represent a logical contradiction, but on the level of true meaning they point to the same thing. Since it is not the task of the present writer to interpret Krishnaji — having no intention to betray him — it is left to the reader to work these things out for himself. No doubt books could be written, and undoubtedly will be written in the future by scholars, about the "evolution' in meaning of some of Krishnaji's terms, which will then probably be called "concepts". This writer will have none of it! Suffice it to say that the life of the spirit, as soon as the mind comes in, is riddled with paradox.

The intellectual who has worked through Krishnaji's recorded

Talks from beginning to end as though it concerned the academic study of a law book or a science textbook, will undoubtedly be greatly irked and the word inconsistency will probably not be far from his mind. But it is just this almost casual, playful attitude towards words, which is a very essential part of Krishnaji's teaching; it means that man is master of the word, and not its servant, as is now generally the case. It is also part of his unequalled pedagogic technique, for it forces us to be on our toes all the time, and really listen with fresh minds. And is it not the familiarity with the association of words used again and again in the same fashion, which reduces the mind to sleep and staleness?

It is not necessarily what Krishnaji says that matters most, but what one can read between the lines which is really precious. After all, words and grammer have their limitations, and on that level there is only the intellect that can respond.

Who would not marvel at the truly scientific exactness and perfect economy with which Krishnaji uses words, his complete mastery over them, and notwithstanding their limitations, his ability, to convey to us a glimpse and a taste of the Infinite? In this respect, too, has there been any other teacher like him? It is this fact, above all, his sheer artistry and the incredible beauty of expression, which compels many people to attend his Talk year in and year out. This is not felt as just another gratification, but the very act of listening to Krishnaji confers a blessing!

To at least some of us the spectacle of Krishnaji unrecognized by the world, giving a public talk is the true world-changing event, and not the latest crisis manufactured by the politicians. Although these few gentlemen are playing with unclear fire, and are capable of killing large numbers of people effecting vast physical destruction, from Eternity's view-point all this is nothing. Worlds, civilizations, may come and go, but consciousness remains as before, and it is here that the real crisis unfolds.

Although in the various convulsions of mankind's evolution this diseased consciousness may undergo certain modifications and adjustments, these are of no avail in resolving the acute crisis. This crisis cannot be done away with by doctoring with the mind in the forms of psychoanalysis, organized religion, moral rearmament (sic), so-called better education or by raising the material standard of living. It is mutation, a complete breaking away from any pattern of the past. This seems to me the true significance of Krishnaji's presence in the world today and his ministry, that some of the momentum of the mechanical process of evolving consciousness may be gathered and utilized as essential energy in this mutation, the explosive shattering of consciousness.

Whilst the author does not expect everyone to share his views on the significance of Krishnaji's ministry as a historical event of the very greatest order, he is convinced that it is essential to be sensitive to his words from the very beginning and see their utterly revolutionary nature, if one is not to waste one's time completely. Those people who say: Oh, he is not giving us anything new, it is only applied Christianity or applied Buddhism — and the author knows that there are quite a few of them — might just as well occupy their time more profitably elsewhere. They are not missing a spiritual opportunity, for obviously they are not yet ready to receive the naked truth, with all its beauty but also with all its upheaval — being still satisfied with a continuation of the comforting pattern of the past. It is perhaps not altogether surprising to observe that generally people either click at once or don't at all with Krishnaji's teaching, and there appears to be no in-between.

It is common for organized religion to emphasize to prospective converts the importance of the right attitude towards a particular cult. With regard to Krishnaji it seems to the writer of the utmost importance to have no 'attitude whatsoever, to come to the man with empty hands; otherwise we shall not meet him at all. This means to have no foreknowledge about him — the approach of a child. Also, we should not even expect to get the slightest thing out of the teaching. Normally, a teaching implies a means to an end, whether the end be 'virtue', 'holiness', 'salvation', or something else. Krishnaji's "No-Teaching", however, is not to be applied, and it does not 'get you anywhere'. It has basically no utilitarian value, although in practice one may find it does, in an indirect way — but by then this is no longer seen to be of very great interest. One must love it (in the true sense of the word) for its own sake.

Having said all this, we find we are still interested in Krishnaji, we may have been able to eliminate those who go to him for the wrong reason (i.e. with an attitude), and we may really listen to him without any motive, with attention that is undivided because there is no pressure from the mind.

We shall then perhaps find that when there is this total attention a state of 'pure listening' has come into being, a stillness in which there is no effort, no application of any kind, yet something happens *immediately*. Then maybe, the miracle takes place: we shall be given richly — and we shall know who he is.

Krishnamurti – A Critical Study
by I. De Manziarly

The dissolution of the Order of the Star by Krishnamurti is surely a gesture which characterises the Krishnamurti of these later years. The desire is for freedom, for deliverance. Clearly, the young Hindu declares that his only desire is to liberate the individual unconditionally, to deliver man from all those things which imprison him within, which mutilate him, which limit him, to the end that the Life which is within him may find its free, creative expression. His work is therefore essentially spiritual, and therefore incomprehensible to those who — deprived of spirituality — would give another meaning to his words. In their language, liberty is often the equivalent of license.

Krishnamurti, as head of the Order of the Star, abolishes it because he believes that Truth cannot be organized, and because he will not himself belong to any organization having a spiritual purpose. Confusion has arisen and impertinent questions are being posed. This assertion only definitely takes account of organisations of a spiritual character, but that does not prevent the public from accusing Krishnamurti of being against all organisations, which has obliged him to declare that he necessarily makes use of the post and the telegraph.

A thoughtful conservative will nevertheless see in these

declarations an anarchist tendency, whereas an extremist of the opposite party will exploit this declaration, badly interpreted in favour of his convictions. But Krishnamurti is not concerned with the destruction of public institutions. He concedes to the state the care of the material administration of a nation, but he refuses to accept it as a moral force: he demands for the individual the right to choose freely and without the intervention of an external authority, the direction which he desires to follow within. Revolt, deliverance, liberty, are those of the spirit. For him to revolt, to become free, does not mean to attack primarily the legal institutions of a country, but to dispense from within with all crutches, with all help, with all shelter, with all authority. The first gesture must not be external but a destruction of our own prejudices, of our own limitations, of our own desires to dominate. That is the starting point.

Having reached the moment of his deliverance man will become a new being for whom the world will have taken on a new meaning. What this new being will do when that moment has arrived only he himself can tell; to prophesy or to guess would be a vain speculation. Let us occupy ourselves with the future, yes, but only in so far as it is contained in the present moment.

The individual (which means each one for himself) here at the present moment, thus is our preoccupation and our task clearly defined. We are not permitted to evade the issue by postponing it to a nebulous future where everything will be miraculously arranged for us. Neither have we to concern ourselves with the duties of our neighbours towards ourselves. It is our conduct, our attitude, our daily life that must be made perfect, brought to that point where the transitory is in harmony with the eternal. And it is precisely the transitory which will allow us to recognise the eternal. Simplify. Not embarrass ourselves with useless speculations, but go directly from one essential point to another essential point, without losing ourselves in the labyrinth of sidepaths.

The life of the spirit demands its rights with as much insistence as that of the body. A starving man does not ask what the Africans of Timbuctoo are eating at this moment, nor what he himself will be eating ten years hence; he wishes to eat immediately. If the hunger for truth is equally cruel; it will make us reject everything that distracts from and everything which postpones its satisfaction. We notice here how Krishnamurti insists upon the necessity of making clear to oneself the application of the word "essential", and then deliberately to choose. He invites each one to examine what really seems to him to be of primary importance. Is he seeking material wealth, popularity, glory? Or spiritual perfection, liberation? Above all, do not let us confound them with each other or try to attain or to play with both. As every being is completely free, as no judge is going to pronounce on his merits, he can in all security seek to discover his true tendencies, without lying to himself in order to acquire an illusory tranquillity of mind. Let him therefore determine the object of his search and then pursue it with all ardour. The only real evil is to lie to oneself, to attempt to reconcile the irreconcilable. The wisdom of Krishnamurti shows itself in this straight line without compromise, in the convergence of all tendencies toward the essential point. A burning desire is the only necessity for such concentration. It depends on us, and no spiritual guide can assist us in this. Established rules of conduct, systems, can only satisfy one who is looking for an answer from without. But experience lived can alone give an answer from within which will be of lasting value. It is this discovery, this intimate revelation which must direct us, it is our alert vigilance, which must be our true guide, warning us throughout the day of the errors which we have committed. There are no pre-established laws to guide the spirit. The spirit makes its own laws and blows where it will. The accomplishment of our task will prove to us that we have known how to perceive this voice of Life. Truth must be discovered: no beaten track leads to it. The world of Truth is, in each individual case, a world not yet discovered. That does not mean that this exploration is necessarily doomed to chance, chaos, or anarchy. On the contrary order governs it, but its own peculiar order and static, temporary values are replaced by eternal values which are dynamic.

It is the present moment which holds them. It is in this moment that we shall discover the world of Truth, invisible and yet real, near, yet inaccessible to the one who lives absorbed in the past or lost in the future.

...

What is new in what Krishnamurti is saying?

The expression of his experimental discovery. But it loses its sense of novelty unless it is seized upon by minds ready to make an analogous experiment. Old bottles contain new wine, and those who have "grown wise in childish things" are incapable of perceiving this new freshness. Only those who are rebels in spirit, who can only be satisfied by the destruction in themselves of the ancient order, will be able to respond to this new breath of the eternal spirit.

This is what Krishnamurti himself says on the subject:

"Those who wish to understand my point of view, who have a desire to attain that which I have attained, can in no manner compromise with the unrealities, with the unessentials that surround them. Through their own ecstatic desire to attain they must impose on themselves the self-discipline of which I am going to speak. I want this perfectly understood. Of what use is a vast horde of people who always compromise, a vast number who are uncertain, vague, frightened, doubtful? If there are three who have become a flame of Truth, who are a danger to everything around them that is unessential, those three and I will create a new understanding, a new delight, a new world. I am going to find one or three or half a dozen who are absolutely certain and determined, who have finished with all compromise. The rest will follow leisurely at their convenience, because they needs must suffer more, learn more.

"Man being free, is wholly responsible to himself unguided by any plan, by any spiritual authority, by any divine dispensation whatsoever. As he is free, he is, by that very freedom, limited. If you were not free, you would have a different world from that which exists at present. As the will in everyone is free, it is limited, and because the self is small, without determination or purpose at the beginning, it chooses, it discriminates, has its likes and dislikes. In the removal of that limitation, which is self-imposed lies the glory of the fulfilment of the self, the freedom of the self.

"This attainment is not brought about by ecstasy, nor does it lie in the abandoning of oneself to work or to meditation, or in the blind following of another, or in the immolation of oneself to a cause. Because the "I", the self, is in process of achieving, it is creating barriers between itself and its fulfilment, by its eagerness, its struggles, through fear, through innumerable complications. To remove these barriers of limitation, you need constant awareness, constant watchfulness, constant self-reflection, which must be imposed on yourself by yourself, never by another. But if you discipline yourself unconsciously, without knowing where you are going, that self-discipline itself becomes a barrier. Understand the purpose of life, and from that very understanding will arise self-discipline. Self-discipline must be born out of the love of Life vast, immeasurable, whole unconditioned, limitless, to which all humanity belongs. Because you love that freedom which is absolute, which is Truth itself, which is harmony; by the very force of that love, your self-discipline will make you incorruptible; so you must nourish that love. The incorruptibility of the self is the perfection of life.

"Till man is made incorruptible by himself, he will know no happiness, he will be held in the bondage of friendship and the fear of loneliness. The wariness of strife will still hold him. Men must be created who are great in the serenity of harmony. Such men must be born in you. Such men must give rise to new transformations, must become a flame to burn away the dross danger to all unessential, childish things.

"To become such men you must live in the eternal now, in that moment of eternity which is neither the future nor the past. In you must be concentrated that understanding, that immense power which shall destroy the unrealities, the unessential things that surround the self. Such men by their lives will create a new world, a new understanding. It is your life that matters, what you do, what you think, not what you preach, not in what manner you cast a shadow on the face of life.

"All this may seem immense, vague, uncertain, impossible to achieve; but you must go after it, even though you are weak, these are all small as compared with the everlasting."

Part II

Conversations

Chapter   8

With C.L. Nahal

I am meeting Mr. Krishnamurti for the second time in five years. The first time was in 1959, when, after listening to one of his talks, I had gone and spent a few minutes with him. He comes in, not much changed since 1959, looking neat and handsome, erect in his bearing in spite of his age, his grey hair properly groomed, and his face sincere and open, his eyes big and penetrating. He folds his hands in greeting.

Krishnamurti: Please sit down.

I sit on the bed. He draws a chair near to me. I explain that since 1959 I had never felt the need to come and personally see him. That his message, or whatever he wanted to communicate, was so simple and direct that it had made its impact on me and I did not think I needed a further explanation from him.

Krishnamurti: What has happened now, sir?

I can't really tell him that there is no special reason, that I just wanted to be with him.

—It is very peaceful here, sir!

Krishnamurti says nothing to this. He smiles, leans forward and gently touches me on the knee, as if to tell me to relax. He does not ask me about the purpose of my visit.

—But it is very peaceful. It was like this, when I met you on the former occasion — equally peaceful. Many of your other visitors have also spoken of it, the calm and harmony that suddenly descends. . . . (Giving a definite shape to my thoughts) Is there any element of hypnosis in it Sir?

Continuing after a brief pause I say: You know persons like Gurdjieff and Mme Blavatsky were accused of hypnotizing their listeners, paralysing them so to say, and inducing in them a state of wellbeing. I should like to know if the peace that I am experiencing this moment is by any chance on account of some controlled effort on your part. Or is it there independent of both of us?

K: I assure you, sir, I do not practise hypnotism nor have any faith in it.

—What is this tranquility then that I am experiencing? From where has it arrived? How?

K: Is your experiencing of this particular feeling you refer to dependent on our first finding an answer to its origin?

—No, I don't think so. Still I should like to know, I am interested in discovering the causes which affect and change our consciousness. Are you aware of the experiments to alter human consciousness with the use of drugs?

K: You mean mescalin and that kind of stuff?

—Yes. (and then, remembering something) Your friend, Aldous Huxley, also experimented with it.

K: (waving his hand, impatiently): Well, Aldous used to discuss it with me, but of course the whole thing is meaningless. Why go so far? We all know that human consciousness can be disturbed with stimulants. An alcoholic drink will do that much for you. But then you are back next morning where you were before, when the effect of the drink is gone, feeling worse and miserable for your experience. Truly great experiences are those which happen on their own, without any effort on the part of the individual to manipulate them — for himself or for others.

—Would you apply this to experiences gained through Yoga? What of the yogis who claim to go into trances, or who practise developing a super-conscious state of mind?

K: The same, sir. These experiences, however profound they may appear to be, remain within the sphere of time. For me hypnosis, drugs or yoga are all attempts at self-delusion.

—Some time back I saw a book by you in a British library, where you speak of leading others to light, provided they followed you. It was published in 1926.

K: (With a reminiscent smile) Ah. yes. That was when I was associated with The Order of the Star in the East. But I've moved away from that position. I don't offer to lead any one now.

—Why did you break with that Order, sir? Was it a change of attitude in you? — I'm sure Mrs. Annie Besant must have been heartbroken!

K: It was not a change of 'attitudes'. It was a total change which I experienced, if I may put it that way. I felt that the truth about life had to be discovered by each individual for himself. The whole concept of Gurus and Followers became unreal to me, and I had to step aside from a position which I realized was a false one. (smiles, leans forward and holds my hand). No, Sir, Mrs. Annie Besant was not heartbroken! (looking sad and continuing to smile) You know, I was like a son to her. She actually agreed with my way of thinking. What worried her, and worried her a good deal, was the physical part of my life. The Order was a very rich organisation, and she didn't know how I would feed myself if I left it and went away. But she sympathized with my outlook.

—But you have been teaching all the same, as a Guru.

K: No, sir, no, I have been teaching, but at a totally different level. I am certainly all for sharing one's thoughts with others. In that light, I would be willing to accept any of the great teachers, Christ or Buddha or any one else. I only object to a cult being woven around them where the figure of the teacher becomes more important than his words or his thoughts.

What exactly is your objection to established religions?

K: I think I've partly answered the question. Man's discovery of God ceases to be a discovery if he begins this search with a foregone conclusion in his mind. Most religions impose a certain image of the type of God they would want their followers to worship. Whereas to my mind, in the search for truth, which to me is the search for God, the choice does not rest with us as to what to reject or accept. Truth, God, call it what you will, is an awareness of the totality of existence, of our hopes and desires, our ambitions, our greed, our loves and thousands of other emotions which constitute what passes for the living individual. I believe organized religions stand in the way of this awareness of the totality of existence.

—In your teaching, you do not give the mind a very big place. You say that it plays a dubious role in our discovery of God. One must come to God, you declare, without the conditioning imposed on us by our knowledge and memories. Would you say that animals, who do not have developed minds or memories, are happier than human beings and closer to reality?

K: Of course not, sir. That's ridiculous. Mind has its own place, a unique place in our lives. Without the use of your mind you won't be able to find your way back home, and I won't be able to conduct this conversation without its help. But mind can only move in the sphere of the known, in the sphere of time. Whereas we refer to God as the unknown the timeless. is it not? Till a certain stage, in the three dimensional world, our mind can serve us to our advantage. But to reach the fourth dimension of existence, the mind instead of moving along the horizontal plane, must learn to shoot up vertically as it were and explode for the timeless, for the unknown to be.

—How do you see this worked out in practice, in the routine life of the millions who seek God?

K: In their sensitivity, in their ability to remain open for the new. I do not like the word God: it smacks of anthropomorphism. But in a man's sensitivity to, in his choiceless awareness of the totality of existence, in this alone I find whatever meaning the word God conveys.

—What according to you, is the most important problem of day-to-day living?

K: You speak as if these were two different issues — that for so many hours a week we seek God and for so many attend to what you call day-to-day living. To me, the two are identical. If anything, day-to-day living is more valuable for me, for it is through this that one unfolds the meaning of existence.

—How do you see this day-to-day living properly carried out?

K: In relationships which are moving and not static. That is the most vital issue. We form a relationship and later get into the habit of looking at it from a fixed point of view — whether the relationship is with one's wife, or one's children, or one's neighbours. Such relationships cease to be creative; they become dead. To have a moving relationship one has to be aware of the others as they are, from moment to moment, one has to be responsive to them, in short one has to be sensitive. Habit of any kind dulls sensitivity. We must be willing to accept the change in others and willing to change ourselves. 'Willing' is perhaps not the correct expression. If we are sensitive, we cannot help noticing how time and circumstances modify others and we cannot help being impressed ourselves by the same process. Sensitivity demands the ability to have serene mind, a mind which is not preoccupied with itself, a mind which is receptive, which is an open mind, a mind which is not always getting hurt at what it sees or perceives.

—What about the spontaneous reaction if some one is rude to you? You cannot help being hurt at unprovoked hostility shown towards you, can you?

K: Well, I am not speaking of reaction. If some one sticks a pin into you, you are bound to react — protect yourself, or cry out in pain, or take yourself away from the offending agent — your reaction depending on several factors, varying from man to man, I mean hurt in the sense of nursing hatred. An event is over and for years we keep brooding over it working ourselves up into a state of passion. The challenge of existence ever demands a fresh approach on our part to an issue or to an individual. A mind which nurses hatred, or for that matter nurses joy, long after the event is over, ceases to be sensitive. Sensitivity is my equivalent of meditation, which brings you its own rewards.

—How can one achieve this sensitivity?

K: By being what you really are. By trying to see what is. You see, genetically, or through earlier conditioning, I have acquired a certain type of character. It is there, a part of myself, like my nose or the shape of my chin. Now I must try and see myself as I am, and I must make no effort to be anything else, (Finding me restless). Just listen, I am not advocating self indulgence, that a hypocrite should continue to be a hypocrite or a thief remain a thief. I should not submit to my weakness, but I should not indulge in the opposite of my weakness either as a way of getting rid of it.

(I am on the point of protesting but Mr. Krishnamurti restrains me).

K: I'll make it clear. Let us say I am given to hating others. Now I must not go and start loving them, seeing love as a panacea for my foolish temperament. That way I shall never learn to grow out of my hateful nature. I will only be generating contradictions in myself, running from one conflict to another. What is wanted of me is to accept the fact that I hate others and then go into the cause of this. I should ask myself: why do I hate? Is it that I expect too much from life? Am I in any respect frustrated? what is it that I want? Am I capable enough to get it? I should ask myself all this, and stay in this state of exploration, without making any deliberate effort on my part to get rid of my malady. Suddenly I will discover that a transformation takes place in myself, without any planning on my part, a creative transformation. My sensitivity has now come into play!

Staggered at the enormity of what has just been outlined and seeing at once its meaning, I ask: Will you say something on death, a fear which haunts most of us?

K: It is a fear only, if we see death as an event in time. We imagine death waiting for us far ahead, and in the course of the years we build up a terror of this enemy which is lying behind the bush to pounce on us.

Now the thing to do is to bring death closer to our daily life. Instead of letting it sit there at the other end of our life, let us bring it nearer, to the present day. We will discover then that death is there in everything: in our relationship with others, in the cells of our body as we continue to live, a constant change which is the law of life. If we keep this fact before us and learn the art of dying every day to some part of ourselves, old memories, old relationships, the fear of death will vanish. The art of living to a large extent consists of learning the art of dying. It will then give rise to that play of sensitivity about which I spoke earlier. The actual death of the body one day, as you know, is unavoidable.

—But what do you think of the hereafter?

K: No one knows the answer.

—But do you hold out the hope of some kind of survival of man's personality after death?

K: That is the repetitive desire of holding on to the known, to the familiar facets of life, is it not? The hereafter belongs to the known. Any attempt to affirm or deny its existence will take us away from the truth of it, and the truth is that no one knows the answer.

—Would you agree with those who find affinities in you and Buddhism or Zen or other schools of thought?

K: It is not for me to agree or disagree. But most of these schools, whether it is Buddhism or Vedanta or any other, suggest a "path" — the middle path, the negative path and the like, I suggest no path at all. For a path implies effort or practice, and the immeasurable can only be faced by a person in keeping himself free of effort, in a state of alert readyness for the new, in a state without fear or hope.

You have consistently spoken against ideals, sir. How about the artists, the writer, the painters and the whole tribe of them who are constantly building utopias before us?

K: Artists are mischief-makers in this respect.

—In what respect, if any, are they an asset to Society?

K: In being more sensitive, more alive to life than most of us are. An artist can make us aware of a whole range of new feelings. But (with a look of pain on his face) new feelings do not merely mean new forms of expression. Most modern art, or modern poetry and modern fiction, is bogged down with a craze for novelty of expression. An artist must first have a new awareness, a new something to say, and the form will of its own achieve a newness and freshness. But modern artists seem to be so impoverished and empty, inwardly.

—Did you make a statement recently to the effect that everything Indian is "phoney"? It was in a Bombay journal, some months back.

K: No, I never made this statement. I'm very fond of India.

—Or that "I understand freedom only when I am in the West"?

K: No, most definitely no. I contradict this. Who has been attributing such things to me? I might have said that in the West people have a greater civic sense, or greater freedom from economic want, but I do not maintain that the West is any more advanced in the sum of freedoms than the East.

—May I ask why you decided on settling in the United States?

K: But I am not settled there. I travel around and move from country to country and have not been to the States for the last five years. In fact, a greater part of any years these days I spend in India — about five months in a year. My books are published in the States, true, but that is only because I have a few friends there who help me in editing my manuscripts. I have no home there, no Ashram, or anything of that type.

—I wish you were to make a permanent home here, in India.

K: I've my home in the world.

Chapter 9

With E.A. Wodehouse

During the recent Winter Gathering at Adyar I was fortunate enough to have several long talks with Krishnamurti. We went for two or three walks together to the seashore; once or twice we sat on the verandah of the upper floor of the new Star Office, which had been lent to me as my quarters during my stay. I found Krishnamurti, as always, only too ready to discuss anything that had to do with his teachings. More than that, I think that he thoroughly enjoys the process of what he calls "having buckets let down into his well", and the deeper the bucket goes the more he likes it. At any rate we had some really good talks, and I have felt that it would be a pity not to jot down what I remember of some of them, particularly as, on one or two points, close questioning elicited from him certain rather important extensions of his teaching, which I feel would interest many readers.

...

For present purpose I shall confine myself to one conversation which took place two or three days ago. It was on a rather interesting topic: — namely, What is liberation? Are we to think of the individual liberated as still active in some way or another? or does liberation mean annihilation?

Many people, I said, listening to Krishnamurti's teachings, think of liberation as annihilation. They take it as putting a full stop to life. This is partly because he himself has often spoken of it as a "goal", partly because traditionally (in Buddhism and elsewhere) it is treated as though it meant the end of all things; partly, again, because many people find it difficult to imagine what kind of further activity there can be, when the individual life has become merged in the universal.

Krishnamurti's answer to this difficulty was a singularly full one — not, of course, given as a discourse, but broken up by question and answer and so gradually opening out one point after another. It is wrong, he said to regard liberation as annihilation. It is more truly a beginning. And yet, in one sense, it is not a beginning at all, since pure life is altogether out of Time. Still, for the purpose of answering this particular question, we may speak of it as a beginning; for it is the commencement of True or Natural Life. Up till the point of liberation we are leading a sham life. We are in the realm of illusion. Only after that do we enter upon life, as it is really meant to be. From this point of view, he admitted, it is certainly misleading to speak of liberation as a "goal". A goal it is, for those who are striving to reach it; but in itself it is more truly a starting point.

There is nothing in liberation, as such, he went on, to preclude further activity in the phenomenal worlds. There can, of course, be no compulsion, since freedom from compulsion is implicit in the idea of liberation. But if the liberated life so wills, it can manifest itself in the worlds of matter; and, in so far as it enters into those worlds, it will come under the law of those worlds, which is evolution.

But even if it does so, the growth which will then ensue will be of a different kind from that which preceded liberation. For it will be a growth informed by absolute, or pure, life. Formerly there was (or seemed to be) an Ego, and growth appeared as the unfolding of this. Now there is no longer an Ego; it has disappeared for ever at liberation. What we have therefore to grasp, if we can — and it is no easy matter — is the idea of universal life building up fresh instruments for its self-expression; those instruments being in the world of form and so having, in that world, the outward appearance of individuality. The chief mark of post-liberation activity will be that it is absolutely natural, effortless, spontaneous, unselfconscious. The life thus manifested in the material worlds will have its roots in the Eternal. It will have realised its own universality. And, because there is no longer any sense of separate "I-ness" to obstruct things, its activity will be as simple and as natural as that of a flower.

Will such a life, I asked him, have anything corresponding to that sense of "I-ness" which we now have? That is to say, will its experience be referred, as ours is, to an appreciating centre? Will it preserve any kind of conscious self-identity, or will it, by reason of its universality, lose this completely in its identification of itself with the life of others?

It does, answered Krishnamurti, preserve what may be called a sense of self-identity. It still, so to speak, looks out on the world through its own eyes and refers all its experience to itself. But this "self" is not an Ego. It is that far more subtle thing — individual uniqueness. And here we come to another thing which must almost elude our powers of thought. Individual uniquencess is not a differentiation on the form side, as the Ego is. It is a differentiation inherent in the life itself, and it only comes into full action, if one may put it so, when the Ego has ceased to exist. Such uniqueness is what makes every individual life different from every other and gives it its own centre of consciousness; and even when the universal life has been realised, this uniqueness remains. One may speak of it as that pure abstract "form" of individuality, which remains when all the egoism has been drained from it. It is individual, and at the same time it is universal. The nearest we can go to it in concrete language, is to describe it as the focus through which the universal life is released, and through which it manifests freely after liberation. For a human being there can be no complete merging in the Absolute, in the sense of evaporation into the

Totality of Life. The differentiation, however, abstract and tenuous, involved in this individual uniqueness is everlasting; and it is this that makes possible any subsequent evolutionary growth, which the liberated life may still experience in the world of form, if it so wills.

So far indeed, Krishnamurti continued, such uniquencess disappearing or "evaporating", is really the supreme gift which each one of us makes to life. For, when once it has been purified of all egoism, it becomes, one may say, a new window through which the universal life can realise itself. Every individual life, in this way, multiples the universe, for it gives to the Absolute a fresh world in which it can discover and recreate its own Being. And the point at which this gift is handed over to the universal life is what we call liberation. For it is then that the Ego relinquishes that which it has helped to build up; and a greater life takes this over. To put it another way, the Ego dies in order that Life may live.

And here, Krishnamurti pointed out, we can see that to talk of so-and-so "obtaining liberation" is a misuse of terms. That which is liberated is always life, not the individual. Indeed it is at the expense of the individual that such liberation is achieved. Life alone benefits by the transaction. It is true that the individual uniqueness, which persists on both sides of the liberating process, finds that, instead of belonging to the Ego, it has really all along belonged to the life universal. But that discovery is made at, or after, liberation. The process towards liberation must always seem like the killing out of individuality — hence its painfulness. The old saying, "Thou must die in order to live", still remains true. Liberation, then, is the liberating of life by the destruction of separateness, so that this life can thenceforward function in its fullness through the pure form of individual uniquencess. And this is the Natural Life, referred to before, which is established, and which first comes into possession of itself, at liberation.

Is there any mark, I asked him by which this "Natural Life" can be easily distinguished from the life which is manifested while egoism still persists? — any thing which can give us a concrete idea of what it is like, without necessitating an appeal to metaphysics?

His answer was that there is one simple mark, which holds good for every manifestation of pure, or universal, life. It is that it acts but never reacts. Until we have got rid of the Ego, most of our conscious life is made up of reactions. Take love, for example. This is, in most cases, a reaction set up within us by some person who happens to attract us. A person who does not happen to set up this reaction, we do not love. But after liberation, when pure life is at work, what occurs is quite the reverse. Then love becomes a life-force going out from ourselves. It may be compared to a searchlight, which renders loveable all on whom its beam may happen to fall. It is thus independent of its object, since the light can be turned just as easily upon one as another. And the same thing is true of everything else in the liberated life. Wisdom, for instance, is not knowledge derived from anything outside. It is a light which, going forth from ourselves, illumines everything which it may touch. It is pure life manifesting as cognition. And here, incidentally, we can see the meaning of the statement, so often made by Krishnamurti, that the liberated life means the poise of love and reason. The explanation is that, after internalizing the characteristics of pure life, people become positive, acting outward from an inner centre, are never driven back to their 'reacting' selves.

The impossibility of thus being driven back is the "poise". No impact from outside can disturb its equilibrium; on the contrary, it is ever ready to leap forth in any direction, as soon as the impulse comes from within.

The great thing that we have all to do, therefore said Krishnamurti, is gradually to change our reactions into actions. Every movement of the life within us must become self-originating. We must cease to be stirred either by attraction or repulsion from without, and must set up an outward-going life which will bestow its own qualities upon the world about it.

Such substitution of pure action for reaction is true detachment; for it is, of its own nature, indifferent to objects. It is also liberation; for the sole life of the Ego — which itself is the sole obstacle to freedom — consists in reactions. Abolish the reactions and substitute pure actions and the Ego automatically disappears. Here then is one way of working for liberation. As regards the question from which we started (that of post-liberation activity) this formula of "action without reaction" may help us to understand a little of what life after liberation must be like. It will be a life of pure action, devoid of reactions: and we can fit this in, in thought, with any kind of activity on the form side.

One further point, he added, can be linked on to all this; and that is the point which started the whole discussion — namely, the statement that liberation can be reached at any stage in evolution.

Liberation, said Krishnamurti, is independent of evolutionary growth in this sense — that, of two persons at different stages of evolutionary growth, the one less evolved may well win liberation before the other, if he is more prepared to do the essential thing; that is, to destroy utterly the sense of the separate "I". This, and not the development of vehicles, is the real pre-condition of liberation. On the other hand, it may be true — probably it is — that a certain amount of evolutionary growth will be necessary before anybody will have the real wish in him to make this ego-annihilating effort. The statement, therefore, that liberation can be reached at any stage should be modified. What is true in it is its assertion that liberation is a matter of the life and not of forms; that, given the capacity to make the effort, attainment need not wait upon any long processes of evolutionary growth; and lastly, that the first movement towards liberation can be made at quite an early stage, and that every step along this path is in itself a liberation. In accomplishing even a small part of the task we, in one way, accomplish the whole.

Krishnamurti explained what he meant by this last remark.

Pure life, he said, cannot be subdivided. It knows nothing of more or less. It is an absolute. Therefore, if, in relation to anything whatsoever, you release life by the breaking down of an attachment, you release within that sphere (no matter how small it be) the whole of life. To turn any reaction into pure action is thus, in itself, a liberation just as full in its way as the all-embracing liberation later on. From this point of view the whole journey towards liberation (if one can put it so) is one long liberation. The great thing is to be facing in the right direction. After that, the length of time which the journey may take does not matter. To have "begun liberating" is what counts. For it means that a man has definitely sided with life in the task that has to be done.

The idea that liberation can be won "in moments", and that each such moment has the essential quality of full liberation, is one on which Krishnamurti laid much stress. That is why he speaks sometimes of the necessity of aiming at perfection in all the little things of life. For "perfection" is that quality which automatically supervenes when absolute life is touched. It is the natural and spontaneous expression of pure life. Consequently to aim at perfection in small details is to aim, indirectly, at the release of pure life; and any perfect action, no matter how small, is thus a liberation. By doing this, Krishnamurti said, we can, so to speak, set up a "habit of liberation", long before the final freedom is achieved.

Chapter   10

With David E.S. Young

Though slender, frail, and graying, Jiddu Krishnamurti is intense, extremely alert, and spiritually so awake that what he says potentially illuminates every corner of the human soul. In the presence of this world-famed thinker, lecturer, author, my own awareness and understanding were turned on to such a degree as to change the course of my everyday existence.

In June, 1944, I talked with Krishnamurti at his home in Ojai, California. Our conversation took place in a small, severely plain sitting room, set aside for such purposes and kept separate from the rest of the rambling house overlooking the Ojai Valley. Outside the window there were orange trees, a hive of buzzing bees, a brown cow quietly munching, and a few white chickens, all of which he helped look after. We sat opposite each other: he, completely attentive, using hand gestures and facial expressions to amplify the meaning of what he said; I nervous and excited.

I had long realized the world problem is the individual problem and the conflict without is the result of the conflict within each person. Clearly this inner disturbance must be understood. How can anyone live intelligently and sanely without self-knowledge? And just how well do we know ourselves? Are we fully aware all day and every day of what we're thinking and feeling?

Perhaps a written record of one's mind-heart activities would be revealing.

With these thoughts churning in my mind, I said, "In order to know myself better I've tried writing down my thoughts and feelings. I wrote about the rushing stream, the majestic mountains, the song of the birds — as if writing a letter to someone..."

Krishnamurti responded quickly. "No, not that. What do you *think* of the birds? What is your reaction?"

Still tense, I was unable to understand what he meant. "Please explain more fully."

"It's important to think right in order to release something creative. To think right you must know yourself. To know yourself you must be detached, absolutely honest, free from judgement. It means continual awareness of one's thoughts and feelings during the day without acceptance or rejection, like watching a movie of oneself.

"In order to watch more closely, it's necessary to slow down the mental process. Close examination will automatically do this, like slowing down the movie. It will help at first to write down one's thoughts and feelings. You cannot write all of them, but as many as possible."

"In a short-hand manner, not necessarily intelligible to anyone else?"

"Yes, two words are enough to remind one of a thought."

"I'd be afraid someone might read it. I suppose one could make sure no one could understand it."

"Yes, or burn it. Also during an activity, such as washing dishes, you can't write, but the process of watching is going on. Afterwards you can write down your thoughts."

I was less nervous and gaining in confidence. I said, "Most of us are aware only some of the time. Are you aware, all the time?"

"Not quite that. Now that I'm talking to you, my attention is on you, but the photographic process is continuing. Suppose I say something false, then afterwards I'll say, `By Jove, I said something false to David!"

I was beginning to understand more quickly now. "Then when you're talking to someone you're not aware?"

"When I'm giving a lecture my whole attention is on the audience, but the recording process continues; afterwards I can look at my inward reactions. If I'm talking to someone about something that occupies merely my superficial attention, or if I'm doing something such as washing dishes, then I'm aware of what's going on inside of me; but I can't give my whole attention to think about it until I'm alone."

The quickening of my interest prompted me to ask, "And when we've written down our thoughts, what then?"

"At the end of the day you can read what you've written, honestly and impartially. You begin to see yourself; you can examine all the different samples. At first you'll be ashamed, but that will pass. You'll become interested in trying to see what lies behind these thoughts and feelings."

"Yes, I can see that."

"Once begun and given the right environment, awareness is like a flame." Krishnamurti's face lit up with aliveness and spiritual vitality. "It will grow immeasurably. The difficult thing is to activate the faculty."

A tiny flame of awareness kindled within me and my inner self seemed to be faintly transparent. Was this a momentary state? Under what circumstances would it flourish? I said, "What do you mean by the right environment?"

"Not being too tired; having enough time to be aware. `Work' on it and give it enough fuel — the fuel is one's life."

Krishnamurti paused to see my response. One could tell how keen he was for me to understand, but I wasn't used to such concentrated, dynamic thinking and we had to stop.

The intensity of the interview stayed with me for several days and I worked at the process of self-knowing; however, it was far from easy. Habits of condemnation, justification, and anxiety acted as distraction from awareness and prevented objective observation. I felt I needed more help.

A week later I invited Krishnamurti to a picnic at a resort where we were staying during our vacation in Ojai. We sat on some large, ever-present, white rocks and watched my family swim in the clear blue river.

After lunch I questioned him further about awareness. "In watching my reactions I usually find craving in some form or other, for instance, envy. I see it. It comes and goes, but I don't seem to be able to think any deeper than this."

He looked at me gently for a moment and then said "You're the result of the past — your body, your feelings, and your thinking. Your body is just a copy. Any feeling, for example, envy or anger, is a result of the past. Whatever you do about that envy, such as repression, trying to make it into something, or some other action, is also the result of the past. So you're merely moving within the circle of experience." He drew a picture in the sand to show this, a circle with marks inside, one for the envy and another for the action taken. "You must 'work' on this; think about it, meditate, try to see it in all its aspects — calmly, detached, as looking at a new and unknown animal, you're interested in its shape, its habits and so on; you don't know whether it's poisonous or not so you're not reacting. That's meditation, trying to free oneself from the past, transcending the past so as to discover the unknown, the timeless; otherwise it's merely moving within the circle of the past.

"You must meditate on this until you can feel it throughout all your being, not just one layer, all the layers." Krishnamurti's entire body expressed what he was saying. "Then there will be a great calmness, infinite peace.

"Write this down as I've said it. Then look at it and watch your reactions to it. Think about it. Try to find out what you think about it. It will come to you later."

His words had a quieting effect. There was a long silence during which we sat motionless. Anything one did was useless; yet, there was still an inner movement. I wanted companionship of some kind — personal, impersonal, spiritual, or divine — I just didn't want to be completely alone. I said, "The desire for affection or the fear of losing it lies at the back of many of my thoughts and actions."

"What is it you desire? It's not affection." He waited for my reply.

"You mean it's not affection in my own heart, but something from outside?"

"Exactly. You're trying to fill a void within. It's like attempting to fill an empty, leaky bucket which can never be filled."

"One has to keep putting something in every day."

"And still it fills only a thin layer; it satisfies only superficially. It never completely or permanently fills the whole vessel. So why do you go on doing this?" Krishnamurti gave an inquiring look, carefully watching my reaction. "You're not really experiencing this. If you really saw this you'd be thrilled. You'd have a tremendous sense of relief — `Thank goodness I don't have to go on doing this!'"

I could feel *his* sense of relief, but not mine. "Why do I experience it so superficially?"

"Yes, why?" he asked.

I was determined to be honest with my replies. "Because I'm dull, not sensitive enough."

"Yes. So find out why you're dull. Investigate everything: diet, inheritance, your English background, imperialism and so forth; your activities; perhaps you're surrounded by thoughts about yourself, memories, comparison, escapes, dreams, and so on — examine everything. Really tackle the whole thing. If you just sit back and say, `Well, I'm dull,' and do nothing about it, then you're old." He sat back with a dramatic, nonchalant attitude; then leaning forward and focussing his luminous dark brown eyes on me, he said, "It should be a matter of life and death."

"Why am I dull now?"

"I think it's because you're depressed."

"Yes, that's true. I know why I'm depressed." I was feeling discouraged about my job in a factory which took all my energy. The work of processing food was the most constructive occupation available for me during the war.

"You can easily trace out the cause of it, but the depression doesn't help, does it? So why are you depressed?" He smiled as he waited for me to put the question to myself. "Directly you ask yourself `why?', really look at it, then it's gone. You're on the mountain top."

"One clings on to the depression. Why is that?" I felt the depression going, but part of me seemed to hold on to it.

"Because it's better than nothing. You don't want to be empty. David, why don't you really tackle this question of the void within? Why do you continually fill it with sensation — comforts, beliefs, comparisons? If you have a leaky, broken bucket, what do you do with it?"

"Throw it away!"

"Yes, sir. You don't go on using it!"

This dialogue had a tremendous impact on me and even now as I write I find the words still very much alive.

What I didn't like was the atmosphere of the factory, but it gave me the opportunity to watch the effect of awareness on my life. As I disentangled myself from the past, I first shed college conditioning, then school influences, and later some of my childhood fears. As I faced things and began to look at myself honestly, I became less nervous; yet, there remained other layers of conditioning, particularly inherited unconscious ones of my English and Scottish background.

Towards the close of 1945 we moved to warm and sunny Ojai with its wonder, its beauty, and its growing group of people interested in Krishnamurti's teachings. I wondered whether it was possible to live completely free and enlightened in the manner indicated by him; it seemed very difficult to support a family and at the same time be fully awake spiritually. I had experienced enough awareness to be eager for a great deal more.

At my first opportunity I went to see him and opened the interview with what was uppermost in my mind "I'm aware sometimes, but most of the time I'm not really conscious of my feelings and thoughts."

"Do you notice the times when you're more aware?"

"Yes, but I become completely engrossed when teaching or dancing."

"Isn't there part of you which remains aloof and watching?"

"Only at moments."

"Are those moments increasing in duration?"

"Yes."

"Therefore you're more awake, however imperceptibly. Do you not find fundamental discussions such as this illuminating?"

"Yes, I find them stimulating."

Sitting very erect and speaking with great clarity and affection Krishnamurti said, "Do you find them just stimulating or are they illuminating? There's a distinct difference between being stimulated and being awake. Being awake is like a flame illuminating everything within." He waited patiently, yet alertly. "Do you really see this? First see it verbally. Then feel it out — being stimulated and being awake. Now go into it deeply, seeing its full significance." His whole being spoke to me.

"I see the difference, but other things come into my mind."

"Never mind about the other things. Really look at this. Really see the difference between illumination and stimulation."

There was silence. My nerves were calm. I felt the touch of something vital and tremendous. "I'm afraid there's much resistance inside me."

"Yes, but just see the enormous importance of illumination, even if it's for only a second."

During the silence that followed I became aware of an aliveness which seemed to exist quite apart from either of us. The expansion of consciousness which took place was too much for me and as a result I almost fell asleep . I asked, "Why is that?"

"You're not used to this concentration."

"I do see the importance of illumination, but there're other things coming into my mind I had prepared to ask you. I'm always doing that — preparing for the future. It's because I'm anxious, but it hinders seeing something new such as you're presenting now."

"All right, you see the futility of the mind always preparing. After this you'll be less inclined to do so much. The thing that matters is to see the importance of light."

My mind was still burdened with questions which I thought I had better expose even if they were 'wrong'.

"Is it better to meditate with the eyes open or closed?"

"It depends. But the thing that matters is to see the importance of light."

I could see the truth of this, but I wondered whether I'd always do so. "What makes one dull again after being aware?"

"Your mind is already greedy for more. It wants to hold onto the light."

Once more there was silence. I saw that in worrying about how to keep alert my mind was seeking a continuation of the experience and that this action was itself a cause of going to sleep. In this way the interview was a meditation, a process of self-knowing. There was an intensification of hearing, seeing, and feeling and my questions felt like interruptions during a concert or sunset. "So you just watch awareness, watch it grow, and never mind about the other things?

"Yes. Experiment with it for a while. Be interested in light apart from David Young. You're more awake than you think you are." Krishnamurti leaned forward and looked straight at me; when he spoke his intense eyes were filled with compassion. "When you do something such as teaching, gardening, or dancing, you don't give all your attention to it — perhaps thirty per cent. What happens to the other seventy per cent? If you don't know, it must be hidden."

"One notices one's reactions and other people's."

"Yes. In other words this watching is going on all the time."

"A continuous meditation?"

"Yes, Listen as if listening to the rain." It was pouring rain. "Suppose we call this phenomenon concentration: hear what it has to tell you, rather than your speaking to it. It will tell you much more than you can tell it. Of course there must be some tension on your part; there must be interplay. For example, you work on your own and then you come to hear what I have to say. If you didn't work at it, anything I said would be just a waste of time. When you listen, then do so without trying to get something out of it."

"We want something, and that hinders us from truly listening and watching."

"Yes. You're reading a book. Read every page. If you read a book on science, it tells you more than you can tell it; doesn't it?"

"Yes."

"Then whatever it is — greed, craving, anger — see the whole process. For instance, read the book of sensation; read it all — about the villain as well as the hero, and not just about the hero — so you'll know all about it. How else can you know the whole story? Find out the whole story of pain and pleasure. Look and see when you're sensuous."

"You mean sex?"

"Sex is just one small part of it. Take sensuality in its most general sense — eating, sense of power, achieving, taking sides — in fact craving in all its forms. We have to watch very carefully all the time."

"In other words, look at craving or whatever it is as if it were not part of me?"

"Yes. It's absorbingly interesting, isn't it? Suppose we look at a picture; we judge it, criticize and so on, instead of really seeing what it has to say."

As a result of this interview, I developed a much better understanding of how awareness operates. It became more of an actuality to me — to gather information about oneself is merely to accumulate memories, but to observe the movement of action is a living process.

By listening very quietly when alone and unoccupied, not only to outside sounds but also to my inner being, and by watching very carefully and feeling, any scrap of light, however small and apparently insignificant, I discovered a luminous intensity which existed quite apart from the busy mind. At the same time I still felt as if I were groping in a fog, so I had the urge to see Krishnamurti again in February, 1946.

As soon as we were alone together I plunged into the heart of my problem, "After watching my mind and feelings, I seem to reach a fog or veil — something blocks my going deeper."

He understood instantly and said, "Doesn't the veil recede a little bit each time?"

"Sometimes." There were circumstances when it was much harder to be aware. "Doesn't alertness depend upon one's physical condition? If one is ill one isn't so awake."

"Of course it does. If there's pain naturally one can't think of anything else."

"Or no energy . . . ."

"Yes, that's it; one lacks energy. So one has to watch one's physical condition, being careful about diet not getting too tired and so on."

"You mean try out the effect of each food?"

"Yes, experiment with foods and watch the body's reactions to different kinds."

"If one is tired?"

"Then push the alertness."

"You mean in spite of one's condition?"

"Yes, but one can go only just so far and then the body cracks up."

Going back to my original thoughts I said, "How can I make meditation more intense?"

"What do you do?"

"I watch my feelings and thoughts and listen to every inner movement."

"So one watches the emotions and the mind with all its wanderings. To do that one has to be very alert doesn't one?"

"Is one aware of everything at once, or does one's attention wander quickly from one thing to another — thought, emotions, actions, sounds?"

"This thing is difficult enough as it is. Don't make it any harder. One has to be alert, physically, emotionally, verbally, mentally, everything all the time. It's like a house with different rooms, different activities going on; yet all are one unit." Krishnamurti's face expressed affectionate concern for me. "I think you need time to yourself in the morning, and then again in the evening, perhaps a walk. When I say alone, I mean alone. If you haven't a room to yourself, go out under a tree somewhere."

"The difficulty is to use the time properly."

"Expose all your problems. Spew out everything, jealousy, everything. Play with it. Then you'll no longer be nervous or angry; you'll be awake, alert, quiet inside."

As always I was deeply affected and I left feeling I had a lot to work on, for a long time.

As it turned out, his interview had to last me several years. I became extremely involved as a teacher in a new independent school and I seldom took a day off. Even in the summer, instead of resting I'd have to earn money teaching, swimming. There was an endless pressure of everyday problems and at night I'd lie awake worrying about all the things that ought to be done. It became increasingly difficult to find space in my life for freshness. Youthful vitality was all too soon beginning to dwindle.

The necessity for finding inner freedom from pressures and influences was urgent. Perhaps a better understanding of meditation would help. Fortunately, in June, 1952, Krishnamurti was back in Ojai and he was kind enough to find time for a conversation with me.

After we had exchanged greetings, he sat quietly and waited for my question. I said, "I've experimented with meditation, and for me the most effective time seems to be when I genuinely inquire, but too often the mind wanders unwatched."

"Since you've experienced this creative release of genuine inquiry, why don't you do it all the time?"

"That's my question."

"Yes, but we're doing it now. Why don't you do it more?" He waited for me to put the question to myself.

"Is it because you're lazy?"

"I suppose that's true; there's inertia. Much of the time my mind is concerned with problems or I'm preparing for the future; occasionally I'm lost in fantasy."

"Let us look at the facts that are preventing the genuine inquiry. You think of problems which could be done later; you're lazy, sluggish, waiting. Those are the facts. Never mine about any explanation as to why you do these things. Let the facts tell the story; the explanations won't alter the facts. Here." using his hands in a typical manner, "are the things which are preventing inquiry and over here is the fun of investigation which you know. Just look at the facts. Really see them."

"Especially when I'm alone, meditating."

"Yes, intensify the inquiry. Of course you can't inquire all day, but you can be alert. You'll find lots of energy. Push the inquiry so you're really vital, not so David Young can be somebody, but for the sake of inquiry itself. Would you like to go for a walk?"

I accepted the invitation as I have on many other occasions. We walked at a brisk pace through orange groves and talked about world conditions, but for the most part we enjoyed nature silently. Together we looked out over the beautiful valley and at the setting sun. Always at this blessed hour there's peace — opportunity for meditation.

On first listening to Krishnamurti I had the impression paradise was just around the corner and if we did as he said we'd be there. The inclination was to use his words as a formula to be followed and to be improved upon as he used new phrases. The task, however, proved to be impossible. There was a constant conflict between what should be according to the formula and the actual. Obviously I was going about it the wrong way.

Then one day I discovered the ability to look at a feeling without judgment, without doing anything about it. This opened a whole new world and indicated a meditative process quite different from the usual practices.

Generally, meditation means repetition of a mantram, a phrase, a chant or else concentration on an image such as that of the Christ or Buddha or on an idea such as goodness, peace, or love. These methods are not without results but they are mechanical in nature and eventually deaden the mind. On the other hand, inquiry into what is, a perception of the truth, is ever fresh, ever vital.

Most of my life I've depended psychologically on Krishnamurti's light and I needed to see him from time to time. This was helpful and at least led me to see the importance of being a light unto myself. Now I realize I must rely on my own light, however dim it may be. Instead of merely reacting to events and circumstances, instead of looking to experience, to music, to gurus, or to some other influence to shock the mind into a different state, I see the mind has to be its own challenge.

There is new energy, I'm no longer getting old too fast, and even though I'm sixty I feel eager for another twenty years of work.

Krishnamurti has given the modern world a clear, simple expression of the truth. As far as my own life is concerned his teachings have stood the test of time. I've found them to be universal and timeless.

With Leopold Stokowski

Editorial Note from "The World Tomorrow"

A journal which deals intensively with concrete social problems is all too likely to overlook the arts and their distinctive, tonic force in the advance of civilization. Here is art, exploring the art of life; a conversation, apparently casual, yet flashing with insight into questions with which all alert minds labour. We are permitted to print the conversation, informally, as it took place at Castle Eerde, Ommen, Holland, between J. Krishnamurti and Leopold Stokowski, famous conductor of the Philadelphia Orchestra.

STOKOWSKI: Every art has its medium of expression. The dramatist — stage, actors, lights, costumes, decoration in color and form. The sculptor — stone or wood; the poet— words; the painter — canvas and pigment; the musician — air vibration. It seems to me that music is the least material of the arts, and perhaps we could even conceive of an art still subtler than that. I was very impressed by a light-color organ called the "Clavilux", invented by Thomas Wilfred of New York. He has developed what seems to me a new art of color in form and motion, and it occurred to me that there are aspects of music that are extremely immaterial, that are almost pure spirit — and that some day an art might develop that would be immaterial, pure spirit....

KRISHNAMURTI: Don't you think that it is not so much a question of comparing one art with another as of the evolution of the individual who produces that art? With regard to the possibility of evolving an art still more subtle than music, isn't it the question of inspiration? Inspiration, according to my idea, is keeping intelligence, enthusiastically awakened.

STOKOWSKI: I feel that inspiration is almost like a melody or a rhythm, like music that I hear deep, deep inside of me, as if it were a long way off.

KRISHNAMURTI: Because you are a musician you will hear that intelligence to which you are awake all the time, and will interpret it through music. A sculptor would express that intelligence in stone. You see my point? What matters is the inspiration.

STOKOWSKI: But do you think inspiration has much "rapport" ......

KRISHNAMURTI: ....Yes, connection .....

STOKOWSKI: ......with intelligence?

KRISHNAMURTI: In the sense in which I am using it, yes. After all, Sir, that is the whole point. If you are not intelligent,you are not a great creator. Therefore, intelligence, if fanned and kept alive, will always act as a medium for inspiration — I do not like the word 'medium', because it is used in so many other senses; if you keep intelligence awake all the time, it is searching for ideas, for new rays of connecting itself with life, and that is what I call inspiration. You get a new idea because you keep your intelligence awakened.

STOKOWSKI: This is not the sensation I have inside at all. I can describe it this way: When I have an inspiration, it is as if I remember, become conscious of something which five minutes or ten minutes ago somehow came into my brain. It was there before, but had not come into my consciousness. I have the feeling that it has been there in the background a long time — I do not know how long — and that it has just come forward.

KRISHNAMURTI: I should say it is intelligence which is working to get this idea after all, sir, please let us take it concretely: a being without intelligence would not be inspired in the highest sense of the word.

STOKOWSKI: Not in the highest, no.

KRISHNAMURTI: I feel inspired when I see a beautiful thing, beautiful scenery, hear beautiful music, or hear someone recite poetry, because my intelligence is all the time seeking. I am keeping my intelligence awake, and if there is beauty, I want to translate that vision into something that people will understand. Isn't that it?

STOKOWSKI: That is one form of expression.

KRISHNAMURTI: And there are hundreds of forms. I am only one form in the sense that we are discussing, and there may be the form of a poet, a sculptor, a musician and so on.

STOKOWSKI: What is the relation between 'intelligence' in your sense of the word and 'intuition'?

KRISHNAMURTI: You can't divide intuition from intelligence in the highest sense. A clever man is not an intelligent man. Or, I should rather say that a clever man need not *necessarily* be an intelligent man.

STOKOWSKI: No, but often there is a great distance between an intelligent man and an intuitive man.

KRISHNAMURTI: Yes, because again it is on a very different scale. Intuition is the highest point of intelligence.

STOKOWSKI: Ah, now I feel entirely with you.

KRISHNAMURTI: Intuition is the highest point of intelligence and to me keeping alive that intelligence is inspiration. Now, you can only keep alive that intelligence, of which intuition is the highest expression, by experience, by being all the time like a questioning child. Intuition is, the apotheosis, the culmination, the accumulation of intelligence.

STOKOWSKI: Yes, that is true. May I ask you another question? If, as you say, liberation and happiness are the aim of our individual lives, what is the final goal of all life collectively? Or, in other words — how does the truth, as you enunciate it, answer the question as to why we are on earth and towards what goal we are evolving?

KRISHNAMURTI: Therefore the question is: if the goal for the individual is freedom and happiness, what is it collectively? I say, it is exactly the same. What divides individuals? Forms. Your form is different from mine, but that life behind you and behind me is the same. So life is unity; therefore your life and my life must likewise culminate in that which is eternal, that which is freedom and happiness.

STOKOWSKI: In the whole design of life you do not find any farther-on goal than freedom and happiness, any farther-on design or function for all of life?

KRISHNAMURTI: Now, Sir, isn't it like a child who says: teach me higher mathematics! My reply would be: it would be useless to teach you higher mathematics unless you have first learnt algebra. If we understand this particular thing, the divinity of that life which lies before is, it is not important to discuss what lies beyond, because we are discussing a thing which is unconditioned with a conditioned mind.

STOKOWSKI: That is perfectly answered, clear and brief. People remember something better when it is briefly conveyed.

It has always seemed to me that art-works should be anonymous. The question in my mind is: Is a poem, or drama or picture or symphony the expression of its creator, or is he the medium through which creative forces flow?

KRISHNAMURTI: Sir, that is a point in which I am really interested.

STOKOWSKI: Now, you are a poet and I am a musician. What

I am interested in is to compare our sensations when we are creating in our respective mediums? Do you ever feel a total stranger to what you have written?

KRISHNAMURTI : Oh, surely.

STOKOWSKI: I do.....and I wake up the next day and say, did I write that? That is not like me at all.

KRISHNAMURTI: Now I say that is inspiration. That is your intuition, the highest point of your intelligence acting suddenly. And that is my whole point. If you keep your mind, your emotions, your body in harmony, pure and strong, then that highest point of intelligence, out of which the intuition acts....

STOKOWSKI: ...... will act constantly ......

KRISHNAMURTI: .... and consciously

STOKOWSKI: And one can live by that ....

KRISHNAMURTI: Of course. That is the only guide. Now take, for instance, poets, dramatists, musicians, all artists: they should be anonymous, detached from all that they create. I think that is the greatest truth. To be, to give and to be detached from what you give. You see what I mean? After all, the greatest artists of the world, the greatest teachers of the world say: "Look here, I have got something which, if you really understand it, would forever unfold your intelligence, would act as your intuition. But don't worship me as an individual — I am not concerned, after all." But most artists want their names put under the picture, they want to be admired. They want their degrees and titles.

STOKOWSKI: Here is an old old question: is the Truth relative or absolute? Is it the same for all of us, or different for each one?

KRISHNAMURTI: It is neither, sir.

STOKOWSKI: Then what is it?

KRISHNAMURTI: You cannot describe it. You cannot describe that which gives you inspiration to write music, can you? If you were asked: Is it absolute or is it relative, you would answer: "What are you asking me? It is neither." You see, you cannot say it is the absolute or the relative. It is far beyond matter, time and space. Take, for example, the water in that river out there. It is limited by its banks. Then you might say, looking at the water: "Water is always limited", because you see the narrow banks enclosing it. But if you were in the midst of the ocean where you see nothing but water, you could say:' "Water is limitless."

STOKOWSKI: That is a perfect answer.....you do not need to say any more — that is complete.

Is there a standard or criterion of beauty in art, or does each person find his own beauty to which he responds? The question is related to the question of taste. People are always saying, this is good taste, that is bad taste. By what authority do they say that?

KRISHNAMURTI: I should say, by their own experience.

STOKOWSKI: That is a personal response. Then can any authority say what is good or bad in art?

KRISHNAMURTI: No, yet I hold that beauty exists in itself beyond all forms and all appreciations.

STOKOWSKI: Ah, then that is an everlasting thing.

KRISHNAMURTI: Like the eternal perfume of the rose. Sir, you hear music and I hear music; you hear a whole vast plane of vibrations, I only hear that much — but that much fits in with all your vast plane.

STOKOWSKI: Yes. It is a question of personal absorption, experience. So the answer is like that to the other question. In itself it is both relative and absolute, but for us it is relative.

KRISHNAMURTI: Must be!

STOKOWSKI: We see design in life, in the arts, in our body, in machines and everything, and the design of an automobile is made always with the idea of its function. What is the function of life, of all life?

KRISHNAMURTI: To express itself.

STOKOWSKI: How does order come from your doctrine of freedom?

KRISHNAMURTI: Because, sir, freedom is the common goal for all — you admit that. If each man realizes that freedom is the common goal, each one then in shaping, in adapting himself to this common goal can only create order.

STOKOWSKI: Do you mean that, in living up to the ideal of freedom, the ideal of beauty, we must all finally come to the same goal?

KRISHNAMURTI: Of course; is that not so?

STOKOWSKI: ....and so order will come?

KRISHNAMURTI: At present there are you and I and half-a-dozen others who have all got different ideas as to what is the final goal. But if we all sat down and asked: "What is the ultimate aim for each of us?" — we should say, freedom and happiness for one and all. Then even if you work in one way and I in another we still work along our own lines towards the same goal. Then there must be order.

STOKOWSKI: How should Society, organized in freedom, treat the man who takes the life of another?

KRISHNAMURTI: At the present time Society, working without a goal, puts him into prison or kills him; it is a just vengeance. But if you and I were the authorities who laid down laws for Society, we should keep in mind all the time that, for the murderer, as for ourselves, the goal is the same, which is freedom. It is no good killing him because he has killed someone else. We should rather say: "Look here, you have misused your experience, you have killed life which was trying to grow through experience towards freedom. You also want experience, but experience which injuries another, which interferes with another, cannot lead to your ultimate happiness and freedom." We should create laws founded on wisdom, which is the culmination of experience, and not on the idea of vengeance. If you had a child, and that child did something wrong, you would not promptly put him into a corner. You would make him see the reason why he should not act in that manner.

STOKOWSKI: But what would you do with a child before it could speak and before it could understand what you were saying?

KRISHNAMURTI: I would protect him from things which are harmful to others or to himself. After all, a murderer is only a child ....

STOKOWSKI: Yes, you would take the murderer and guard him from hurting others and himself, and educate him...

KRISHNAMURTI: Yes, educate him.....

STOKOWSKI: What is the highest and ultimate ideal of education?

KRISHNAMURTI: Teach the child from the very beginning that its goal is happiness and freedom, and that the manner of attainment is through the harmony of all the bodies — mind, emotion and the physical body.

STOKOWSKI: When the child falls below that ideal and hurts itself, or somebody else, or destroys beauty of some kind, how would you describe to the child what would be the ideal course of action, instead of the destructive course that he has followed?

KRISHNAMURTI: Put him into conditions where he will see the ideal. That is, precept, example ...... Sir, if you are a musician, and I am learning from you, I would watch every movement that you make. After all, you are a master in music, and I want to learn. Don't you see, that is my whole point — the example is lacking ....

With Carlo Suares

It is absolutely and urgently necessary to produce a radical revolution in human consciousness, a complete mutation in the entire psychological structure of man.

— J. KRISHNAMURTI

KRISHNAMURTI: What do you want? Real facts or erudition? A survey of my lectures? A synthesis of opinions? Ideas?

SUARES: This is not what is wanted. We need change....

KRISHNAMURTI: Psychological mutation takes place only when the process of accumulation ceases.

SUARES: You have used the word 'mutation'. It is being used often nowadays, but in the sense of a change in the world which will lead to an inner change in man, while you demand an immediate and total revolution in consciousness which cannot and should not be the result of an evolution in time.

KRISHNAMURTI: We all know how explosive is the present epoch. Man's resources, which remained stationary for thousands of years, have suddenly increased million-fold. We have now electronic computers with performances improving at a fantastic rate; soon we shall be able to go to the moon or further; biology will soon unveil the mystery of life and even create life. All the postulates of science are being questioned; established theories collapse one after another and the nest brains exert themselves in search of the new. We know all this; we do not need to go over it again. Among the universal confusion man seeks material security which only technology can give. Religions have become obsolete; they no longer influence the course of events; but the fundamental questions remain without answer. The questions of time, pain and fear.

SUARES: We all agree that everything in the world is undergoing a fundamental change; why should we not expect a commensurate change happening in our minds?

KRISHNAMURTI: Of course we should expect it. But what will be the mutation? Will an electronic brain do? Consciousness is not only brain.

SUARES: It is not merely a question of brain. Our consciousness has expanded to the size of our planet; it reaches out to the very end of the world.

KRISHNAMURTI: Yes, I know.

SUARES: The burning Buddhist monks, the African rebels....

KRISHNAMURTI: Of course they are all parts of ourselves: the terrible poverty of Asia; tyrannies everywhere; cruelty, ambition and rampant greed the numberless conflicts — all this is ourselves. Bear all this in mind and you will see at how deep a level the mutation is needed.

SUARES: In France at present the view is spreading that since world affairs have become infinitely complex, a collective mental effort is required which would assemble and integrate the tangled strands of our knowledge. There is also the problem of religions. Can we think of a religion of the future, based on all we know about the universe and on the deepest feelings of the human heart? And also the question of fear which lurks in every modern man, be he old or young. Could you tell me what are you aiming at?

KRISHNAMURTI: I want to decondition the totality of human consciousness.

SUARES: Which means that each one of us must decondition completely his own consciousness. But what puzzles us most in your teaching is your insistence that such total mutation of consciousness does not need time.

KRISHNAMURTI: Evolution needs time, not mutation. Mutation is sudden.

SUARES: The man who has changed completely will still carry his past with him. While he influences his surrounding, his surrounding will influence him.

KRISHNAMURTI: It is not exactly so. Man affects his surrounding and the surrounding affects only that part of him which depends on his surrounding. It cannot affect the whole of him, the deepest in him. No outer pressure can do it; it can affect only the surface of his mind. Nor can psychoanalysis cause mutation for all analysis needs time. Nor will it be precipitated by experience, however exalted and 'spiritual'. On the contrary, the more it takes the appearance of a revelation, the more it is conditioned. Whether the change is caused by subjective analysis or external pressure, it will not lead to a deep transformation of the individual; he will be merely modified, shaped and adjusted to fit into the social frame. In the case of a so-called, 'spiritual' experience, it either conforms to an organized belief or may be quite personal. Yet it is always an escape into a symbol; in each case the change is under pressure, moral or social and caused by a sense of contradiction and conflict. Society always contradicts itself. It demands effort from its members and creates conflict. But contradiction, conflict, effort, competition are all obstacles to mutation, for mutation is identical with freedom.

SUARES: Hence escape into symbols.

KRISHNAMURTI: The unexplored parts of the unconscious are full of symbolic images. Even words are only symbols. One must go beyond words.

SUARES: What about theologies?

KRISHNAMURTI: Leave them alone. Every theology shows immaturity. Let us not lose the point. We were talking of experience and that an experience always conditions. Every experience, not only the so called spiritual experience, has its roots in the past. All that I recognize as my experience, be it of God or of a man, implies a bond with the past. A spiritual experience is merely a response from the past to my anxiety, pain, fear and hope, a compensation for misery. My consciousness arrogates the opposite of itself, and imagines the opposite to be reality, happy, exalted and consoling. The Catholic or the Buddhist builds and protects the image of the Holy Virgin or of the Buddha and these constructions create intense emotions in the same unexplored layers of the unconscious, which have been responsible for the visions and now take them for reality.

The symbols or the words become more important than reality itself. They stay as memory in consciousness which says: "I know, for I had a spiritual experience". The words and the conditioning by words give life to each other in a vicious circle. The memory of an intense emotion, the impact of an ecstasy, create the desire for a repetition and the symbol becomes the supreme inner authority, the ideal towards which all the efforts converge. The re-capture of the vision becomes the goal of life, aspiration and ceaseless discipline — the means. But thought itself creates a gap between the individual as he is and the symbol or the ideal. Mutation is not possible unless we bridge this gap. Mutation can happen only when all experience ceases completely. The awakened man is free from experience. But everybody seems to be in search of ever deeper and vaster experiences. We are all convinced that the more experiences we have, the more we are alive. But we do not live reality; we live symbols, concepts, ideals and words. We feed on words, our spiritual life has become a perpetual conflict, because we live by concepts like the hungry man who eats bits of paper with `bread' written on it. We live by words, not facts. In all walks of life, whether spiritual or sexual, in our work or leisure, we are stimulated by words. Words organise themselves into thoughts and ideas; they excite us and the greater the gap between reality (what we are) and the ideal (which we are not), the more intensely we imagine ourselves to live. And thus we destroy all possibility of mutation.

SUARES: Let me repeat. Mutation is not possible as long as there is in consciousness a conflict of any kind. As long as the authority of the Church or State rules our minds, there can be no mutation. As long as your personal experiences create the inner authority based on memory, there can be no mutation. As long as we adapt and imitate, there can be no mutation. As long as there is evasion of any kind, there can be no mutation. As long as I strain in self-discipline, or believe in a revelation, or have an ideal, however exalted, there can be no mutation. As long as I try to know myself through psychological analysis, there can be no mutation. As long as we cling to images, symbols or ideas, there can be no mutation. I would even go beyond. As long as there is thought, there can be no mutation.

KRISHNAMURTI: Yes, exactly so.

SUARES: What then is this mutation of which you speak all the time?

KRISHNAMURTI: It is a total explosion in the unexplored layers of the unconscious, an explosion at the very core, at the very roots of conditioning, a demolition of time.

SUARES : Life itself is conditioned: How can one abolish time without destroying life?

KRISHNAMURTI: If you want to know, you must die to time, die to the entire concept of time, to the past, present and future. Die to systems, to symbols, to words, for they are all factors contributing to corruption. Die to your own psyche, the maker of time which has no reality, the time of memories and hopes.

SUARES: When consciousness has lost its bearings and is deprived of the very notion of its own identity, what will remain then but despair, anxiety and fear?

KRISHNAMURTI: You ask this question because you have not travelled that far, because you have not crossed to the other shore.

SUARES: What you tell us frightens us. And I am prepared to admit that at its very depth consciousness needs that fear. This explains why it always sought food and shelter in religions. Religions tranquilize and distract to save man from seeing himself as he is. Between reality and consciousness they build walls of verbalized theologies.

KRISHNAMURTI: This problem of fear is both deep and vast. Let us tackle it from all directions. Fear is thought, fear is time. We are giving continuity to fear as we are giving continuity to pleasure, by thinking. It is very simple — thought gives continuity to the thing which gave us pleasure and to the thing which caused us pain and fear. If I am afraid of you — or death — or anything, I think of you or of death and perpetuate my fear. But If I can face the thing that frightens me, fear ceases.

SUARES: How can it be?

KRISHNAMURTI: I am talking of psychological fear, not of the fear of a physical danger we want to avoid, which is but natural. Look at the fear of death. What is it made of? We divide the totality of existence into life and death. Life is the known and death the unknown. Are you afraid of what you do not know or do you fear to lose what you know. Life and death are clearly only two aspects of the same event. Once we stop considering life and death as separate, all conflict ceases.

SUARES: May I ask if there is such a thing as pure fear, fear by itself?

KRISHNAMURTI: There is no absolute fear. Fear is always of something. Look at it carefully and you will see. All fear, however unconscious, is the result of a thought. All fear, of the outer or of the inner, is basically the fear of extinction, of not being. Not being this or that, or just not existing. We know that all existence is transitory and, yet we crave psychological permanence and thus craving is the origin of fear. To be free from fear we must explore to its very roots this idea of permanence. The man without illusions is without fear. Which does not make him cynical, but indifferent.

SUARES: It means he has seen that the psychological structure with which he has identified himself is merely verbal, not real.

KRISHNAMURTI: So we are faced with a major problem: death. To understand it, not verbally, but as a fact, to penetrate into the reality of the fact of death, we must free ourselves of all belief, notion or speculation with regard to death, for every idea we may have about it is born from fear. When you and I are free from fear, we shall be able to state the problem of death correctly. We shall not be asking what will happen 'after' death, but we shall explore death as a fact. To understand death, all begging in darkness for survival must cease. Are we in the state of mind which does not seek beyond death, but wants to know what is death? Do you see the difference? If you ask what is after, it is because you do not ask what it is in itself. And are we able to put forth such a question? Can we ask what is death without asking what is life? And can we ask what is life as long as we have ideas, concepts and theories about death. What do we know of life? We know a consciousness ceaselessly struggling among various conflicts, internal and external. This consciousness is torn by contradition, enclosed in the ring of its own demands and commitments, of pleasures it pursues and pains it shuns. Internally we are living in a world which no accumulation of possessions, material or mental, will ever fill. In that emptiness there is no life, so the question of death does not arise. Is our existence life, and our theories about resurrection or reincarnation, do they arise from the knowledge of death? Are they not mere protections of ideas we have about the fragment of existence which we call life?

SUARES: I have a question to ask about religion. The great religions of today were born in times when the earth was flat and the sun was moving across the sky. Till quite recently they imposed forcibly on us a childish picture of the universe.

Compelled by necessity they are now coming to terms with science and admitting that their cosmogonies were merely symbolic. Yet, inspite of all, they still claim to be the sole custodians of the eternal truth. What can you say about it?

KRISHNAMURTI: They continue their propaganda in order to maintain their power over minds. They seek to get hold of children to condition them better. The religions, whether of Church or of State demand from man every virtue, but their history shows a succession of violences, terrors, tortures, massacres, horrors beyond imagination.

SUARES: Would you not admit that Churches now are less militant? Have not the heads of the great religions declared, that human brotherhood is more important than the details of a cult.

KRISHNAMURTI: If brotherhood has become more important than a cult, it is because cults have lost their value even to their priests. But their universalism is mere mutual tolerance, the bearing with each other under certain conditions. All tolerance needs the background of intolerance as non-violence of violence.

It is a fact, that nowadays religion, the true communion between man and what lies beyond him, has no place whatsoever in human affairs. Religious organizations, on the contrary, have become instruments of politics and economics.

SUARES: Are they quite unable to lead man beyond himself?

KRISHNAMURTI: Quite unable.

SUARES: Let us leave alone the religious institution and turn to religious urge as such. In a universe of Einstein are we not more able to commune with reality, because we know more and better?

KRISHNAMURTI: Whoever wants to enlarge one's outlook can pick up any of the sciences that suits him. To imagine that the knowledge of atoms and galaxies will enable us to commune with the universe is like maintaining that the study of books on love will give us the insight into and the power to love. And did the modern man, so conversant with the latest discoveries in science, lay bare the universe of his own unconscious? For as long as the smallest part of his mind remains unconscious, it will project words and symbols which will create the illusion of communion with something higher.

SUARES: Still, we can have one day a religion based on science.

KRISHNAMURTI: Why talk of some future religion? Let us see rather what is true religion. An organized religion can produce mere social reforms and superficial changes. A Church exists only within the framework of a society. And I am talking of religious revolution which will take us beyond the psychological structure of society, of any society. A truly religious man is free of all fear, for he is free of the patterns created by the many civilizations over thousands of years. He is also free from the past, personal and collective and his future is not distorted by the pressure of his own actions.

SUARES: Such a man, being free of his own content, which, in a way, contained him, must be extremely free....

KRISHNAMURTI: He is free, vital and totally silent. Silence is important, which is a measureless state, knowable as beyond experience, beyond words, beyond thought, an uncreated energy. Without this creative silence there can be no brotherhood and peace and no true religion.

SUARES: All religions talk of prayer, of some method of contemplation in order to commune with a higher reality, whatever its name, God, Cosmos etc. What is your religious activity? Do you pray?

KRISHNAMURTI: The repetition of sacred formulas calms the agitations of the mind and puts it to sleep. Prayer is a sedative which enables us to continue in our psychological prison without feeling the need of bursting it open and destroying it. The mechanism of prayer, like all mechanisms, gives a mechanical result. There is no prayer capable of piercing through the ignorance of oneself. All prayer addressed to the unlimited presupposes that the limited knows the unlimited and how to contact it. It has all kinds of ideas, concepts and beliefs about the unlimited and is enclosed in a system of explanations, locked up in a mental prison. Prayer binds, it does not liberate. And freedom is the very heart of true religion. Religious organisations deny man this essential freedom, inspite of their assertions to the contrary. Self-knowledge is not prayer, it is the door to meditation. Freedom is not based on a set of psychological theories nor is it a state of surrender in the expectation of grace. It destroys the constraints imposed by religion or society. It is a state of total attention, and not of concentration on the particular.

SUARES: Will the thought, the intelligence of mankind, having absorbed and assimilated the conquests and discoveries of all the sciences, be able to help humanity to grow towards sanity?

KRISHNAMURTI: The evolution we know, from bullock cart to spaceship, is only a limited part of the brain. Even if this part develops a million times, this will not answer the fundamental question which man puts to himself about himself. The evolution of science and technology will go on — it is necessary, inevitable and irreversible. But the remainder of the brain is there unawakened and we can put ourselves from now onwards to the task of bringing it to life. This waking up is not a question of time. It is an explosion, a sudden acceleration of the evolutionary process which takes place at the very source of being and prevents the crystallisation and the hardening, of the psychological entity. It is an explosion in lucidity, in insight, which takes up every problem as it arises and thus the importance of the problem becomes secondary and unless this burst of intelligence, which has its own source of energy, which is neither personal nor collective, takes place, the world will know neither peace nor freedom.

(Translated from the French)

Part III

Man, Nature, Reality

Chapter 13

Man, Nature, Reality in the teachings of Krishnamurti
by E.A. Wodehouse

The peculiarly intuitional method of teaching adopted by Krishnamurti in which every question that presents itself is dealt with, not by any process of discursive reasoning, but by the direct appeal to some central standard of Truth, even available for instant reference — is one that cannot but be impressive to those who have watched it at work. It is this perhaps, as much as anything, which has led many to set him apart as a Teacher, giving to the word, as applied to him, that special and exceptional sense which we instinctively signalize by writing it with a capital letter. Here, people have felt, is no ordinary teaching. The stamp of greatness is upon it. It belongs to the tradition of the Master-Teachers of the race.

But it has this inevitable disadvantage, so far as others are concerned that it is something which it is quite impossible for him to pass on. And this becomes felt a real difficulty when, as occasionally happens, any student of Krishnamurti's teachings is asked by friends to give them some idea of the main outline of his message and to single out its fundamental truths. For anyone, who is thus challenged, makes an immediate discovery. And that is that, in order to present the teaching to others, a technique of quite a different order is needed from that which works so admirably, and withal so effortlessly, in Krishnamurti himself. When Krishnamurti is speaking, the very fact that he has his own living Truth always, before him communicates itself in some mysterious way to his hearers, and causes many things to seem easy which are really far from being so. And this is what the would-be expounder at once finds out. Connections, which seemed so obvious when one was actually listening to him, have now to be painfully translated into logical correlations of thought. Points, which seemed almost to go without saying when he made them, have now to be reinforced with arguments, if they are to strike home. What, to Krishnamurti himself, is a living unity, immediately apprehended and fusing all the teachings into an organic whole, has now to be displayed as an intellectual interdependence. In a word, what is needed is just that framework of order and system, with which he, being what he is, can dispense. Otherwise the exposition will be a sorry one, and the inquiring friends will go away empty-handed.

The present writer had this uncomfortably brought home to him just under a year ago, when a friend, whom he was particularly anxious to interest in Krishnamurti's teachings, asked him what was the new thing, about the teachings, which separated them from others. When, in future ages, people come to look back upon Krishnamurti's life and message, what, in my opinion, would they point to as his great and outstanding contribution to the philosophy of the spiritual life?

I forget what my answer was, but I know that it was hopelessly stumbling and inadequate. I realized that, after some years of fairly close contact with Krishnamurti and his message, I had no synthetic grasp of the teaching as a living interested whole. And I thereupon determined to do my utmost so to grapple with them as to get them into some sort of perspective. In this I took the question that had been asked me as a test case. It was one, I felt, to which any serious student ought to be able to give an intelligible answer. Moreover, it interested me. Like most other students, I had felt the newness of the teachings. Indeed, I had always had the feeling that, if the whole secret of them could be laid bare, it would be found that Krishnamurti had done something no less epoch-making and far-reaching, in his own sphere, than the revolution wrought by Einstein in the domain of physical science. But what exactly he had done, I could not say.

I had been turning over the problem in my head for some months when I came in June 1930 to spend the summer at Castle Eerde. One morning, about three weeks after my arrival, I was working as usual in one of the summer houses overlooking the moat, and had written two or three desultory sentences with no very clear idea in my mind. When, however, I came to glance through these, I found, with a very real thrill, that they contained a hint of the thing I was after. Since then I have been at some pains to develop the possibilities contained in the hint, and the present brief study is the result.

Needless to say, no authority is claimed for these lines, and I should be arrogant indeed if I imagined that they had opened up the whole truth. They are purely a student's exercise and, even as such, only touch the outskirts of a great subject. All that I can claim for them is that the central thesis, which I have tried to work out in them, has been illuminating to me personally, and that it has helped me to get a little nearer to an understanding of the teachings as a whole. This study may be taken as an experimental attempt to give an answer to the question just quoted: — What is the great new thing about Krishnamurti's message? What will future ages be most likely to point to, as his outstanding contribution to the philosophy of the spiritual life?

Man the Exile

Every individual in the world, as he looks about him, is conscious of himself as a living unit, surrounded on all sides by a vast enveloping Scheme of Manifestation, which in turn he feels to be dependent upon an Ultimate Reality beyond it. And he feels too that this Reality, if it could only be understood, would explain the meaning; and purpose of manifestation and, in explaining this, would make clear by derivation his own meaning and purpose as part of the whole. An all-embracing spiritual Truth would, in other words, correlate these three terms in the order given, as parts of one organic synthesis. It would explain, Nature in terms of the Ultimate Reality manifesting in and through Nature, and it would explain Man in terms of Nature herself by relating him, as part of Nature, to the significance of Nature's own life. And in this way it would find a home for Man in Nature. She would become his Mother, not a stranger; and the very processes by which her life was being worked out would be the processes of his own spiritual self-realization.

For such a genuine Nature-philosophy everything poetical and mystical in Man has always yearned. There has ever been a deep instinct in him which asked for a Truth which should not be at the expense of Nature, but should include his life in hers. Man, in his heart of hearts, has no wish to be an exile within Nature's Kingdom, even though to be such an exile would be interpreted as a sign of superiority.

Stronger than any pride of aloofness has always been the call of the Great Mother. What the innermost soul of Man demands is a philosophy which will interpret his own self-fulfilment in terms of natural life. Not in spite of, not outside of Manifestation, but within and because of it, must he come into his spiritual heritage.

The Answer of the Religions

But how have the religious and spiritual-teachings of the past helped him towards his desired goal? Without exception, they have divorced him from Nature, because they could not (or did not) translate the workings of Reality, in and through Nature, into any terms which seemed applicable to the problem of Man. Instead of correlating the three terms — Reality, Nature and Man — into a living and organic sequence, making nature dependent on Reality and Man on Nature, they have cut the Gordian Knot in a kind of despair, and have sought to relate Man directly to the Ultimate Reality, leaving him fundamentally unrelated, or only negatively related, to the intervening Scheme of Manifestation. One and all, they have preached Man's spiritual self-realization as something to be achieved in opposition to, or outside Nature. They have taught mankind to look for the true life, not to the manifested order of things, but to the primal Reality outside and beyond Manifestation. Briefly, they have abolished the Natural Order as the intermediate term between Reality and Man. The one ideal synthesis, which could have harmonized the three fold ordering of experience as a whole has been broken in the middle. What should have been an organic Truth, descending through Nature to Man, has been short-circuited. Man no longer receives the gifts of the Spirit from the hands of the Great Mother. He is told to seek them from Reality directly.

The Reason

And why has this been so? It is because, in all the great spiritual teachings of the past, the relationship between Reality and Nature has been so formulated that there was nothing in it which could be handed on from Nature to Man. It has been the defect in all these teachings that — although they recognized that spiritual self-realization, for Man, meant spiritual happiness, and that no solution of life's problem could be accepted which negated, or disregarded, his deep instinctive demand for bliss — they failed to recognize that there can be no genuine Gospel of Happiness which does not flow from a fundamentally happy view of Manifestation. One and all they have made Manifestation an unhappy thing, and so have preached happiness, not because of, but in spite of it. Nature, for all, has been an enemy and not a friend. And thinking in this way they have destroyed the organic continuity between Reality, Nature and Man. They have linked up Man with Reality; but Nature has been left outside.

The Doctrines of Neutralization and Escape

That this is true needs little argument. At the root of all the accepted religions has been a repudiation of the actual in favour of the unrealized and the remote. All alike have started from the assumption that life in form and matter is, fundamentally, an imprisonment, that Manifestation is a burden, and that, therefore, not in the world of Things as They are, but in some other ordering of existence, is happiness to be found. And thus it is that, by all of them, spiritual self-realization for Man has been preached in terms of neutralization or escape. He can either neutralize the burden, by setting up some active principle within him, strong enough to prevent him feeling its weight, nor can he throw it off and break free from it altogether. Under one or other of these two representative solutions all past spiritual teachings can be grouped. The religions of neutralization have preached that a man may love so strongly that he will not feel the burden of existence, or that, by regarding the burden as a discipline, he may welcome it in its utilitarian aspect as a preparation for some different kind of life. The religions of escape have been far more uncompromising: "Break free now", has been their watchword. "Turn your backs on the whole order of Manifestation, and seek your fulfilment in the realm of pure unmanifested Being."

Space does not permit illustration here. But most readers will, I think, agree, as they glance back over the world's religions, that this feeling of the inherent burdensomeness of life in form and matter has been, throughout the ages, the keynote of the world's spiritual life. At the root of that life has been a profound pessimism about the This, the Here and the Now; and whatever hopes mankind has had of the possibility of the attainment of happiness have all, in one way or another, translated themselves into the language of the That, the There and the Hereafter.

Mysticism and Occultism

In this basically unhappy view of the Manifested Order, even schools of thought so unlike each other in their conceptual programmes of self-realization as Mysticism and Occultism have made common cause. For the Mystic and for the Occultist alike, life in form and matter is the very negation of freedom; and both of them have sought, each in his own say, to escape from it into the world of the Unmanifest — the extreme Mystic, by repudiating the world of external objects altogether; the Occultist, by a series of progressive repudiations, whereby he mounts steadily from one order of Manifestation to another, rejecting at every step the order that he has just left, his aim being to press ever upwards into regions of Being, where the burden of Manifestation is less insistent and matter subtler and less stubborn; and in this way, eventually, to emerge into freedom at the top. For both, liberation, in its ultimate or metaphysical sense, can only be attained by complete escape from Manifestation. There can only be one true freedom, and that is outside the prison-area. The Mystic seeks this freedom by endeavouring to break through the walls; the Occultist by climbing from story to story, of his prison-house until at last he steps out on the roof. The distinction is one of method only. Both reject Nature, or the Natural Order, and see the fulfilment of life outside it. Both, in the last resort, are active protests against Things as They Are.

What is it, then that all these philosophies of neutralization and escape have done?

The Exile of Man

They have made man a wanderer and an exile in Nature by separating him from the Natural Order; for they have interpreted this Order as antagonistic to his own spiritual life. As a dweller within this Order. he looks around upon all the wonder and the beauty of Manifestation; he sees the process of the seasons and all the changing wealth of field and wood and hill; he sees the pageantry of the heavens above him and the pageantry of the earth at his feet — upon all this he looks, and perhaps, in the hidden places of his heart, in the depths that are deeper than the philosophies, there leaps upon some buried instinct of kinship, and he feels, "Of all this I am a part". And then he remembers his philosophy; he recalls what his religion has taught him; and sadly he says: "No. Physically I am a part, but spiritually I am an alien. For the Absolute Life, which I am seeking, all this is but a burden and an imprisonment. From the point of view of that Life, in its free and unmanifested condition, this manifestation in the flower, in the tree, in the stone, is an unhappiness; for in entering into them it negates its own freedom. And since I, too, am seeking freedom, for Life in its absoluteness, what I seek cannot be found here." And so he turns away from Nature. In spite of every filial instinct, he cannot see in her a Mother; he cannot find in her his spiritual happiness. Her very being is the unhappiness of Life.

Such is the result of these philosophies. Seen in their light, Reality cannot transmit its bliss to Man through Nature; for Nature is the negation of that bliss. It cannot transmit through her its freedom; for Nature has taken that freedom away. And so, in the world of Manifestation he dwells as a spiritual stranger. He is the disinherited of Nature, for the simple reason that Nature has nothing to give.

Had Things been Otherwise

And yet, if things had been otherwise; If only Manifestation could be seen as a joyous thing, instead of as a descent into imprisonment; if only the Absolute Life could be found, in all its purity and freedom, within the conditions imposed by form and matter, instead of merely in the void; if only the workings of that life in Man could be shown to be but the carrying on and fulfilment of the workings of life in Nature; if only it were because of Manifestation, and not in spite of it, that the ultimate happiness could be achieved, and if that happiness belonged not to remoteness, but to the This, the Here and the Now — then indeed all would be different. The continuity of things would then be unbroken, and Nature would take her place once more as the middle term between Reality and Man. Through her Reality would flow to him; and in achieving his own spiritual self-fulfilment he would achieve her own aim for him. Then would dawn the real Nature-Religion, the Religion of Things as They are. For the philosophy of Rejection would be substituted the Philosophy of Acceptance. At last would become possible that Natural Life of which the poets and idealists have dreamt.

For the first time in spiritual history, Nature would have become Man's home.

What Krishnamurti has Done

Now, it is just all these things that the teachings of Krishnamurti has done for us, if we go down to its fundamental principles. The new thing about Krishnamurti's philosophy — the thing which, I feel, will be recognized in time to come as having marked a new era in spiritual thought — is that he has restored the organic sequence of which I have been speaking; that he has re-enthroned Nature, or Manifestation, as the mediate term between Reality and Man. And he has done this because, with the true instinct of spiritual genius, he has found a formula which does for us every one of the things which have just been mentioned as desiderata. It shows us why, from the point of view of Life, or Reality, Manifestation is a happy thing. It shows us how the Absolute Life — which other philosophies have been able to find in its freedom, only outside and beyond Manifestation — is to be found in all its purity within it. And it shows us how the spiritual self-realization of Man, so far from having to be worked out in opposition to Nature, is to be achieved simply by his taking over from Nature, and carrying on by transmission, something which is already at work in her. Above all, it shows to us how that ultimate or metaphysical happiness and freedom, which the Spirit in Man knows as its birthright, is a thing which can be won in the world of Things as They Are; how, indeed, it is only in and through the conditions of life in form and matter that its winning becomes possible at all. The absolute liberation, preached by Krishnamurti, is not a freedom from Manifestation; it is a liberation into it. Thus, in Krishnamurti's teaching, all the currents of Being are flowing in the same direction, and what Reality is doing through Nature it is also seeking to do through Man. There is no need, therefore, for Man to look outside Nature for his salvation. He is incorporated in her very being. His aims and her aims are one.

How the Change has been made Possible

How has this enormous change in the whole conception of

Manifestation been brought about?

It has been made possible by the simple substitution of one formula for another in the description of that Ultimate Reality which may be thought of as the basis of all manifested existence.

It has been customary in all spiritual thinking, which has sought to found itself on a Metaphysic, to conceive of this Absolute Reality as an infinite ocean of Being in a state of utter purity and stillness, of Being unsullied by a single qualification, unruffled by a single ripple of movement; and so to regard what we call Manifestation, or the emergence of life in matter and form, as an incursion upon this absolute stillness and purity. From this point of view all Manifestation is a limitation, since it robs that original Being of all that made it what it was. Infinity gives place to finitude; absoluteness is lost in particularity, formlessness is cramped and conditioned by form. The Unconditioned is now the captive of a whole host of conditions; the Unqualified has taken on the innumerable qualities of things. And so, in the very act of entering into Manifestation, Reality ceases to be itself. It has lost something — nay, everything — in its passing from Being to Existence. Conversely, the Life that is imprisoned within the Manifested area has to be thought of as regaining or rediscovering something (or everything), if and when it ever passes back out of Manifestation into its own primal state.

Manifested Life a Burden

To all philosophies of this kind life in form and matter is necessarily a limitation; and if they by descending degree of matter, ranged below each other in order of increasing density, each successive ensoulment by the informing Life becomes therefore an ever more stringent imprisonment, until the final darkness of incarceration is reached upon the physical plane. The effect of this is to leave Man — in his character of a physically-clad being living amid physical conditions — stranded, so to speak, on the very ultimate shores of limitation, with all the intervening strata of manifestation to pierce through if he would get back to that lost purity of Being which he feels to be his spiritual birthright.

To escape from this nightmare theory of Manifestation, to rescue Man from his *ultima Thule* and to restore his immediate contact with the purity and absoluteness of Life, it is clear that no partial measures will suffice. It will be necessary to go right back to the beginning of things and to reconstruct our whole conception of manifestation. Obviously, the "limitation" view must go. The primal relationship between Reality and Existence must be restated — and restated in such a way that any idea of "loss" or "imprisonment", as occasioned by the transition from the one to the other, must be shown to be false. The Absolute must lose nothing by self-manifestation. Matter must be shown to be no limitation. The purity of original Being must be shown to remain unchanged. We must construct, in short, a theory of absoluteness in the Manifestation instead of the accepted theory that such absoluteness can only be found outside and beyond, or antecedent to, the universe of matter and form.

The question is : how is this to be done?

There is only one way. Only one type of formula can give us what we require; and this is the formula which is the basis of all Krishnamurti's philosophy. Our ultimate of ultimates must cease to be static and become dynamic. We must set Reality in motion. For the formula of Pure Being, as described a moment ago, we must substitute the formula of Pure Creation.

Krishnamurti's teaching reconstructs the universe upon a fundamental principle of Creativeness. Life or Reality, he tells us, is not to be thought of as Pure Being; it is Pure Activity. At the back of everything — out and beyond the whole universe of Manifestation — we must conceive, not an ocean of stillness, but an eternal movement; and that movement is Creation. Creation is Life: to be is to create; take away creation and Life itself ceases to be. Consequently what we called Manifestation, which is only Life actively creating, is not a disturbance or a limitation of Reality : it is Reality in self-expression. It is creation releasing and so realizing, its own creativeness. It is the impulse to go forth creatively, set free as an actual going forth. And if we ask why there should be this impulse, Truth has no answer. Creation for the sake of creation is the last word that she has to say. Beyond this even the profoundest metaphysic cannot penetrate; for there is no beyond.

Now the significance of the formula of "Life of Creation" is that it possesses, of its own nature, an enfranchising power, which liberates, at a touch, the whole universe of Manifestation from the burden under which it has hitherto groaned. Into the world of form and matter it admits the fresh breath of Reality, allowing this to sweep through every nook and corner of it and cleanse it of all limitation. In Krishnamurti's universe the Absolute is no longer some remote abstraction dwelling in however many strata there may be of ever-increasing material density; for by such progressive densification creativeness, as such, remains untouched. To understand this, let us once more revert to our sculptor.

Creative Activities

The sculptor creates in marble. But there are other creative activities, which work in materials much less hard and stubborn than this. Let us arrange a few of these in an ascending order, starting from the "densest". The sculptor creates in marble, the painter in pigments, the musician in sounds, and the philosopher in ideas. But is the "creativeness" of the sculptor any less than that of the painter, or that of the musician any less than that of the philosopher? In other words, does creativeness diminish as density of materials increases? Surely not. A great sculptor is, in his own way, just as creative as a great musician. The difference is solely one of technique, conditioned, as all technique must be, by the materials in which it works. Again, is marble, as a creative medium, any less "liberative" to the sculptor than words are to the poet, or colours to the painter? Is it less effectual in giving release, through self-expression, to his shaping and creative ideas? The obvious answer is, No. The release is the same in all ceases, and is independent, in itself, both of the special technique and of the special materials employed. And so in a manifested universe also. If we start from the formula that Life is creation, then Life must remain equally creative, and therefore equally itself, in every gradation of material density with which it may have to deal. All that these amount to is a series of different creative techniques; and the difference of technique, as we have seen, leave completely unaffected the creative "release" which takes place at all levels, whenever a creative purpose finds expression in matter and form. This is the answer to that "nightmare" view of materially metaphysical aloofness beyond the utmost confines of Manifestation. It is not simply some pallid Universal, into which the host of particulars can be resolved, or dissolved. It is here, as a living Energy, in every concrete object. Pluck a leaf, and it is there; pick up a stone, and you hold it in your hand. The world about us is no longer a prisonhouse; it is open to the wind and the sky. Reality has ceased to be a stranger, it has come, in all its purity, to our very doors.

Life as Creation

To understand how the formula can do all this, and how it has been worked into the very fabric of Krishnamurti's philosophy, let us seek help in a very humble and ordinary illustration. The illustration in question will, I think, show how the simple change from "Life as Pure Being" to "Life as Creation" abolishes, at one stroke, the whole "burden" theory of Manifestation which has so long infected our spiritual thought and how, through this abolition, it opens up to us a programme of spiritual self-realization altogether different in principle from those two alternative methods of "neutralization" and "escape", which were the only two logically possible under the older view.

The Instrument of Release

Take a block of marble. For the man who is carrying it upon his shoulders, the block is nothing but a burden and a weariness; and he can obtain relief from it only in two ways. First he may have so strange an emotional incentive for carrying it that he ceases to feel its weight. Thus, he may be bringing it to someone who needs it urgently, and whom he loves so deeply that any service, no matter how irksome in itself, becomes a delight. Or, if we like, he may be carrying it to save that other person from carrying it — his motive here being the same. Or again, he may be shouldering it as a physical exercise, in order to develop his muscles; in which case he will put up with the immediate burdensomeness, for the sake of the ultimate good that it will do him. All these belong to the way of "neutralization." The burden is still there — the salient facts about it will remain its mass and weight — but this aspect of it has been counter-balanced and, so, effectively cancelled by something else. The other method is simpler and more direct. It is to untrap the block from the shoulders and let it fall to the ground. This is the way of "escape". Even here, however, it should be noted that the mass and weight remain the relevant facts. The block is no longer being carried, but it was because of its mass and weight that it was dropped.

One person, however, is there for whom the block is neither a weight nor an impediment; for its relevance to him is totally different. For him it is the very means and instrument of release. That person is the sculptor. Give him the block of marble, and the self-same qualities that made it a burden to the other are seen as the essential conditions of his art. The hardness and massiveness cease to be restrictive or oppressive; for it is precisely through these that he is able to create. All, therefore, that was felt as "burdensomeness" by the carrier of the block, becomes a liberation, when the block is looked upon, not as something to be carried merely, but as something to be fashioned creatively. It is still the same block, but its nature, or relevance, is entirely transformed.

Effortless Achievement

And so it is, with Manifestation. Substitute a creative relationship between Reality and Manifestation — cease to regard form and matter simply as things to be "carried" by the manifesting Life

— and at once we have a total revaluation of the universe. What seemed to be limitations now become essential conditions of release. We get a "free" universe, where formerly there was nothing but a burdening and an imprisonment. And the freedom remains, graduated Manifestation, to which we referred a few moments ago. From the point of view of Life-as-Creation, all such degrees are irrelevant. In all, it remains equally creative; and the release through creation is the same in all.

And now, since we are speaking of "release", let us ask ourselves a further question. What, in terms of creation, constitutes an absolute, or complete release? Surely, so far as the end or purpose of creation is concerned, it is when the creative idea, or intention, working in the material employed, and in terms of the special technique which this material necessitates, achieves its own perfected self-realization. For this means that between the idea and its fulfilment no obstacles have intervened. So far, on the other hand, as the creative process is concerned, the highest degree of such freedom will be when the creative energy works with complete effortlessness and spontaneity — achieving, with unerring ease, that at which it aims. Effortless and spontaneous achievement of perfection is thus the full formula of creative freedom. And so, in our philosophy of the manifested universe, if we can show that Life is creating within it with effortless and spontaneous perfection, this will be the same thing as showing that within that universe Life is, creatively speaking, free. The freedom in question will be creative freedom and, will be, in every case, realized in and through the materials in which Life happens to be working and the technique which these materials impose, yet without losing thereby its own purity and completeness. And this purity of freedom will be the freedom of infinite or absolute Life. In every such perfect achievement Life-as-Creation will have realized its own absoluteness. Wherever there is perfection, there the Absolute will have to be thought of as having found release.

Before, however, we leave this subtle and difficult question of "perfection" as freedom" — which plays so great a part in

Krishnamurti's philosophy, there are two further points that need to be brought out. One of them concerns the particularity of all perfections. The other has to do with the relation between any given perfection and the totality of Life. In both cases, our sculptor may once more serve us for illustration.

Perfection is of the Particular

Is the sculptor (we may ask) to be regarded as failing in perfection, if his statue — perfect in all other respects — has not the functions of a living man: if it can not think, or move, or speak? Clearly, no. The perfection of a statue is a particular kind of perfection, special to the art of sculpture and including only what is proper to that art. Again, supposing that our sculptor is engaged upon a realistic figure of an old beggar woman, is he to be thought of as having fallen short of perfection merely because the figure, when perfected, in terms of this intention is less beautiful than an idealized figure of Pallas Athene or of Aphrodite? No, once more, because the perfection of any given work of art is the perfection of that particular work; and nothing more than this is demanded of it. Every such perfection is a unique thing, and between it and other perfections there can be no comparative valuation based on superior or inferior dignity of subject matter. The perfect statue of a goddess is not, as such, any more "perfect" than the perfect statue of a beggar. We thus get the important generalization that perfection is always of the particular. To each thing its own appropriate perfection, and every such perfection is sufficient unto itself. And so we come back once more to the idea of an Absolute, which is realisable within the scope of the particular creative act, without losing anything of its own absoluteness. The idea is a difficult one, but it has to be strenuously clung to; for it is one of the most important that flow from the formula of "creativeness".

Further — does our sculptor, considered a living creative individuality, put less of that living individuality into a statuette than into a statue, or into a work of humble genre than into a figure in the grand style — provided, of course, that in each of these works he is striving for perfection? Surely not. Into every one of them he puts the whole of himself. He creates as an undivided personality, and the finished work — no matter how small in size or how humble in subject — stands as the expression of the whole man. Regarded, moreover, as the "release" of a creative idea, every such work, great or small, is an equal and similar release. In each case there is a total liberation, if the work be perfectly achieved. And so we get another very significant generalization of far-reaching philosophical value:— namely, of a Creative Life which realizes and releases the whole of itself in every creative act, yet remains, in spite of this, eternally unexhausted and undiminished of an Absolute which can enter wholly into the particular, imparting to this its own absoluteness, and yet is able to enter equally into countless millions of other such particulars at the same time. We have, in short, laid bare that profoundest yet most illuminating of truths — that, in a universe translated into terms of Creation, the particular is the Absolute, if it be only the perfect embodiment of the idea that it is meant to express — that, in such a perfected particular the whole of Creative Life is realized and, in thus realizing itself, achieves freedom.

We have now only to gather up the results of the last few paragraphs to hold in our hands the key-principles of Krishnamurti's retranslation of the universe. For it is by the application of these principles to Life in creative Manifestation that he is able to show us that this Life, in spite of every apparent limitation of form and matter, remains, as it ever was, absolute, pure and free. Nature, he tells us, is not the prison-house of Reality; it is rather Reality, or Life, set free. As the block of marble was to the sculptor, so are form and matter to Life-as-Creation. They are indispensable conditions of self-realization and release. Nor does increasing density of matter affect this creative self-liberation. It may impose a difference of technique, but the creative release is the same. In other words, our physical plane Reality is no less a Reality than that which is found on higher planes. In the world of physical things about us, Life Creative is just as fully present, and just as fully liberated, as in some world of infinitely subtler matter. For Liberation, in its creative aspect, is always independent both of the material that is being used creatively, and of the technique which this material involves — and is equally true and full in all.

Only one thing indeed can make or mar creative freedom; and that is the realization or non-realization, in all its fullness and purity, of the informing creative idea. For Creation, perfection is the only freedom — and the highest freedom is perfection spontaneously and effortlessly attained. And this, Krishnamurti teaches, is exactly what we see about us everywhere in Nature. In the perfection of every natural object, the manifested world around us proclaims (in the language of creativeness) the absolute freedom of the Life of which it is the expression.

Look where we may in Nature, we find a Creative Artistry achieving, spontaneously and without effort, the perfect embodiment of its own creative ideation. And here, Krishnamurti is careful to point out, we must not confuse this concept of perfection with things that do not belong to it. A beautiful thing is not thereby more "perfect" than an ugly thing; a more evolved thing is not thereby more "perfect" than one that is less evolved. Perfection, in every case, consists in a thing, or creature, being perfectly and exactly that which it is intended to be — in its own place and according to its own kind. What was said above about the sculptor should here be carefully remembered. This may now be slightly paraphrased, in order to bring out its application to Manifestation as a whole.

In considering "nature perfection", Krishnamurti teaches, and by "natural perfection" is meant the perfection of any object in living Manifestation, we must not ask of it that it should be more than it can be; for its perfection will consist in being exactly what it is, and no more. Thus we must not condemn the stone for not being a plant, nor the plant for not being an animal. The "perfection" of each is according to its kind. Nor again must we condemn anything, in respect of "perfection", because it is coarser, or less beautiful, or less pleasing than some other thing.

The flint has its own perfection, although it is not a diamond. The daisy has its own perfection, even if it be not a rose. To each thing, as was said above, its own perfection; and this perfection is sufficient unto itself. In Nature, therefore, we must not look for one perfection, nor for any general standard of perfection based upon objective qualities. We must look for an innumerable host of perfections, each of them proper to the object, or the kind of object, of which it is the perfection. And every one of these perfections we must regard as complete in itself — owing nothing to any other perfection and resisting, absolutely, all attempts at comparison or classification. Each, in short, is an Absolute. Into each the whole of Life Creative has entered, finding its realization and release therein.

Naturalness

And what is this but to say that the perfection of every single thing in Nature consists in its "naturalness" Every created object becomes perfect in being what is naturally is. The daisy realizes its "naturalness", becomes "perfect" according to its kind. And so, right up through the whole gamut of Nature, from the grain of dust to the very threshold of humanity, we find "naturalness" and "perfection" going hand in hand. Only in humanity does the rule fail, or seem to fail, for the first time — but that is another story, and we shall come to it in due course. Suffice it to remark, in passing, that the rule does not really fail. It is because something else in Man, which is in opposition to Life Creative, renders him temporarily `unnatural' that the continuity seems to be broken. Later on, when the alien element has been transcended and the Creative Life, in all its purity, has once more been set free within him — then, when he has attained what is called "Liberation", will he become "natural" and so, perfect once more.

The Dynamic view of Life

Such is the conception of "naturalness" as "perfection" which we find in Krishnamurti's teachings. To bring out its full meaning, one would have to write of it at great length. But we are concerned, at the moment, only with its bearing upon the general relation of Reality with Nature, or Manifestation; and enough has perhaps been said to indicate what this relationship is. Life, or Reality, Krishnamurti teaches, is free and absolute in every corner of Manifestation, for the simple reason that every created object, within the Natural Order, is the pure expression of its own informing creative idea. Simply by being what it is, simply by fulfilling its own "naturalness", it is, for the Creative Life that fashioned it and informs it, a manifest and achieved perfection and so (in the language of creativeness) a freedom. Meta-physically. every such object is an ultimate. It manifests, in absolute purity, the freedom and the fullness of Life.

And so our universe is set free. The exchange of a static for dynamic conception of Life has, so the speak, loosened up the whole structure of manifestation and let in light and fresh air where, before, all was darkness and suffocation. The burden and pressure of limitation, which made Nature an obstacle between Reality and Man — hostile to his spiritual aspirations, alien to the deepest instincts of his being — have once and for all been abolished. It is no longer necessary for Man to plan his spiritual self-realization in terms of the neutralization of a burden; for there is now no burden left to neutralize. He need no longer plan an escape; for there is now nothing left to escape from. The Reality that he seeks is no longer a stranger. It is here, all about him in the natural perfection of every created object. All that the poets have ever dreamed of Nature has made true. She can now take her place as the middle term in the great organic synthesis of Reality, Nature and Man.

Absolute Value

Such, therefore, is the universe into which Man must be conceived as being born, when he makes his appearance in Nature — a universe made up of innumerable single perfections, each an absolute in itself and each the product of a unique creative act, concerned wholly with bringing that particular perfection into existence; a universe, consequently, of which no relations can be posited except the simple and primary relation between the object and the Life that created it, and the simple relation of all such objects to each other, as manifestations of one and the same life; in which, in short, Life is itself the only common factor and the only possible relation. This is Nature, as she exists for Reality — a world free through and through, because every object in her is a sign and token of an absolute creative freedom and because, as a totality, she is the aggregate of such objects. And so, in a world of this kind there can be literally nothing that binds, nothing that can impair, in even the slightest degree, the integrity of the single object: no groupings of objects together in respect of qualities, no classifications of them in terms of value, no binding of them together in respect of some purpose that they are supposed to subserve.

No Gradation of Value

Life, as it looks upon the Nature of its creation, sees no common qualities, only uniqueness. It sees no gradation of value, since every object possesses its own absolute value simply in being itself. Nor does it perceive a purpose, binding any of its creations to any other, since one and all alike have only one purpose, and that is to express Life itself. And this can hardly be called a purpose, any more than it is the "purpose" of water, released from a height, to seek its own level, or of a solid body, similarly released, to fall to the ground. Life creates because it is Creation: that is all that we can say. There is thus, between it and its own Manifestation, no more purposive a rotation than there is between me and my reflection in a mirror. I am in front of the mirror, and therefore my reflection is there. Life is Creation, and so Nature is there. But it intends no more by its self-manifestation than I intend by my image in the glass.

And now, having endeavoured to describe the universe — purposeless, relationless, discrete, and having no further meaning for Life than that of simple manifestation or expression — which is Man's true home (if he only knew it) and in which he has to play his appointed role, let us now pass on and consider Man himself. What, let us ask, is this role? and how does he become, by virtue of it, the third term in our organic triad? We have seen Life as Creation passing, by its own inherent impetus, out into Manifestation. We have now to see, if we can, what further necessity it is that carries this Life, by the same process of organic self-unfoldment, out and beyond its simple manifestation in Nature, and sees it working for Man.

In the "free" universe, of which he have been speaking, the perfection of the created object marks the completion, or consummation, of the simple creative act. Thus the act which created this particular flower, or stone, that I happen to hold in my hand, must be thought of as having realized and completed itself in the perfection or naturalness of the object in question; and so on, right through the whole innumerable host of "perfections" in Nature. In every case, the Life impulse, that went into the bodying forth of uniqueness of the single object, comes to rest in the perfected accomplishment of that which (in the human idiom of "purposiveness") it set out to do. Every such perfection, from this point of view, represents a finality. It corresponds to the finished picture on the easel of the artist. And it is precisely here, if we think closely, that we shall see what is lacking in Life-as-Creation, even when it has created perfectly — and what no number of such creative perfections can ever supply. We shall see that there is something else, which has to be added to the perfection of the created object, if the Life that has achieved it is to find full metaphysical self-realization and self-release — the fact being that, in the very act of creating perfectly, something has been lost to it, which is just as essential to it as the purity and freedom which the perfection attests.

The loss of mobility

That "something" is its mobility. The purity and the freedom remain, but the creative momentum has been arrested; so that what went into the object as Life-as-Creation, dwells thereafter in it, not as Creator, but as pure Being. What has happened to it is just what happens to the creative impulse of the sculptor, when he has succeeded in expressing perfectly his own creative idea: — the impulse ceases to be creative and becomes thenceforth the indwelling "life" or "being' of the statue.

The perfection of all natural objects, therefore, must be looked upon as signifying two opposite things for Life. As the perfected realization of a creative act, it must be regarded as giving "creative" freedom to the Life that fashioned it; at the same time, it must be thought of as holding up the movement of that Life. Everything else that belongs to the absoluteness of Life still remains in it; only the onward impetus is of the very essence of Life-as-Creation, it follows that, in the very act of achieving a perfected self-objectification, this, Life, in its aspect of a vital movement, ceases to be itself.

The craving for restored movement

Thus seen, the world of objective Manifestation, or Nature, is both the release and the arrestation of Life — is both its affirmation and its negation. In relation to the creative process which brought it into being, it is a release. As an aggregate of perfected objects, remaining in existence after the perfection has been achieved, it is an arrestation — since the Life that was active and creative in the making of these is now, so to speak, locked up in each of them as pure Being. And this being so, it becomes clear that the simple act of self-manifestation in the object cannot give ultimate satisfaction to Life. There must be, on the contrary — at work within every such manifested object — a profound metaphysical "craving", on the part of the Life arrested within it, to recover that lost impetus, that onward movement of creativeness, which is of its very essence of Life. Full self-realization can only be opened up to it, when it shall have become creative and active once more.

The recovery of creative impetus

This, then, is that missing factor, the instinctive reaching out to which has to be thought as carrying our organic synthesis of Reality, Nature and Man, out of its second term in search of the third. Just as it was an inner necessity, inherent in a Life conceived as Creation, that carried this Life out into self-manifestation in Nature, so it is a further inner necessity, also belonging to it as Life Creative, that propels it on this further quest. Somehow or other Life has to recover for itself the creative elan, which the perfected object, as such has arrested. And not only has it to do this, but it must recover it in all that boundless fullness and freedom which belong to an absolute creative Life. Pure creativeness, in a world, has to be re-established; for only then can the Life, locked up in the world of objects as pure Being, become Life-as-Creation once more.

Its recover through the object

And it is here that we come to a difficult part of our subject. For when we ask: How is Life to do this? the answer has to be, that the momentum can be restored only through the agency of the very thing that now obstructs it. The lost elan cannot be re-started at the expense of Manifestation. The object cannot be abolished, in order that the Life, arrested in it, may find release; nor can Life recover its metaphysical momentum by the simple device of withdrawing from Nature and starting to create afresh. For one thing, this would negate the very "onwardness" that belongs to it as Creation. For another, even if it were to create afresh, it would still end by being locked in its own creations, and so be no better off than before, Only one course is open to it — and that is to go forward. Life must somehow or other press onward into its own world of Manifestation and find release by breaking through. It is on the further side of the object, and not by retreat from it, that it must seek to set itself once more in motion and, in this way, to extricate itself from Being into Activity. And this, it is clear, can only come about, when it has succeeded in creating an object which shall not simply arrest its movement, but shall permit it to flow through; an object, in other words, that shall be not a terminus, but a focus, of creative Life. Then, and then only, will it have forged the instrument of its own enfranchisement. Through such an object-focus alone will it be able to unlock itself from the world of its own creations and become creative beyond.

Man as object-subject

And to be brief — such an object it finds in Man. In the organic unfolding of Life-as-Creation through Nature, Man emerges as the third term, because it is in and through him that this metaphysical need is fulfilled. It is through Man that pure Being is once again released into creativeness, for the simple reason that he is what nothing else in Nature has yet succeeded in being — namely, object and subject as well. Janus-faced, he looks back into Nature as an object, and out from her as a subject; and it is by virtue of his subjectivity that he is able, so to speak, to draw the Life, that went into him as an object, out of Being into Activity, and to express it creatively on the further side. And to say that he is subject as well as object is only to say that in him, for the first time, the Life in Nature flowers into self-consciousness. "Man" in the sequence of Reality, Nature and Man, stands for the point at which Reality awakens into self-awareness and is thus set free to become Life-as-Creation once more.

The organic nature of the sequence

Such, in the purely algebraical language of our formula, is the significance of Man in the metaphysical unfolding of the World-Process. And we can now see why the process has been spoken of as "organic". It is "organic", because each stage is vitally linked to the others, and because the whole thing unrolls itself by a profound inner necessity. It was natural and inevitable for Life, being Creation, to express itself in Manifestation; and it was equally natural and inevitable for the Life — imprisoned as it were, in the very perfection of its own manifested world of objects — to seek release by piercing through these, in order to restore that mobility which is its essence as Creative Activity. Life being what it is, all this had to happen and so, in the working out of the vital sequence, each term both anticipates the next and gathers up into itself all that has preceded.

We have now, therefore, to follow the unfolding into its next stage — just as inevitable and as natural as the two which we have been considering — and to see how the eternal story of Life-as-Creation completes and rounds itself off. We have arrived at man, as the third term of the synthesis; it remains now to see what, in the teaching of Krishnamurti, is the part that he has to play in the great unfolding, and how all that has gone before is gathered up and consummated in him. And in order to make this as clear as possible, let us pause for a moment longer on the subject of the last few paragraphs, and try to state in a little more detail, what in the light of all that we have been saying, Man is.

What is Man?

He is, in the first place, — in his ultimate spiritual uniqueness — an object in that world of "free" and "simple" Manifestation (which we have already discussed). Every single human unit exists metaphysically for Life-as-Creation as a separate perfection, or naturalness, among the uncounted hosts of such perfection, of which objective Nature is made up. And because he is a perfection, he is also an absolute — a thing wholly unique, and removed by this uniqueness out of all relation or comparison to any other perfection. And we have only to remember what was said about all such creative perfection, to see that into every such living unit, just because it is perfect the whole of Life Creative must have entered. Every man therefore, as an object in Nature, is perfect by virtue of his uniqueness and is, for the same reason, the expression of the whole of Life; and this Life, in so far as he is an object, is locked up in him and dwells within him as his Being. Purely as object, consequently, Man is all that he can ever be. At the root of his nature is absolute Life, or Being — Being, which is, at the same time, universal and unique. And this Being we may regard as his permanent capital — as the infinite fundamental wealth that belongs to him as Man, but which, so long as he is object merely, remains vault-hidden and dormant.

But he is subject as well as object; and because he is a subject, he can become creative. And this means that he has it within his power to draw his hidden riches out of Being, or latency, and to set them once more in circulation. And this is precisely what, in terms of our formula, he is meant to do. For to be creative is nothing else than to translate his inmost Being into Activity. Every act of creation is thus to realize a dormant asset; it is to convert into creative energy something of what he already is. And so we arrive at the generalization that Man, as a metaphysical being, has not to become anything, for he is already in absolute essence; he has simply to express what he is — to release it and to convert it into current coin. And the end will be attained when he has transferred the whole of his Being on the other side of the equation — when, in other words, the Life that is in him is wholly released as Creation; when, from absolute Being, it has become absolute Activity. Then he will have become one with Life in the fullest and purest sense. Life-as-Creation will have realized itself through him in all its original purity, with the added glory that it is now self-conscious. And the way in which this has all to come about is that he should learn to create with the freedom, the perfection, and the effortless spontaneity, which Life itself exhibits in its own primal self-manifestation in Nature.

To become absolute Life-as-Creation is thus the end of every human being; and it is by becoming this that he completes the circle of the Life-process and leads it home to where it began. We have now therefore to ask ourselves what is meant by "creation" in this context. When we speak of Man 'creating", what do we mean by the word?

Man's creation

The creativeness of Man cannot be the same as that of the Life at work in Nature, for the simple reason that it moves in an opposite direction.* The primal creation was that by which the

---

NB: * The change of direction is really that which we find in a circle. The downward arc, and the upward arc, of a circle are, from one point of view, in opposite directions, yet the latter is only the continuation of the curve set up by the former.

Life displayed itself in all the infinite multiplicity and variety of the manifested universe; and its movement may therefore be described as starting from Life and ending in the object — for the object represented the completed realization of that which the movement set out to achieve. But now a change has taken place. The object has become creative subject; and so what was the terminus of one creative process becomes the starting point of another. That which went forth from Life and found its end and realization in the object, now goes forth from the object (turned subject) and finds its end and realization — where? Obviously, only in Life.

The creation of significance

The new creativeness ends in Life, as the other began in Life. It has to create, not objects, but Life itself. And how can it "create" Life? Quite simply, by rediscovering it. Its task will be, in other words, to deal creatively with the vast complex of objects which, in its totality, constitutes Man's environment — and which, of course, includes all other human beings like himself — and by so doing to re-create them out of their seeming objectivity and externality into what they really are: namely, expressions of Life itself. And this is only another way of saying that it has to translate them back into terms of their own original and fundamental reality — that it has to discover what they mean. Life, on the further side of Man, has to be recaptured in terms of significance. All that went into the object in the original act of simple creation — and which made it the unique perfection, or naturalness, that it is — has now to be recovered, and referred to its Source, through a process of laying bare its meaning.

Creative interpretation

And so "creation", as it emerges upon its new adventure in Man, become what may be more accurately called "creative interpretation". Such creation does not disturb the Natural Order, nor does it add to it. It merely transforms it by kindling it through and through with significance — by investing it creatively with the value and meaning which are already implicitly there. If we can imagine an artist who, by the working of some divine automatism, has created a number of masterpieces without knowing what he has done, and who then, awakening amid his own works, comes gradually to perceive their wonder and their beauty and learns, rejoicing, of the miracle of his own genius we shall have some idea of what happens to Life when it awakens into self-consciousness in Man. In the original Creation — in the bodying forth of that universe of separate perfections, or uniqueness, which we have referred to as the world of simple Manifestation — Life created perfectly because, being Life, it could not create otherwise. But the artistry was unconscious; it was as natural and spontaneous as the putting forth of leaves by a tree. And so, although the beauty and perfection were there, they were without significance; for there was no conscious mind to appraise them. Once, however, there emerges an intelligence, capable of appreciating and understanding all this wealth of perfection, then the whole universe of objects is transfigured. Then, so to speak, Manifestation is lit up from within. Everything remains objectively what it was; but at the same time everything undergoes a vital change, because value and significance have been born. Then begins Life and true ecstasy of creation, which is the bliss of the creative rediscovery of itself.

Reversed creation

It is into such a reversed creation, then, that Life is released, when, having at length fashioned an object which is also a subject, it escapes through the focus thus provided and enters upon a fresh creative career beyond — a creation that unravels every thread in the fabric of Manifestation and transmutes each into a golden strand of significance. The writer of the Book becomes its Reader. The Maker of the Song emerges as its Singer. Nature ceases to be a world of objects merely, and is revealed as a treasure-house of infinite meaning; and in penetrating to this meaning, Life comes into knowledge of itself. If, then, we would seek a formula wherewith to define Man's place and function in the world-process, it would be roughly this:— Man (we might say) in the organic synthesis of Man, Nature and Reality, is the living instrument through which Life-as-Creation, awakening into self-consciousness, comes into realization of itself by the creative interpretation of its own works.

Every individual a focus of creation

And when we say "Man" here, we mean, not Man in the abstract, nor humanity as an aggregate, but every concrete unit of the human race. For Life's work of creative interpretation takes place, and must eventually fulfil itself, through every individual alike. Each, in turn, must serve as a focus for that great process of self-discovery.

The Goal

And the end will be reached when, through the medium of any human self-consciousness, the vital creative principle comes to work with the absolute effortlessness of perfection which it knew in its original free state — when, in the whole vast universe of Manifestation, there remains nothing that it cannot instantly and unerringly interpret into terms of its ultimate significance, or truth. Then, in that supreme consummation, the individual becomes one with Life; for the whole of his being has been transmuted into pure creative activity. And when this happens, the three terms of our synthesis cease to be separate and are gathered up and fused into one. For Life, in interpreting Nature, reclaims her; the two become incorporate and pass into organic self-identity. And, by the very same process, the "I", within which the interpretation has unfolded itself, knows itself, in that final fulfilment, as the "I" of Life. At the end of the great cosmic story stands the man who has realized himself as Life Creative, and for whom Nature is the living organism which he has come to ensoul. Each, in that supreme illumination includes all other individualities within himself. For each, alike, "the universe grows I".

Every interpretation unique

But is this process of self-realization, then, identical for all? Does every human unit merely duplicate the experience of all the rest? No. For since every individual is in his essence unique, the interpretation, of which he is the instrument, takes on the character of that uniqueness. Every such rediscovery of itself through Man is thus, for Life, a fresh adventure. The Book is read a million times, but each time in a new tongue. The Life that started forth as Pure Creation, returns upon itself, as Significance, in as many different idioms as there are living units of mankind.

Infinite creation

And surely this had to be so. For the capacity for such an indefinite self-multiplication will be seen, if we think for a moment, to have been implicit from the first in the whole idea of Life-as-Creation. Life, being Creation, and being also infinite, must needs create infinitely. It must go on and on, multiplying itself as it goes; and to this process there can, metaphysically, be no end. And so, having bodied forth that infinite host of uniqueness which makes up the universe of simple Manifestation, it cannot rest here. Each of these must in turn become a centre, from which the whole creative process can be originated anew. Nor is it enough that every such fresh creation should be merely numerical addition; it must be totally new in turn. In this way, the multiplication will be not only quantitative, but qualitative also, and it must go on for ever — an eternity which is made possible by the fact that simple Manifestation itself never ceases. The creation of objects is ever being replenished and renewed and every one of these must sooner or later be urged to the point where it becomes a subject; for the urge is inherent in Life itself. And so, new foci must continually be emerging, — each of them, in the purity of its uniqueness, opening up a fresh self-revelation to Life. We are confronted, in brief, by the mystery of a Life Creative, which multiplies itself to infinity, while remaining eternally the same.

The last few paragraphs have carried us into rather high and abstract regions; but the principle, I think, is clear. It is the function of every human being towards every other human being to recreate the universe about him in terms of its living significance, until he comes to understand it and to feel it in that purity and fullness of meaning which it bears for Life itself.

And when he is able to do that, he will have become one with Life; for there will have been established within him, in full consciousness, that simple relationship to the whole world of manifested objects, which was Life's relationship (albeit unconscious) when it created them. The Eye of Life will have awakened into vision through his seeing; the Heart of Life will have learnt to beat with his. And this is a thing which every man must do for himself, since, being unique, he can look for help to no other. He must offer up his uniqueness to Life as Life confers its universality upon him. He can only begin to interpret truly, when he has become utterly and uncompromisingly himself.

The ultimate verb

And so we see that, in the light of our formula of Life-as-certain, everything in the higher, or spiritual, life of Man has to be expressed creatively — in terms of recreation or interpretation. The ultimate verb in the life of the Spirit is not to be, in the sense of passive Being. It is to make, or create. Man has, in his life of everyday, the capacity for creative interpretation that he is habitually able to exercise. His world is, at any given moment, the degree and quality of significance that he has been able to read into it. In the perfecting, therefore, of his recreativeness lies the perfecting both of himself and of his world. And both of these will have reached perfection, when with effortless and spontaneous certainty, he can translate the whole universe of Manifestation, as it presents itself moment by moment to his experience, back into the infinite depth and richness of its ultimate Beauty and Truth.

In such perfection of creative understanding and feeling lies the final self-realization of Man as a spiritual being. And yet, though final, it is not really an end: it is, rather, a beginning. For it is only when he has thus become a living principle of pure interpretation — when Life-as-Creation flows freely through him and Life-as-Significance lies before him as an open book — that he achieves his full metaphysical Manhood and enters upon his true life in the organic synthesis of Reality, Nature and Man. In the teachings of Krishnamurti, Man only becomes metaphysically "Man" at the moment when he becomes Life.

Part IV

Personal Reactions

Chapter   14

A Letter to Krishnamurti
by Reynold Welvaert

In my last talk with you I have put forth the question: "How to
realise this self-integration, in which our thoughts and feelings
are spontaneously co-ordinated, producing in us the fundamental
unity in which there is total peace?" We know so much of
philosophy and literature, we have so much of our own
experience that for each and every question we have a reply all
ready.

We cannot silence the false expert in our mind, the records of
memory turning out and throwing up endlessly the known. We
know all this and struggle sometimes against the thraldom of
memory and we want to throw overboard the part of ourselves
that presents or hampers living, but then we are in confusion:
without memory we cannot understand, and we end up
frustrated, because in seeking relief from pain we have ampu-
tated the painful limb, we have discarded a part of ourselves.

How to escape duality? How is unity discovered?

Our discussion ran more or less on these lines: —

What are you seeking, asked Krishnamurti,

—I am seeking integration.

—Do you know what is integration?

—No.

—How can you seek a thing you do not know? Can you seek God, Love, Truth, the Unknown? Do you see that such a thing is impossible? Not one of the ways you know will bring you to it. When you have fully understood that your habitual approaches are blind alleys, what are you to do? You are in front of me and I want to understand you.

—What am I to do?

—I look at you, I see your complex mind; I also see your dress. I have to be aware of you integrally, without judging, comparing and so on: then only shall I be able to discover.

When you look at a glorious sunset, what is your state? Full of quiet, able to perceive unconditionally the beautiful and the ugly. Such a state comes when perception shaped by memory has ceased.

It is only when the mind is motionless that the unknown can enter, there is communion, there is love in action.

A mind pacified by satisfaction of desire or stilled by the effort of will or immobilized in the search for and achievement of a result is entirely different from a mind which is free of motivated effort, merely silently perceiving, giving attention and choicelessly, spontaneously concentrated in the Now. There is deep quiet in a consciousness altered by the urgent need of insight into the present moment.

It is a state free from dreaming, free of our habit of total commitment, neither exclusively emotional nor exclusively intellectual, neither observation nor abstraction. In that state we feel completely free and yet one with every passer-by. We are serious without being affected, we are disengaged from all conditioning. This quiet is not a habit nor the result of a method, a technique, but a revolution ever renewed, a vital urge perennially understood and expressed. It is a state of fluid perceptivity, neither crystalized nor dogmatised, but so acute, so penetrating, that all our powers, mental emotional and of action are balanced and move in harmony. The goad of the unknown keeps our thoughts and feelings still.

The intensity of the present integrates the many layers of our consciousness. The wall between our desires and the opposing ideas is no more and we have a view of the whole of existence in a manner we could never had expected. This new insight into the unknown brings in a great silence which is also extreme alertness. And all so disconcertingly simple to a mind habitually lost in its complexities. Things, events, life itself are seen in their naked simplicity, without the covers our illusions throw over them. A drowning man needs being hit violently to make him see his condition and shake off the paralysing fear. Similarly the self holds on to false values until life wakes it up to reality by facing it with the unexpected.

The psychological 'surgery' (which I resented so much) was applied to the unexplored part of my unconscious rather than to the daily 'surface' consciousness. A new state came into being, of freedom from all self-identification with feelings, words and ideas, a state of such subtlety and fluidity, of such flexibility and richness of expression, that it is exceedingly vulnerable, for there is nothing automatic in it; it disregards nothing.

Suddenly, clearly, effortlessly we see ourselves to the furthest depths. In the beginning we try to escape by a vigorous display of memory and erudition to block the contact, to look away from reality. But growing pain makes poignant the tragedy of our condition, the misery in which we vainly seek complaisance. The drama of our existence grows on us and we seem to witness it more terrified than ever, yet in the depths of us we feel an extraordinary peace.

The surface anxieties and fears are mere habits of thinking, which refuse to die and prevent us from seeing the real as it is.

In the clarity of the present moment all valuations, comparisons and judgments are burnt up. We are fully aware that we are in prison. We feel the weight of conditionings, made up of automatisms, of reactions of self-identification with sensations, with greeds and lusts begetting thoughts, shaping our illusions. Our self jerks madly, feeling its end coming. We drink our bitter cup to the last drop, we go round our prison for the last time so that we may feel and understand fully what is illusion, separation and sorrow.

And suddenly the curtain splits. We understand our entire being, we feel one with all, at least for a moment. Then the curtain falls, we are back in our former state; we try to find a way to a repetition and we find that we have no control. All we can do is to watch the illusions we keep on creating as well as their creator and the day will dawn when the unknown will come to us.

(Translated from the French)

C h a p t e r   15

There Is
by Carlo Suares

There is. This is a statement. There is — this is my first statement. There is — light, There is — many lights. There is — Earth and her breathable air. There is — life. There is — movement. There is — consciousness of all there is. There is a human consciousness facing all there is, compelled to state: — there is. There is — and that is all. There is — and no more. Why no more?

Because 'There is', whatever is, is un-understandable. There is — the simple fact: there is — that there is something — is un-understandable. There is a grain of sand — and the mystery of it is beyond all power of imagination. The very discovery that there is fills me with wonder. I am so full of it that in me there is no place for anything else, for any religion. My many friends, Christians and Jews, Musalmans and Hindus praise their own religion as the only true, the truly revealed. Each claims divine origin for his own. When I study these revelations, I find the mystery of mysteries, the pure *there is*, unfathomable, untranslatable being triturated, masticated, cooked and sieved and made assimilable by weak minds which are afraid to admit that we all live in an un-imaginable, unthinkable, universe. The mystery of 'there is'? How simple! The universe is a double mystery, created by a triple mystery. (You did not know? Yet it is so!) The triple mystery of the Para-Brahman dreams up the world's double mystery (you did not know? Yet it is absolutely true!), which explains the simple mystery of 'there is'. This is what we get from religious revelations: They pile mystery upon mystery and their childish explanations put us to sleep. The mystery which is real, immediate, actual, constant, present with us, day and night the *there is* is being pushed down and hidden in the obscurity of the sanctuaries, thrown into a no-more past (the world has been made — it is over, why think of it?) or into a not-yet future (when you die, you well know!). The less clear, the more convincing are the explanations. But the cause is in its result, is here, now in the present. My will is indestructible and lucid: I do not want to be drugged by explanations. There is no first cause — the true cause is now, living, active, never as active as now. There is no effect, all is cause of the simple fact: *there is.* Tell me that the universe is two billion years old and infinitely finite within its curvature. Tell me that what happened happened two billion years ago when there was nothing not even space. Tell me the universe having a beginning, must have an end and therefore, may be, it has no middle! I am not going to be obstructed by what happened two billion years back. There was, there will be — all this meant or will mean: *there is. There was is there is* no more, *there will be* is *there is* not yet. Let the universe expand for two billion years and then explode into-being and recommence after some more billion years — it does not reduce my wonder before the mystery of 'there is; (a grain of sand). The presence of the smallest thing contains the mysterious totality which is un-imaginable. I can see and understand as everybody can see and understand, that all that men have invented to think about the un-thinkable and explain the inexplicable is childish or plain silly worth only to be thrown away. Hence my statement which is simple, bare, un-disputable, truly universal: *there is.* I am bent on seeing the fact of *there is* in all its wickedness and forbid myself every escape every idea, every concept, all that makes up for thinking; my pure and simple awareness of the fact *there is* is made possible by the acute perception of my utter incapacity to go beyond my mind. This awareness of *there is* is in fact, the end of all seeking and all knowing. It brings out the creative spark in a mind left alone to face the fact.

The statement *there is* is neither subjective nor objective. There is awareness of *there is,* not the consciousness of my saying so. No. 'I think there is' or 'I know there is' are no inventions of mind but just *there is* in its inexhaustible fullness. From generation to generation men continue their endless disputations about consciousness; some find in the mind the origin of nature, some seek in nature the origin of the mind. Amidst their wranglings they forget what comes first — consciousness or nature or may be, just the illogical, un-understandable *there is.* Some take the mind to be thought only; some take thought to be the product of the mind. The wretched problem of the subjective and objective, the 'me' observing and the 'thing' observed is born of evasion of the simple naked fact: there is.

I say: 'there is', I do not say: 'I think there is'. To make a statement, I must think, but the fact *there is* is beyond thought. I know why it is beyond thought: in *there is* time and space are united in a way which I cannot conceive, while light, reflected and dispersed, makes visible the world in which we live, and so does our consciousness, reflected and dispersed, scattered among sensations and perceptions, thoughts and feelings, creates our inner, subjective world. I know it, for to know it I need only to look at my mind. Consciousness either is determined by its content based on sensations and memory traces or it is independent of content (denoted by the unimaginables like Absolute, Eternity, Infinity, God etc.). Unimagined, hence void. Yet this void is myself, the negation of myself, and therefore a reflection of myself as I know myself — the sum total of all 'there is' experienced up to now.

All experience being based on the separation of time from space, on measuring time and space in different units, I conclude that all things and thoughts are caused by this separation of *there* is into *where?* and *when?*

(Translated from the French)

Chapter   16

The Basic Challenge
by Vimala Thakar

The awareness of "something beyond" dawned upon me at the age of five. The traditional concept of a personal God had become a living reality. So the search started at that early age. By the time I was twelve years old I had read the biographies and life stories of nearly all the leading Indian saints. Ramkrishna Paramhansa, Vivekananda and Ram Tirtha had captured my mind. At the age of fifteen the Personal God was replaced by "Soul Force". Those were the days of intense intoxication and I used to move about, without the slightest regard for what was going on around me.

While at University I studied Logic, Ethics, Psychology and Metaphysics. That widened my horizons. I came to learn that Hinduism and the Hindu concept of Atma were not the only attempts at fathoming the depth of Life. Plato and Aristotle, Hegel and Immanuel Kant took me into a romantic new world. Sufism thrilled me. The Life of Jesus Christ nearly possessed me. General study of Buddhism was sufficient to make me see very clearly that there were no absolute categories in Reality and that it was necessary to postulate a fixed and static truth as the foundation for meditation.

Then came the journey to the United States of America. My

short stay in the States and England made me aware of the impact of scientific and technological advance on the human mind. It inspired me to apply a new scientific approach to total human life. I returned home and wiped out all the ideas and ideals regarding spiritual life. The urge to attain liberation or Moksha in the traditional sense of the term melted away.

By that time Vinoba had launched the Bhoodan Movement. Its undaunting faith in man's innate goodness and its nature of a romantic adventure to bring about a radical change in the very structure of human society as well as a radical revolution in the very substance of the human mind attracted me toward that movement. I worked in it for eight long years. The Movement made me visit practically every State of India. I crossed the country up and down addressing public meetings, organizing training camps for workers, collecting land donations and distributing land to the landless labourers. It was quite an experience to face the living India.

The work introduced me to different systems of political thought. In those days I mentally travelled with the pioneer socialists in Europe and United Kingdom and was fascinated by their intense desire to bring about a qualitative change in the human mind and to change the total evaluation of human life. I went to Yugoslavia and spent six weeks there. I could feel that the qualitative change had not materialised and the old values were still lingering, though in disguise. My second visit abroad took me from Yugoslavia to Italy, Switzerland, Scandinavia and the United Kingdom. Those six months brought the realization to me that the human mind was still in bondage. Nationalism, racialism, and such other exclusive loyalties had estranged man from man.

I awakened into the consciousness that one must get over the outmoded divisive concepts of Nationalism, National Sovereignty, which were only euphemistic names for racial ego, ideological ego. And I also realized that one must get the better of the mind itself which was a creation of different types of conditioning. I was fortunate enough to come into contact with J. Krishnamurti.

He helped me to sharpen my reason and refine my sensitivity. He helped me to see that Humanity was facing a terrible challenge. The challenge consisted in the need to jump out both of the conscious and the unconscious mind. Either the human being jumps out of all the layers of the mind, wipes out everything ruthlessly and pushes back the frontiers of consciousness on all sides or he rushes headlong towards the precipice of total destruction. In the light of that realization my interest in creating a nonviolent society faded away. I felt very deeply that no human problem could be tackled on the canvas of one country. That would deprive me of the right perspective and would drag me into a fragmetary approach. Every problem was, thus, essentially a World Problem. Only that mind which had ceased to belong anywhere, could understand the full implications of the world problem. The mind which was entirely free could fearlessly proceed to think afresh about human life.

It is not easy to analyse the state of mind which this staggering consciousness had created. That consciousness played havoc with my inner life. With the dropping away of conceptual thinking all the cherished symbols and ideals were thrown to the winds. The ego was torn to pieces. Nothing can describe the pangs and agony experienced in those days. The pitiful condition of the mind which turned to every refuge, visionary and imaginary, defies description.

Soon after my return from abroad I become seriously ill and had to spend eight months practically in bed. That illness gave me sufficient leisure to go deep into myself. The same illness compelled me to go abroad again in 1961. This was my third visit to the man in the West.

I saw that he was completely disillusioned, that he was haunted by the fear of a World-war, that he was frightened by the apprehension of complete annihilation. I saw that the United Nations was becoming less and less effective as an agency for resolving international conflicts and tensions. The co-existence of the communist and the non-communist blocks had changed the complexion of both of them.

Moreover, I found that some of the most eminent psychologists in the West were dissatisfied with the knowledge they had obtained about the human mind. That the collective unconscious is indestructible and that the residue of racial unconscious cannot be unravelled completely, did not satisfy me any more. Yet it must be admitted that the psychologists of the West were foremost in realizing that psychological transformation is the basic challenge of today.

Thus I arrived at the turning point. Thus did I feel obliged to respond to the terrible challenge. The compulsive urge to respond led me to the study of the nature of the challenge and its implications in every aspect of life.

Chapter   17

What Krishnamurti has meant to Me
by H.W. Methorst

I find it extremely difficult to answer this question without falling into theoretical generalities, for the first meeting with Krishnakmurti's ideas did not mean for a change-over. I had nearly written "unfortunately not", for so much have his words been in accordance with my own mental picture of the world that I have agreed with him from the very beginning, perhaps too much. And my attitude has not changed since then. Over and over again I agreed too much with him mentally, though on re-reading his books (often when translating them, for example) suddenly a new aspect revealed itself, so that words already well-known at once became completely new for me: but never a shock or conflict.

Yet from the very beginning, but much more consciously during the last few years, I have sought to acquire the necessary distance from his word. When writing, I carefully — though quite unconsciously — avoid quoting his name, in order to try, for heaven's sake, to say what comes from me, instead of trying to parrot him. Quotations would present Krishnamurti, as well as myself, in a false light to the majority of readers; I would become a disciple and he a leader. The regrettable result of this is, that it becomes more and more difficult to make his words and ideas more widely known; thus Krishnamurti remains relatively unknown. Whereas, one would like to say, if possible: "This is so tremendously true, please take serious notice of it." But there remains an invincible diffidence or shyness lest the other person's reaction reveal misunderstanding — inevitably putting the whole question on the wrong level: "He uses propaganda to get me round to his own movement or opinions."

The way in which Krishnamurti has been important to me will show itself naturally in my words, for every personality "influencing" us, including Krishnamurti, means a door opened onto the sphere of our individual task, our problem, our keenest interest. He who approached life originally from the religious aspect, will discover in his words an attack on religion or a renewal of his religious feeling; the socially inclined will appreciate his change of focus from the social to the individual, the philosophically inclined, the shifting from philosophy to the purely human; while those interested in psychology will realise the great difference from professional psychology, the change from analysis to synthesis from the methodical approach to spontaneous interest in the living moment.

As I was in agreement with Krishnamurti from the beginning, the group-discussions which he held had by far the greatest importance for me; not somehow by a 'tradition of personality", however activating this may temporarily be (I did not come originally from a Theosophical or other spiritual movement), but simply because when discussing one is more active inwardly than when listening or reading. In discussion, even when one is not oneself speaking, one is continually prepared to answer, to take sides; thereby revealing oneself naturally. Unexpected answers and reactions from one of those discussing may hurt, shock and unbalance us, giving us an unexpected vision of one of our own 'sore points". This kind of thing has nearly always meant very painful consequences for me, and although I could live on this level only a few hours a day and was then nearly exhausted, I felt also that this was extremely vivifying and intensifying because it threw new light on my own reactions and habits, which was the more helpful and honest since it was unintentional. For nothing in Krishnamurti's way of speaking indicated the will to influence, to admonish, to be tendentious. No light is more effective than the one falling unintentionally by impersonal, unbiased examination (I avoid the wrong and often misused word "objective" — for every living discussion is highly subjective also, surely)....

What strikes me personally is the highly paradoxical and grandly contradictory nature of his expression. which makes for a better approximation to truth and a more adequate avoidance of illusions and anchorages than anyone has been able to give since Lao-tze. And this not by relativating everything either...nor by robbing life of the intensity of shock and absurdity... not even that.

I can most definitely say that Krishnamurti is not Oriental in this respect — certainly not. The typical mentality of the Oriental is to be found, for instance in a (to me very unessential and mediocre) book called "The Vedanta for the Western World," with its characteristic "using the higher to conquer the lower", typical Western mentality, perhaps, in the great mathematician, philosopher and educator, Bertrand Russell — the "mystical" person versus the "reasonable" one. Krishnamurti has as much or as little affinity with the one as with the other — that is, none. In him I find a synthesis, which, like every true synthesis, is essentially different from the two poles of the opposition: Western-Eastern; philosophical — psychological, mystical-mental; social-individual; masculine-feminine. His word is paradoxical, because it belongs to a state of being which does not yet exist and which our language cannot express. If what great mystics or thinkers meant or experienced was, perhaps, the same un self-conscious that Krishnamurti tries to express by means of the negation, then this has never shown forth sufficiently clearly from their words; it was much too mixed up with an old, misleading terminology, or coloured by the gratefulness of memory.

Still, it is possible to make these things felt by those who hear or read. It is not only a question of language or way of expression, and we need not blame our language for the misunderstandings in the world; it is chiefly a question of interest and understanding.

Another difficulty remains which is more serious; the fact in itself or writing an article or giving a lecture or holding a discussion creates the impression on both sides that "something has to be done" — we are high and ought to come down, or we are low and ought to climb — the origin of all tendencies, of all idealism, I think this is what inspires important contemporary writers (e.g., Sartre, Camus, and others) to give only facts, to give the real psychological and social situation without a conclusion or moral.

One of the most important and necessary innovations in the field of education (now that modernity has in many ways prepared the ground) is that the child will have the possibilities of full experiencing. Such a development enables him to live fully with his senses, his emotions and his intellect — and not only spontaneously, intensely but subtly, so that the less striking inner voices of the soul have a chance and are not first buried for a period of ten, twenty or even fifty years.

Chapter 18

How I understand Krishnamurti
by M.F.

From time to time the multipersonal entity that is mankind produces a man of wisdom and compassion. He knows the hearts of beings and the Truth beyond the fleeting. In himself he bridges the gap between the apparent and the real and calls everyone to use him for crossing the chasm of beginningless illusion.

Krishnamurti is one such. The Truth he wants to take us to is as ancient as the heart of being, but the way he shows is supremely adapted to the present state of the human mind.

We have lost all confidence in whatever the past has created. Our religions, cultures and civilizations have betrayed us. We are at the brink of the abyss between nuclear warfare and overpopulation. And we do not know whom to trust, whom to follow.

Krishnamurti says: trust nobody, follow nobody Doubt — question — see the false as false and the so called true too as false. Distrust even your own capacity for doubt, till your mind realizes fully that not only it is unable to reach the true, but it creates illusion ceaselessly. The understanding of the perverting nature of the mind is all the mind can reach. Total self-distrust leads to a state of infinite despair. The mind has nothing to turn to and yet cannot stand the agony of nothingness. Having nowhere to go it does what it never did before — it goes within along a new dimension and meets at last the power and the loving wisdom of the Fact.

Krishnamurti has an enormous reverence for facts. To him the fact contains all that is needed to deal with it creatively and happily. All that we need is a mind able to meet a fact in humility and obedience. We do it in science and in love and in pure action born from reverence for truth and life.

Part V

Comparative Studies

Chapter 19

Way of the Paradox
by Luis S.R. Vas

The theme of this paper is the paradox: an occurence more wide-spread than is usually realised. It is a tendency in the whole universe, of things to behave in precisely the opposite fashion to what we might reasonably expect them to do. Beginning with the physical world of matter, as illustrated in Heisenberg's princi-ple of indeterminacy according to which, if you know the veloc-ity of a sub-atomic particle, you cannot know its position at any given time and conversely if you know the position you can't know the velocity; from there it extends to the animal kingdom as when a donkey who refuses to move forward at any price does so readily when pulled back by the tail; and exhibits its most curious varieties in the human organism and mind.

Consider the case of Homoeopathic medicine. The underlying principle was discovered by Dr. Samuel Hahnemann of Germany while translating Cullen's 'Material Medica'. The unfamiliar claims made for some herbs in the book, provoked Dr. Hahnemann to swallow a sample of cinchona bark which has fever curing properties.

To his astonishment he found himself running a temperature. After more tests the doctor was inevitably led to draw the startling conclusion that substances causing the symptoms of certain diseases in healthy men cure those affected by the same ailment. "Similars cure similars" is how Dr. Hahnemann worded the law which makes homeopathy work. The `similar' drug merely heightens the symptoms, thereby giving enough stimulus for the organism to be led to the `opposite', that is to say towards health. The only precaution needed is to "do no more than stimulate the diseased part upto the normal level." This is relatively simple, since the smaller the quantity, the more effective the result. Vaccines in allopathic medicine show a similar property.

What happens in the mind appears to be no different than the peculiar reaction of the body. Victor Frankl, a noted Austrian psychiatrist and originator of logotherapy discovered the use of 'paradoxical intention' to cure neurotic compulsions. To those stutterers whose malady has psychological rather than biological roots, he advises the course of trying to intensify it instead of attempting to reduce it. The patients generally find themselves unable to do so and speak normally.

Insomniacs are asked to keep awake for as long as they can. They find that each night they can keep themselves awake for shorter periods until finally they are able to sleep normally. A patient suffering from neurotic fear of heart trouble, following Frankl's suggestion would say to himself: "Yesterday I had one heart attack, today let me try and have two." He can hardly help being struck by the humour of the situation and would undoubtedly laugh at the absurdity of his ailment. This would restore him to health.

Even Freudian psychoanalysis illustrates the psychological boomerang. When we try to forget unpleasant memories, we merely succeed in burying them deep in our unconscious where they upset our mental balance. until brought back to light by free-association and dream analysis and are met face to face. The meeting and simple recognition of the cause resolves the problem.

The eminent Indian thinker, J. Krishnamurti, shows how various psychological and spiritual problems can be tackled in this way. Left to ourselves, we usually try to escape unpleasant emotions like hate or boredom by cultivating the opposite emotions. We try to find excitement when bored; try to be loving when hateful. With the result that conflict is implanted in the mind. We are torn between what we are and what we want to be; between boredom we feel and excitement we want to feel. This only worsens our condition.

Krishnamurti, on the other hand, tells us: "If you have nothing to do, if you are bored, why not be bored? Why not *be* that?...If we accept what we are, then we see that the thing which we dreaded, the thing which we called boredom...despair...fear, has undergone a complete change." We begin to look at it from an entirely new angle and it ceases to be boredom, despair or fear and we no longer want it to leave us.

Alan Watts in his book 'Wisdom of Insecurity' pleads for a similar attitude in dealing with our obsessive craving for security. The feeling of calm and poise will come, he maintains, when we whole-heartedly accept the fact that security and redemption from peril are unobtainable in the essentially transient nature of life on earth.

We shall discover then that such a security would not be worth having at all.

In Japan the art of defence called Judo also follows the way of the paradox in encouraging the enemy by giving him the upper hand and then using his effort to one's own advantage.

The Zen sect of Buddhism employs a similar strategy to open its novices to enlightenment. The instrument it has perfected for the purpose is the Koan, a logically insoluble riddle which can be deciphered only when rational thinking is suspended and intuition takes over. The novices rack their brains to the point of exhaustion to solve the Koan, to no purpose, until in complete desperation they give up. At this point the solution comes to them in a flash and they attain Satori (enlightenment). Zen thought, language and practice make a consistent display of paradoxes, whose aim, again paradoxically, is self-integration which leaves no room for wavering between 'to be and not to be'.

The paradoxical nature of man is also discernable in a somewhat different guise when he passes from the state of nature to the state of 'grace'; from savagery to gracious living. This transition which involves the acquisition of enough affluence as to be assured of his livelihood, entails the reversal of means and ends.

He who used to eat to live, begins to live to eat. He who used to hunt to survive, hunts for sport. He who used to face dangers to forestall greater dangers of death to himself and his tribe, now enjoys dangers for their own sake in mountain climbing and motorcar racing. Arnold Toynbee describes the growth of civilization in terms of challenge and response. One would have thought that one's capacities would develop if unrestrained by external agents. The opposite is in fact the case. Only when sufficiently difficult obstacles stand in our way can we gather enough energy to overcome them.

Eric Hoffer has shown how radical changes in society are carried out not by the strong and the powerful as we might expect but by the weak and the discontented. America is the product of the persecuted, the misfits and the undesireables of Europe.

Witness also how revolutions which imply the breaking of the law are masterminded by lawyers whose business is to preserve and protect it: two outstanding cases in point being the French Revolution and our own struggle for independence.

Paul Tillich calls the phenomenon under discussion, ambiguity. "It is my conviction' he said once, "that the character of human condition, like the character of all life, is 'ambiguity': the inseparable mixture of good and evil, of true and false, of creative and destructive forces — both individual and collective....He who is not aware of the ambiguity of his perfection as a person and in his work is not yet mature; and a nation which is not aware of the ambiguity of its greatness also lacks awareness". The paradoxes cited above, thus point to the essentially perplexing quality of human and non human nature. Their moral for us — finite beings groping for the infinite; living in the present, yet planning singlemindedly for the future; whose `greatness is in what we can do with our petty grievances and joys'; for whom, whose life is worth nothing, nothing is worth their life — the lesson for us is that our way of life should meet requirements of the `struggles for existence' by waging a kind of tactical warfare which uses the enemy's powers to our advantage, rather by engaging the adversary in a pitched battle, fought and lost in prehistoric times by the dinosaurs in their bid to survive. We have to learn that we live no more by logic alone than by bread alone and that in our time madness may lie, not so much in our loss of reason as in the loss of everything except our reason, to borrow a phrase from the greatest paradox maker, G.K. Chesterton.

Chapter   20

Zen and Liberation According to Krishnamurti

by Robert Powell

Zen may be true, but is it necessary? And if so, for what and for whom is it necessary? It may be a need with the Buddhist, or with the individual who has a penchant for exotic cults; but is it essential for the ordinary human being seeking liberation from sorrow? For if Zen is Life — and this is how the author sees it — do I then still have to bother with it? For as little as I can avoid Zen, and any conscious preoccupation with the word "Zen", or what has been said about it or in its name, must be superflous.

On the other hand, if Zen is not Life, but a mere fragment of it, a special discipline, or pattern of action, it can't be true. Then it is just another "ism", an invention of the mind anxious to find security, or it may be merely an intellectual pastime. In that case the question starting off this article would not arise at all.

To enquire from a particular point of view, according to a certain ism — whether Communism, Roman Catholicism or Zen, is immaterial — is no enquiry at all; for what I find will in some way be dependent upon my premises. Moreover, it is not Zen either.

It is important that the reader be fully aware of the contradiction involved in the last paragraph, on the verbal level. If Zen is the Nothingness of Life, then what more is there is say! Then surely, the moment I utter one word — that is, a word *about* it — I have betrayed, I have cut up the Wholeness of Life. And is it not this which is taking place in the world today and has happened from times immemorial whenever an individual caught a glimpse of the Truth and tried to communicate it to another?

Because only very few understood and kept their tongue tied, the Truth was so-called "passed on" by the "followers" and in the process "interpreted" *i.e.*, twisted and stepped down, so that it was born, with its philosophy, its meditation exercises, koans, etc., to be greedily snapped up in the twentieth century by the ennui'd intellectuals of the West, who are ever looking for some new stimulant, some new fad to cover up the barrenness of their minds and the emptiness of their hearts. And so it came about that Zen Buddhism became a factor in increasing the confusion in a confused world.

Now, the person who really clearly perceives this, is at once free from all flirtation with words, isn't he? Having seen that all intellectualization, all speculative philosophy is a betrayal of what is true, he will have none of it. To him the issue is not whether or not to embrace Zen, but to live totally, to face one's immediate problems with intelligence, knowing that this intelligence cannot function as long as there is a dependence on an authority or the following of a system.

To cling to Zen, or to any other technique, approach or circumscribed path is to deny Life, which is a pathless land. To find this Life, to discover whether there exists anything beyond thought and experience, one must deny Zen as well as any other school of thought; as Krishnamurti once expressed it so pointedly: "You can only find everything by abandoning everything."

The denial of everything that stands in the way, *i.e.*, this whole intellectual process of analysis and synthesis, deduction and induction, must be made with passion, with intensity, which springs from an instantaneous perception of the fallacy of any positive approach. Thus, there is only the negative approach, which is not an 'approach" in the accepted sense of the word because it is not a movement in time, not progressive, but the seeing of things in a flash. The destruction of all false values in one's outlook on life. Let us first do that, before seeking "positive values". Maybe then we shall find that all "positive" values are false —"values" being ideas or ideals — and that their total denial brings into being a positive state which is not a reaction to the false — a form of being which may be said to have "virtue". But the above implies that what is referred to by the word "state" is a being without "continuity"; it is the dynamic process of denial, which requires a great deal of energy and passion and alertness.

This revolutionary approach to an investigation of true and false values cannot be learned from another, it cannot be mastered through the acquisition of information, which is adding to one's store of knowledge and therefore the cultivation of memory. It comes into being the moment that thought becomes aware of its own conditioning, and thus of its incapability of ever freeing itself. After all, to find out if there is the Eternal, the Unlimited, the mind must first be unlimited, have destroyed its own frontiers, for can the limited ever find the Unlimited, the Immeasurable? And how can the mind destroy its frontiers when it does not even recognize them? There are really two questions involved in this problem, namely: can the mind know its own limitations; and if so, can it then proceed to destroy these limitations?

If we go into this problem for ourselves and experiment a little, we shall discover that the mind *can* become aware of its own limitations; and that this very awareness signifies at once the destruction of these limitations. So in order to go beyond thought, I am first to go strenuously with thought as far as it will go; and to pursue thought in this manner to the very end, I should be able to think straight, with accuracy and patience. In this awareness comes to light the chain of cause-and-effects leading to the exposure of the mind's conditioning and which is therefore rigidly determined. This perception is the first stepping into freedom, but it is also the last step; it is truly an explosive shattering of the prison of the mind: the birth of the First and Last Freedom.

Chapter   21

Krishnamurti and Modern Thought
by Rene Fouere

One of the features of modern mentality is a sort of aggressive individualism. The individual, instead of being a centre of affection and intelligence, has become a pattern of insistent and excessive demands. A vociferous declaration of human rights.

Such demanding individuals are the natural results of an outlook which makes human growth less important than the ever growing possessions, both material and intellectual. Once such an outlook is accepted — and it seems to be so universally, openly or by implication, one is brought to believe that the quality of a civilisation is measurable by the quantity of material or intellectual goods it is able to produce. No wonder that another feature of contemporary thinking is its obsession with efficiency, both physical and mental, based on scientific and admittedly very fertile technology. The breaking of records has become a passion. Science is now entirely utilitarian, industrial efficiency grows by leaps and bounds, the individual is increasingly regimented, governed and controlled by the modern superman, the expert. All thinking has become deeply specialised. The individual is now only a cog-wheel in the social engine. His life is atrociously hollow and barren. His inner poverty makes him crave possessions and distractions, for once a thing is divorced from its legitimate use, it becomes merely a source of entertainment. Literature is now mostly a source of violent emotions or of verbal sedatives. Stimulation and evasion have become universal, human thought is devoted to amusements and escapes. An ever growing demand for things accelerates still further an industrial development already excessive and man is crushed under the burden of his own accumulations, yet asking for more more and more. People fight viciously for raw materials and markets, for territories and political power to the point of being threatened with the terrifying prospects of nuclear annihilation. Man seeks in the excess of property and pleasure an intensity of life which may end too quickly and in nameless horror.

The total mechanisation of human existence proceeds rapidly, gaining impetus from its own results. Man has become increasingly automatic in his actions, increasingly demanding in his distractions, for he cannot find any meaning in his cog-wheel existence ruthlessly conditioned and controlled by all around him, threatened with a sudden, atrocious, and meaningless death. Both literature and art reflect the universal anxiety and distress of humanity without values and without fervour, engaged in endless filling of some bottomless buckets.

Science, incredibly successful, has acquired prestige in the eyes of the masses; the worship of science is now almost idolatrous. All is expected from its constant and rapid progress, from its adventures in the depths of matter and of life. We hope that science will resolve all our problems and put an end to the conflicts between individuals themselves and between man and society. We expect a well qualified technocracy to bring order even into the universe of human relations. We are convinced that new institutions, the result of careful investigation, will succeed in controlling behaviour by a judicious system of pressures and enticements and will weld people together into a harmonious unity in which everybody will find his happiness. In such an approach to transformation of mankind, primary place is given to ideological constructions, the mental models shown to the crowds for believing and following. These ideologies are social myths and we seek among them the supreme, the most satisfactory, myth. No wonder that modern thinking is all centered around ideologies.

Science and ideologies both undergo a process of development which seems to aim towards a perfect individual in a perfect society as the inevitable outcome of a historical process. Thus perfection becomes a matter for the future, not for the present. We sacrifice the living generation to a definite but distant goal. The man of today is sacrificed to the superman of tomorrow.

Along with the material progress, the moral development of man is taken to be the result of a historical process. In a society devoted to production efficiency confers merit and social distinction. Social morality has been identified with the art of holding on to the top of the social ladder, the rings of which represent the hierarchy of conventional distinctions.

In literature, as in life, love appears to be felt as a mutual dependence, a search for each other's company, a craving for mutual possession, in which the desire to possess and to be possessed merge. The greater the mutual dependence, the stronger the bonds that bind, the more perfect love is considered to be.

Rational thought, the mother of science, is believed to be the only instrument for finding the ultimate truth, which could be formulated and impressed through education on the minds of the young as and when it suits the experts.

In the same manner, happiness must be found on the cross-roads of historical development and social (or religious for some) organisation. Man is predestined to be happy provided he believes, obeys and follows. Naturally, the individual rises in revolt whenever his own little scheme of happiness is threatened and creates within the bigger world of society a world of his own. Similar to the ever expending universe of the astronomers are our individual expansions. Every individual wants to expand, to accumulate more and more, physically and mentally, at the cost of everybody else. He may include within the circle of his egotistic urges a few of his family and friends, but the rest of the world is his legitimate prey. The individual has become the cancerous cell of the social body which rots and tears because of his blind and lawless urges. The more so when all the cells of the body social are diseased, when each preys on others. The collective organism grows beyond all sense and measure and crumbles under its own weight, entangled in the enormous complexity of its functions. Such is the picture of the modern world and the ideas that made it. Modern thought is filled with the self-assertive rebellion of the individual against a society arranged for supplying mass produced and mass controlled happiness to every man, provided he fits into a pattern. Man is either taken to be a member of a group, identical with other members or entirely separate, separate in his morality, his values, his merits, his uplift, his security, his continuity and his historical development, which is endlessly postponed.

What is Krishnamurti's attitude to modern thought? He rejects it almost totally. It has condemned itself by the world it has created and its blood-drenched chaos in which we live.

Krishnamurti will not accept the definition of the individual as a focus of multiple demands to be satisfied and made happy by an ideological formula, however scientifically worked out. To him happiness is not the result of accumulations, material or mental, nor can it be found in a resurrected past nor in an ideal future, but only in the immediate present and by a man who has taken sole and total responsibility for himself and his life. To Krishnamurti morality has nothing to do with merit, with disciplines suggested by others, with following a pattern of behaviour. Morality is merely the way to reality, it has no value, in itself. He says that no amount of scientific research will establish harmonious relations between our fellow men that a truly human world, self-correcting and therefore stable, will come only when temporal gains will give place to eternal values. Such eternal values will not be found in some imaginary heaven, but in the quality of human relations, which in themselves are their own eternal value. Escape from human relationship is escape from reality.

Truth is, to Krishnamurti, something living and indescribable and not an abstract proposition compressed into a formula.

According to him, the sense of 'I' is the very source of suffering. To him all self-increase, all search for power for one's self is merely vain escape, foolish and cruel. He says that rational thinking is valuable only when it leads to an experience which is beyond thought. Such experience may still be called 'Thought', but it is thought of a different quality, fluid and pliable, free from all authorities and traditions, from formulas and habits, from all slavery to words, such thought never repeats or imitates itself, it is always creative, eternally renewed, ever fresh. It is also real love. This love flows in motiveless action, not in the self-seeking, utilitarian and spectacular activities of the world. The man who loves is neither bound nor does he bind. His is supreme intelligence. He alone can solve all problems, individual and social, which are fundamentally the same. Such love cannot be born from a ritual, an ideology, from admonitions of another or some self inflicted violence. It is the flowing of our inner clarity and silence. It is its own eternity. Not the eternity of continuity of some idea, hope or desire, but a stream of living moments, each complete, each a timeless, but perfect expression of love itself. Such eternity can be realised any moment by a kind of vertical jump out of the horizontal grooves of common, time bound thinking and of the feeling in the 'like-dislike don't care' pattern. Love is not cumulative, it is not a product of evolution. We cannot find it in the course of time, for in time only the 'I' grows. Nor can it be put together by a clever reassembly of materials and capacities already at our disposal. Love comes into being spontaneously when thinking, the creator of problems, calculating, aiming, striving, has seen that it is unable to resolve the agonising problems it has itself created. When the mind is fully convinced that all its activities are sterile, it stops and the moment of perfect silence is suddenly flooded by that eternity of love, of which Krishnamurti speaks. When all comparisons, choice, accumulations and intentions are given up, when the mind ceases to draw on the future which was but a projection of the past, man finds his own eternity, which is also the reality of the world around him.

Chapter   22

Transformation of Personality According to Krishnamurti, in the light of Psychoanalysis

by Luis S.R. Vas

Briefly the kernel of Krishnamurti's analysis of Personality is as follows: We are normally the result of past experiences. We see the present only in relation to our past and plan the future too with the data gathered from it. The unknown we see only as a variation of the known. The past, the known, the experienced form a pattern and against this frame of reference we fashion our life. Consequently the newness of present experience is soiled and our perception is distorted.

Moreover we label the bits of our past experience variously as 'pleasant', 'unpleasant', 'indifferent'. As we scan the present we tend to act with a view to collect more pleasant material, which we like to accumulate in our storehouse of memories, and tend to avoid the unpleasant. Having once tasted good food, received praise for our intelligence, things which delighted us, we seek these things again in the future.

Emotions rise in us and provide the potential, which Krishnamurti calls 'capacity' to acquire, by checking with our accumulated knowledge, what we deem to be desirable and to reject what is not. Our behaviour, then, is largely automatic and much of it hardens into inflexible habits, addictions, obsessions. Even worse, this conditioning produces dilemmas which can in the end cause sizeable emotional conflicts. For instance we may regard a certain commodity such as, say, a high income as desirable. Its acquisition entails the unpleasantness of hard work. There is a tension between greed and laziness. The stronger emotion of course wins but may lead to frustration if results belie the expectations. Or if the contending forces do not appreciably differ in strength, the long hard war can only end in a nervous breakdown.

Is there, then, a way out? Yes; this course of events, so common as to be almost universal, need not necessarily take place. It is an avoidable aberration caused by our lack of understanding of our psychological processes.

Krishnamurti's solution envisages the breaking up of the frame of reference of our past and living only in the present, moment by moment. But since we cannot will our experience into oblivion nor dissolve our emotions when we please, the solution is easier formulated than applied.

To make it applicable, Krishnamurti offers a set of preliminary insights. The first involves the realisation that we cannot solve a psychological problem by a static measure. That is, no formula, no discipline, no practice will serve the purpose. The second insight is that while we cannot erase the factual memory of our past, we can wipe off the 'psychological memory' which is Krishnamurti's term for emotionally charged memories. For instance, if I were beaten up in a certain dark alley, the terror I then felt would keep on recurring every time I passed a dark alley. It is not possible by dint of will to forget the alley or the treatment meted out to me there, but the fear can be made to subside through a state of awareness. This awareness of all our feelings, thoughts, desires, and reactions as they occur should not be tinged either by approval or condemnation. Nor should we try to escape the fears, stop the thoughts, arrest the desires or otherwise change the reactions as they arise in us. This is the last insight.

Total awareness then becomes, according to Krishnamurti, the only way to solve the 'problems', our profoundly unsatisfactory relationship with life, by a total transformation of personality. A few considerations on personality in the light of psychoanalysis will show how.

Psychoanalysis describes personality in terms of two drives — the libidinal and the aggressive which emanate from the psyche. The libido — the psychic source of love — rising from the subconscious in a constant stream is directed, 'cathected' is the technical term, in varying degrees to the ego or external objects depending on circumstances which make either or both receptive to it. The aggressive drive — the psychic source of hate — operates from the superego and varies in direction and quantum in relation to the stimulus provided by conditioning, that is to say, the habits and taboos and customs learnt from society. If, for some reason, the aggression on the ego is weak, then the libido directed towards it is correspondingly stronger. The personality of such a person is said to be narcissistic. If the aggression on the ego is strong, both aggression and libido are deflected to the external world and such personality is aggressive in Freudian terminology .

Personality, according to Psychoanalysis is largely acquired due to early training imparted to the child in its first few years. If the child is brought up with rigorous discipline, a strong superago is formed and an 'aggressive' personality in the process. A permissive rearing of the child leads to a weak super-ego and a narcissistic personality.

P. Spratt who has done a study on *Hindu Culture and Personality*, claims that Hindus are distinctly narcissistic due to a pampered childhood as opposed to the aggressive personality of the Westerner. Of course there are exceptions but these types characterise the vast majority. It should be clear from this summary account that both personalities are to a greater or lesser extent unbalanced, the Indian leaning towards the Yogi, the Westerner towards the Commissar end of the spectrum. Spratt adds that the best kind of personality is that of the projective introvert, that is to say of the man who loves his ego completely and then identifies it with the world. Tagore's personality is described as an example. This balance is not very satisfactory either, since it is a temporary state of an essentially narcissistic person.

Putting Krishnamurti's awareness into operation dissolves the conditioned thinking and does away with the superego, also permitting an unobstructed flow of the libido to the ego and the external world equally. Love, not the super-ego, becomes the lawgiver. The moral consequences were indicated by Aldous Huxley on his foreword to 'First and Last Freedom'. "Love and do what you will...." Huxley wrote "but if you start by doing what you will or what you don't will....you will never love". This aphorism also serves as a nutshell statement of Krishnamurti's thought.

Chapter   23

General Semantics as an Introduction to Krishnamurti
by Luis S.R. Vas

"Man is an amphibian" wrote Aldous Huxley. He is compelled to live on several levels at once — the physical, the emotional, the verbal and other levels. His organism is stimulated by `agents' from all these sources. The `agents' are symbols that have acquired for him some meaning or other. Thus the word `fire' (verbal level) shouted in a cinema house (physical level) may rouse a thousand human beings to panic (emotional level) with all its unfortunate consequences. The illustration demonstrates how stimulus from one level prompts the human organism to react on different levels. The enormously complex interplay of stimuli and reactions flying back and forth from level to level results in a general and hopeless confusion he projects onto the world at large; and his relationships with it and fellow men are seriously infected.

Having established a particularly serious handicap in human condition, it is possible to examine and compare two attempts made so far to resolve the situation. J. Krishnamurti and Alfred Korzybski approach the problem from two not widely different directions. To Krishnamurti it is a problem of freedom versus slavery or of clarity versus confusion. To Korzybski it is essentially the latter and its consequences on human sanity. They have, in other words, many points in common and it is the purpose of this paper to suggest a synthesis of the tow with Korzybski's thought as a spring board to Krishnamurti's philosophy of life. But to begin, let us take the latter first.

Krishnamurti's method is that of mass brain-storming with huge audiences or face-to-face exchanges with individuals. In either case his function is that of a catalyst in a chemical reaction. Employing a kind of verbal shock therapy, he hopes to force his audience to think for itself and be aware, moment by moment of its mental processes and physical reactions. His ultimate purpose is to free a notoriously security-prone mind from the enslavement imposed through conditioning by tradition and society. Krishnamurti provides the first push in this direction with his perceptive analysis of the various concrete situations that corner the mind into relinquishing its responsibility to habits and social norms.

It is difficult to say how far Krishnamurti has been successful. But it is a safe bet that the vast majority of his listeners go back more deluded than they came. The reason is not too far to seek. Krishnamurti is not too careful to define his terms, sometimes using the same terms in more than one context and in senses widely divergent from the common usage.

With Korzybski the case is very different. He has created a system — the very thought of one horrifies Krishnamurti — designed to separate the "levels of abstraction" and to clarify the mind. The blue-print of his system of General Semantics was drawn in his masterpiece, `Science and Sanity', and further refinements have been added by a small coterie of able followers who include S.I. Hayakawa (*Language in Thought And Action*) Stuart Chase (*Tyranny of Words*) Wendell Johnson (*People in Quandaries*) Irving Lee (*Habits in Human Thinking*).

Only a few of their many fascinating techniques can be mentioned here. First, the definitions and the axioms: general semantics is a comparative study of human reactions to words and other symbols with a view to forestall unwarranted, harmful, confused and confusing reactions and to ensure a saner living.

This is possible, if you learn to live on one level of abstraction at a time. When you are eating, for instance, shut off all your thinking; concentrate on the taste of the food. Don't verbalise, don't compare with your memory of another food's taste. With practice one is capable of achieving this for a continuous minute or so at a time. Similarly with the emotions, learn to accept them, without rationalising. Rationalised acceptance or rejection stimulates second order emotions (like hating your hate or being proud of your love) either strengthening the original emotion or causing a conflict between first and second order emotions. It may be remembered that emotions are not *directly* dependent on the will but curiously *"acceptance of that which cannot at the moment be changed, changes it"* (*Levels* of *Being & Existence, Weinberg*).

The verbal level is the most active and the cause of most inter-level confusions. It is also the most important because it provides the main entry into the levels of knowledge and belief.

For clarity here, then, General Semantics prescribes the directive "find the referent" every time a word is used and a statement made. Referent means a concrete, objective, palpable reality. Take the sentence "Capitalists are blood-suckers" — who are the `capitalists' you have in mind; whose `blood' have they `sucked'? Secondly, use quotation marks when the statement or part of it is inferential, not directly observed as shown in the previous sentence. Thirdly, take the help of date, index and `etc'. to qualify and clarify your thoughts and statements and those of others. Thus friend 1, is not friend 2: Two friends need not be friendly in the same way or for the same reason; Indian (income Rs. 1,000 p.m.) is not the same as Indian (income Rs. 100 p.m.); U.S. Foreign Policy (Rusk). Mr. A. is a capable manager (etc)" — `etc' implies that he is in addition, a father, husband, smoker, teetotaller etc. etc. etc. — to remind yourself that no statement is or can ever be complete.

As a substitute to the above techniques, general semantist D. David Bourland Jr. advises doing away summarily with all forms of the verb 'to be'. Since he began practising the precept, his listeners have noticed an increasing lucidity in his expression (Time, May 23, 1969). The reason is that the verb 'to be' freezes the concept of time by emphasising an identity: for instance when you say " 'B' is a thief" you imply (or at least instil the impression) that B was a thief and ever will be a thief. Thus "our language" says Bourland "remains the language of absolutes", while in reality time and movement are inexorable and though you say a rose is a rose in the fraction of a second that a rose is described, it has already begun to alter. The technique has three major advantages over conventional English (i) Questions like 'What is Man'? 'What is Art'? become meaningless (2) Woolly, cliched phrases like "Boys will be boys", "We know that is the right thing to do" are avoided; (3) Factual and inferential observations cannot be confused with one another "Once you realise that everytime you say 'is' you tell a lie," he says, "You begin to think less of a thing's identity and more of its function. I find it much harder to be dishonest now."

With clarity at the conscious level it is far easier to achieve clarity at the unconscious level too. Having separated the various levels of abstraction it is much easier to be aware of the reactions at each level, even if more than one level is operating at a given time, while ordinarily one is aware at only one level at a time, now it is possible to be "living on several planes at once". Self awareness is a highly creative activity, and clarity at every level both sharpens awareness and it is intensified by the latter. The creative and curative powers of conscious attention have been stressed by thinkers other than Krishnamurti and Korzybski. "One hour of conscious solitude will enrich your creativity far more than hours of trying to learn the creative process" says Paul Tillich in "The Eternal Now". Elsewhere he writes "No one can experience depth without stopping and becoming aware of himself. Only if he has moments in which he does not care about what comes next can he experience the meaning of this moment, here and now and ask himself the meaning of life" Here is what Reinhold Niebuhr has to say: "If the self-centered self is shattered by a genuine awareness of its situation there is the power of a new life in the experience".

And as Gurdjieff says "All energy spent on conscious work is an investment that spent mechanically is lost forever".

Chapter   24

Tagore and Krishnamurti
by S. Sivraman

Like all the religious poetry of India, Krishnamurti's poetry also is mystic. Krishnamurti seems to have communed with God face to face, as did the seers of the Upanishads. The living vision of God, which has plunged Indian Saints into ecstatic self-forgetfulness and caused some of them to become oblivious of the world and some others to see all the world as the mani-festation of the One, cannot but be a little incomprehensive to the West, since the West has largely lived its religious life through faith rather than direct realization. But in the East the vision of God is as real as the concretest reality, and consequently yearning and vision have moved the Eastern poet saints to as intense poetry as any earthly vision or yearning has moved the poets of the West. This relation of the individual soul to the Supreme Soul has been so endowed with personality that the religious poetry of the East is not an impersonal philosophy, but is full of the persona; human element in the highest degree required for great poetry. That is why the effusions of the Eastern mystics from the seers of the Upanishads through the saints of the middle ages down to their modern descendants such as Rabindranath Tagore and J. Krishnamurti, are not only highly religious, but also highly poetical.

Since Indian religious poetry expresses the search and discovery of one supreme personality by another individual personality, it possesses a rich, living variety, inaccessible to any poetization of mere philosophy.

Both Tagore and Krishnamurti seek union with the Eternal Beloved mystically, but their ways differ greatly. Some of the former's songs represent the human soul as a lover in search of the beloved. They are, therefore, characterized by a feminine self-surrender. Other songs of his represent God as a companion or a Master, and carry the note of friendship or of loyalty. Krishnamurti, on the other hand, merges himself in consciousness with his Beloved and his poetry looks on life from the serene summit of the Infinite. While in Rabindranath's poetry an individual personality is endeavouring to commune with and delight in an infinite Person who manifests Himself through love and beauty in the universe, in Krishnamurti's poetry the individual personality is endeavouring to become absolutely one with the Infinite. While, again, in Rabindranath's poetry the realization is one of communion and accord through love, in Krishnamurti's it is one of absolute identification with the Infinite. As a consequence, the poems of Krishnamurti have the tranquility and serenity of perfection and Godhood. Rabindranath represents the Vaishnavite's relation to the Infinite; Krishnamurti represents the Vedantin's.

Part VI

Implications of
Krishnamurti's Thought

Part VI

Implications of
Krishnamurti's Thought

Chapter   25

Self-consciousness and Fear
by Rene Fouere

Krishnamurti does not trust ideals. "The ideal is always what is not", he said, ironically, but quite judiciously. Even the ideal of non-violence he questions. (I mean here the ideal of non-violence and not non-violence itself as expressed in actual behaviour). He says that it is not the worship of the ideal of non-violence that will bring peace into the world, but it is the individual who can embrace everything, including violence, in compassionate understanding.

Krishnamurti maintains that he has found the truth; but the truth he speaks of cannot be reduced to an intellectual formula; it is the living present, it is life itself. And exactly because it is living, conscious, it cannot be known objectively. Nor can eternity, which is another aspect of Truth, be known as an object. When we ask Krishnamurti why it should be so, his answer is deep and penetrating.

"You cannot know but what is over. The living thing cannot be known. You cannot 'know', analyze out thought, unless it is no more. You cannot know a living thing which at every moment is alive, vital, creative. Please, see the importance of the fact that Truth is not something that can be known."

All objective knowledge can be only of the past. Even in the world of matter the present moment is impossible to know. And even more so in the world of the mind. All introspection is a form of retrospection. When, in self-consciousness the "I" wants to know itself, it comes to know only its own past. On the level of objective knowledge subject and object are forever separate and they are condemned, so to say, to chase each other eternally, without being able to catch up with the living reality of ourselves. In order to be with ourselves in the immediate present we must be able to know ourselves `on the spot', without the intervention of analytic thinking which always refers us to the past. Intuition, the perception of the full meaning of the fact at the very moment of action and not after, is what Krishnamurti calls awareness, which alone, according to him, can open the doors to the living truth of our being. He has no regard for introspection which is merely an obstacle to action, nor for detailed analysis which destroys instead of revealing. Introspection and analysis cannot liberate us, for liberation is the fruit of complete self-awareness in the present. And he is one with Ramana Maharshi in denying the value of all knowledge which is not based on self-knowledge.

Our vital problems, the problems affecting our behaviour, cannot be resolved in any way except by awakening in us the creative intelligence or intuition, which, by fully grasping the significance of the conditions in which we are, will liberate us from them whatever they may be. Such intelligence is when there is the meeting of thoughts and feelings, of love and reason. It transcends thought and feeling; it is life itself, beyond the subject independent of the object.

The inadequacy of our responses to the ever new situations that challenge us all the time is the result of our thought being divorced from our feelings. We are prevented from living fully, from being totally present, really alive. In other words, we are not whole in our actions; we act with divided strength, distracted by contradictions. Our actions are not complete, not adequate, and leave behind them a sense of frustration. The more we try to do about it, the more our unrest grows. We are forever anxious about our future and waste our life on getting ready to live.

We are wrapped up in layers of the past memories which give rise to all sorts of morbid reactions. Krishnamurti says that these memories form the very substance of the daily 'me', the 'I', built out of failure and frustration, condemns us to slavery to time. It is the residue of yesterday's incomplete actions, which stand like a wall between us and our fulfilment in eternity.

It is a fact that all self-consciousness is painful and is absent in the states of ecstasy and fullness. Krishnamurti says: :When you are really happy, deeply in love, the 'I' is not. There is only happiness, the immensity of love. This alone is real, everything else is false."

We find here a new and striking definition of liberation: it is a state in which all 'I'-consciousness has ceased because the duality indispensable to self-consciousness is no more; the duality being the distinction between the observer and the observed. One can understand why Krishnamurti claims having lost himself at the moment of liberation.

Nevertheless, when we lose the consciousness of ourselves as separate 'I' it is because we become more than conscious of ourselves; we become consciousness itself. "Consciousness itself is the I" tells J. Krishnamurti. Liberation, therefore, is not something terrible, but is the fulfilment and perfection of consciousness.

Before we were a self and self-consciousness apart from it. Now this distinction is no more: being and consciousness have become one; the thinker and the thought have merged; all division, identification or contradiction have ceased. Nothing is lost, all has become one. Only the distinctions are abolished, but not reality. The content of existence is intact, only its capacity has gone.

We no longer are within the field of consciousness, for we have finally arrived; an end has come at last to our travelling backward in time; going into the future, but looking at the past, which is so characteristic of the sense of 'I'. This loss of all self-consciousness is the full flowering of consciousness itself. It is a sign of inner integration, of victory over all division. There is nothing to frighten us in that state; on the contrary, says Krishnamurti, it is a state in which no fear can be. Man has become spontaneously creative and therefore needs no longer to be conscious of himself.

Krishnamurti teaches that the very sense of a distinct and separate existence to which we cling with such desperate tenacity is an obstacle to the fullness of living. But in our ignorance we take the obstacle itself for the fullness which it obstructs. We live by the very wall which bars us from living. Its ugly mass fascinates us because it appears so substantial and immovable, so totally objective. It gives us the certitude of our own continuity.

Krishnamurti tells us that self-consciousness arises only when we are hurt or frustrated. At its root there is the desire for self-perpetuation and self-expansion which ceaselessly sacrifices the present to the future. This desire centered in the future deprives our actions of all intrinsic value and turns them into mere means towards a goal which is never reached. It brings the fear of death, which can always rob us of the fullness of life we seek. The very desire for fulfilment delays it and keeps it back in the future which is never realized.

Krishnamurti shows us the 'I' as an endless process of misery and blindness due to a basic distortion of consciousness, which perpetuates itself by its own errors. It creates a vicious circle dominated by the past which even the most painful experiences of life cannot break. This process of the self is rooted in the fear of not becoming which is the root of all fears and which Krishnamurti calls the fundamental fear.

This fear is the dark and fatal shadow of conscious self-limitation. The self, aware of its own insignificance, feels lost in the immense ocean of space and time of which it itself is the unconscious creator. This perception of its real nothingness, however dim and shunned, fills it with unconscious agony and makes it seek security which eternally escapes. It wants to expand its smallness, to strengthen its weakness and to achieve that, it puts itself to collecting, with frenzied ruthlessness, the most varied materials within its reach; it tyranises others to create for itself an illusion of power it does not really possess. Yet it knows that no possession, however great and absolute, can change the relation between its own nothingness and the immensity around it. All our urge for personal aggrandizement, which has cost the world so much blood and tears, is merely a futile evasion of a fact, an endless search for a non-existing security, an absurd refusal to meet face to face one's own true condition. It is only in the full awareness of oneself, says Krishnamurti, that we can put an end to our self-perpetuated torments and break the lance with which forever we goad ourselves.

(Translated from the French)

Relationship and Love
by Charis Leybourne-White

Relationship, as it is generally lived, is often a source of problems, of conflict and unhappiness. In failing to realise the complexity of our own inner being, we naturally fail to realise the complexity of another human being. We are naive and approach relationship only with ready-made standards, to idealise it or to condemn it. For example, we have a rosy picture summed up in such a phrase as "Mother love", and do not dare to uncover this and look into the real interplay of psychologies between Mother and son or daughter. There is the natural instinct of the Mother to protect her Young, but she is still a human being with her own problems and needs. So, into such 'love' there enters usually the sense of possessiveness and a dependence which is not merely physical but psychological. There is psychological dependence of the older generation upon the younger, the Father's as well as the Mother's clinging to `my' child in a possessive way needs to be recognised and understood by parent and child, if the relationship in later years is to be freed of hidden resentments and antagonisms. But such clinging is mutual. It is very necessary for the younger generation to be utterly clear about the extent and implications of clinging to parents *beyond the point of what is natural*. Attitudes and influences in our childhood or adolescence mark many a life into manhood and womanhood.

But if parents especially were aware of all this and of its implications, the basic relationship of human life, that between parents and children, might never become a problem.

Then, there is the need for understanding somewhat deeply the subtleties of relationship between man and woman. Perhaps one of the facts rarely appreciated, yet basic to mutual relationship between men and women, is that characteristics and qualities most typical of the man are not foreign to or absent from the woman and vice versa. Behind his male rationality, strength, active drive, assertiveness in word and deed, there lie in the man qualities more usually associated with the woman — sensitivity, passivity, receptivity, gentleness, grace, shyness, withdrawal, emotion. And thus, just as there is a so-called female side to the man, so is there a so-called male side to a woman. — strength, activity, verbosity, expressiveness, even aggressiveness, sometimes suprisingly offsetting gentleness and mildness. If men and women realised this in each other, they would not confront each other as strangers psychologically, often with such bewilderment and confusion at each other's behaviour. The relationship between the two could be freed of old misunderstandings and tensions. Furthermore, it would become for each a mirror to themselves. The other's behaviour and reactions and problems would help each of them to see clearly and to understand their own hidden qualities. This would be to bring to the relationship a maturity and a significance normally denied to it. To accept and live in a relationship merely for mutual dependence and gratification and comfort, is to deny it its full possibility, its real flowering. Lived in mutual understanding of the other however, and at the same time of themselves, it is vital and always fresh and changing. As things are, our relationship because stale, is wearisome, if not in open conflict. We have fixed ideas in our minds about 'him' or 'her'. In our attitudes to the others, we imagine we know each other, nature, mind and being; but this is a mere mental image, born out of projection and past experiences of the man or woman. Normally we do not feel the living quality, which is swift and ever-moving and changing. We thus relate ourselves to a dead *idea*, about them.

And consequently the whole relationship becomes devoid of any spring of renewal, it becomes a dead thing, lacking the freshness, wonder, which it had known in its beginnings. There is dullness in such relationship. There is no hope for it unless and until the partners are aroused to deeper awareness of the relationship as complex and subtle, and involving issues which go deeply into the heart of human existence. When such awareness begins to operate, however, it simultaneously begins to free the relationship from its old rut, to transform it into a reborn joy. The relationship becomes full, all-round, as they bring to conscious awareness every aspect of themselves. And mutual respect in the relationship grows. There emerges a full, balanced relationship. It might be possible then at last to come to a ripeness where each was in contact with and was beautifully expressing the whole range of human qualities. Thus, as an article in *Span* recently expressed it. "The creative individuals (men and women) are more able than most to give expression to opposite sides of their nature, to achieve a reconciliation of the conscious and unconscious, reason and passion, rational and irrational, science and art."

Such exploring would inevitably bring the pair to the question which underlies all others in a relationship: what is love. The challenge of this question is inescapable and none unfolds it more profoundly than Krishnamurti. How vital for us he says, for all our lives, to find out what love must be, stripped of all the illusions and pretensions. We say we love, but there is jealousy, we hold and destroy. Is it love to say, 'I love you on condition that you do not forsake me, do not fail to please me, to support me, to comfort me, do not fail to be constant to me.'? Would not most of us feel that it would be indifference, to say 'I love you, but you are free to do *What* you like: I make no claim, no demand?' This does not mean more licence or looseness: but it may mean an act of profound inner discipline and deep respect for oneself and the other. And this, not imposed through some idea — but a spontaneous feeling of freedom for oneself and the other. But if we would, and in general we would think such an attitude indifference, are we not equating love with jealousy? If 'do what you like' were to mean an act contrary to 'me' and 'my' exclusive interests, then jealousy would flame within most of us. And if we were not jealous, the common conclusion would be that our feelings could not be love. Love is also generally synonymous with mutual dependence: I cling and depend upon you — which means I deny you freedom. and you do the same to me. And because we depend, we demand, we demand of love to continue for ever. As Anne Morrow Lindbergh says in her delightful little book, 'Gift from the Sea'. "There is no holding of a relationship to a single form. This is not tragedy but part of the ever-recurrent miracle of life and growth. All living relationships are in a process of change, of expansion, and must perpetually be building themselves new forms." And that very demand, which is in effect *using* the relationship for security, even mutual security, smothers love. What may have been clear, fresh, vivid, spontaneous, becomes dull, prosaic or even destructive. Anxiety about holding the quality of the relationship unchanged, inevitably brings a rigidity, which cramps and may ultimately drive love away. For love is like life and it cannot be held fixed, static. Love has then been killed, reduced to an idea of the mind. Only if each moment of love is fully and utterly lived and then not held on to desperately, as the pattern for the next moment, as a continuity, only then can love live on in a relationship. Why do we normally seek continuity in that which was real and joyous at the moment of experiencing? Is it not a question to be gone into deeply? Not to demand continuity in a certain pattern would be to set love free to be as joyous and bright at the end of a lifetime of companionship, as it was in the morning of its years.

We normally imagine it is easy to love. We regard love as something which blows upon us like the wind and carries us whither it wishes. But do we know what love is? Perhaps if we cared for what it is, loved love, we may say, we would cherish more its true perfume and make our loves sweet, unadulterated by jealousy, or clinging, or any demand. When we really love, is there not an absence of self-centred concern, and instead an outflowing concern and caring for the other?

Where there is love there are expressions, though they are not, can never be, commensurate with the love itself. Often we mistake this and equate love with its physical expressions. We take a sensory satisfaction, and more deeply, we take psychological gratification in being loved. Few of us escape the tremendous sense of belittlement, inferiority, if we are not loved. We scarcely recognise the condition of just loving, without asking love in return. To love without a return of our love is to most of us a humiliation, a threat to our own self-esteem. We seek self-esteem, through our manhood, through our womanhood, through love itself. If this were clearly seen, such clarity would obviously not mistake such self-centredness for love.

That clarity would also be capable of going further. It would perceive that quality of love which is not asking anything what-soever in return, as a quality which is essentially beyond merely you and me. Being selfless, this state is assuredly something quite new, different in essence from all we have known in our accustomed, me-and-you bond in which each one has a very self-centred concern. Then love itself would be important and not merely the object of love. From this it would naturally follow also that such a feeling of love could not and would not be confined to one person alone. In him who was no longer self-centred, in his living, in him there would be love which would not be confined to one alone, but would flow out generously to many, and not alone to the obviously beautiful, gifted and lov-able. Again from Mrs. Linderbergh's Gift from the Sea: "We all wish to be loved alone." "Don't sit under the apple-tree with anyone, else but me," runs the old popular song. Perhaps, as Auden says in his poem, this is a fundamental error in mankind.

> For the error bred in the bone
> Of each woman and each man
> Craves what it cannot have,
> Not universal love
> But to be loved alone.

Is it such a sin? In discussing this verse with an Indian phi-losopher, I had an illuminating answer. "It is all right to wish to be loved alone," he said, "mutuality is the essence of love. There cannot be other in mutuality. It is only in the time-sense that it is wrong. It is when we desire *continuity* of being loved alone that we go wrong." For not only do we insist on believing romantically in the "one-and-only" — the one-and-only love, the one-and-only mate, the one-and-only mother, the one-and-only security — we wish the "one-and-only" to be permanent, ever-present and continuous. The desire for continuity of being-loved alone seems to me "the error bred in the bone" of men. For 'there is no one-and-only," as a friend of mine once said in a similar discussion, "there are just one=and-only moments." How shall such love come into being? To this, there is no simple answer: but perhaps we can all learn to love only by loving — and by loving, love may break its own bounds and intense love for one may burst into the flower of love which is no longer narrow, exclusive.

Thus, if relationship is to be a flower which does not wither with the earliest winds of challenge, and difficulty, it must be faced as a mirror reflecting and portraying to each of us ourselves and our own selfishness. Such portrayal will transform selfishness. Then and then alone, may this quality of love come into being, the quality which alone can transform the travesty of human life devoid of love, into a creative beauty of being.

Chapter   27

Peep into Krishnamurti's Philosophy
by M.A. Joshi

A careful reader and listener of Krishnamurti can at once make
out that he speaks not to the masses but to the individual.
Repeatedly he tells us that he is not going to put forward a
theory of philosophy and is not teaching anybody or trying to
prove his intellectual superiority. What he is interested in, is the
direct or firsthand experience of the living reality. He says that
we must live in the present or, to put it more precisely, we must
always live in the 'now'. What is this 'now'? And how do we
know that we live in the 'now'? These questions apparently
seem very easy, but are very puzzling. By 'now' he means the
present, the ever-living present, without any involvement of the
past or future; the awareness of this moment is what he calls the
living reality. But we are not aware of living reality because all
our activities are determined by the past and future, we always
act from the centre, that is to say, from the memories of the dead
past and the hopes for the unknown and unborn future. To put
it explicitly , we are slaves to the memories of the past and
aspirations relating to an unknown future. And so long as we
are encrusted within the past memories it is impossible to live
in the ever-present reality. For a comprehension of the reality
we must learn to live with the facts. The very nature of fact is
to be dynamic, and unless we become dynamic it is not in the

least possible to understand the nature of reality. For example, I am sitting here and speaking to you is a fact, you are listening to me is a fact, sex is a fact, change is a fact, death is a fact, envy is a fact. All these are facts and our statements regarding facts certainly imply neither acceptance nor rejection, but just a look at the facts. You need not accept or reject what Krishnamurti says, but only to listen to it and it is in this very art of listening one can learn. Listening does not involve any element of choice. If your mind is open, unloaded with what you have heard or read or thought, it is capable of apprehending and comprehending the living present; and therefore it can rise to the higher realms of consciousness. As long as our mind is clothed with ideas, ideals, ambitions, jealousies, hatred and all the rest of it, it must distort our view of reality. When we face any problem we always look at it from the personal point of view. For example, you are preparing for the birthday of your sister and at the same time a poor man is dying without food, what would you do? You will rather purchase a very valuable gift for her. Now both are facts, but you live with only a fraction of the situation Your memory is bound with your sister, not with the hungry man. The moment you are aware of it, you live in the totality of fact at that particular moment.

All our activities are determined by our likes and dislikes, by our positive and negative tendencies. By the term positive and negative, we do not mean opposites, that is to say negative is that which is not positive, and positive is that which is not negative. There is pain in every pleasure and pleasure in every pain; our valuations shift all the time. We are balancing all the time the bigger against smaller pleasures and we waste our precious life in running frantically to and fro. We crave for power, position, prestige, status and so many things. How many of us are free of these petty desires? Then wherein lies our freedom of action? Does it lie in discovering the technique of controlling all these? Certainly not. The only possible key to freedom is to become aware of the entire machinery of the mind. That is to say, we must know the workings of the conscious and the unconscious mind. We must become conscious of our thought processes, our emotions and feelings, we must live attentively from moment to moment. Continuous awareness of one's mind is the key to Krishnamurti's teachings. We have to face some challenge very moment and we have to respond to it rightly. And the problem is how to act. Now, what is a right action? Right action is that which is in accordance with the situation. We are not defining the right action in the moral sense of the term. We are not stating what must the action be. Both are unknown, the situation and the action, yet when the action is a harmony with the situation we live fully from moment to moment. Immediate and adequate response to a challenge is our way to reality and reality itself.

Chapter 28

Krishnamurti and the Problem of Effort
by Rene Fouere

There is a link between the effort to secure, the effort to attain, the effort to achieve and the effort to imitate. Even the simplest desire to possess a thing is the pursuit of the ideal of oneself as the thing's possessor. The urge to acquire and the urge to become are essentially the same urge. There can be no peace and no fulfilment for a man who seeks them on the 'horizontal' levels of 'becoming this' or 'becoming that' and refuses to rise 'vertically' into the realm of pure being which is also pure action.

One would argue that even this realm is, on the level of 'becoming'. But it can be a 'becoming', for it is not an approximation to an ideal. In the state of 'pure being' itself there may be such a thing as pure and spontaneous becoming, a creative, unfolding of life, a 'deathless renewal' in the eternal fullness of the present moment.

Krishnamurti, apostle as he is of complete spontaneity, asserts repeatedly and forcibly, that no deliberate intervention can put an end to the cycle of conditioning, the cycle of self-consciousness and of sorrow. The reason he gives is simple: the desire to break the cycle springs from the cycle itself, from the very conditioning it wants to break; it is ultimately a desire to gain or attain something else and such desire is the very substance of the 'I'.

Such desire can bring about a change in self-consciousness, but not a change away from self-consciousness.

'It is the truth that sets you free and not your effort to be free' says Krishnamurti. 'Seek Truth and Truth will make you free' says Christ.

All conscious and deliberate effort, all self-compulsion by which we hope to reach some kind of perfection is merely an attempt to shape ourselves according to a pattern and shows a complete misunderstanding of our real nature. We are so busy in becoming somebody else, that we have no chance to know what we are. No becoming can bring us to ourselves and so we live in perpetual illusion, born of ignorance of our own being.

Besides, all effort of will ends in creating a rigid pattern of behaviour, which keeps us permanently in conflict with the changing circumstances of life, both outer and inner, and which are altogether beyond our control. We find our patterns being continually destroyed and demand endless and painful reconstructions, calling for ever fresh efforts of will.

When we disapprove of our desires and urges and rigidly suppress them, they only change their shapes and assert themselves in some other way. We do not seek the real cause of our distress and therefore it merely changes its level and expression. All our efforts to end desire must remain fruitless and we shall never cease to struggle with ourselves, to divide ourselves into opposing camps, to scatter ourselves more and more and thus keep alive our inner contradictions, which in their totality constitute self-consciousness.

The idea of complete sterility of all deliberate effort forms an essential part of Krishnamurti's teaching and has been expressed by him with great clarity in his talks. It is at the root of his negative attitude to every form of concentration, to all forcing the mind to some particular and pre-arranged channels. According to him no special faculty of the mind (will, intelligence or feeling) should be specially stressed and developed.

This does not imply that Krishnamurti is against all effort whatsoever. It would be an extreme and mistaken conclusion. To him there are two kinds of effort: one caused by the desire for pleasure or achievement the other — an expression of understanding and love in action. (Here by understanding we mean the understanding of ourselves). When we act from understating and love, physically we may be making tremendous effort, but there is no psychological tension in us for we act with our entire being. We make what outwardly looks like effort, but there is really no effort and compulsion — we just act. Our obstacles are outer, not inner.

(Translated from the French)

The Problem of Suffering
by Rene Fouere

The only thing that stands between ourselves and freedom is our incapacity or refusal to see ourselves squarely as we are. Suffering forces us to face ourselves and there is no other remedy for suffering but to submit to its imperious demand for self-awareness. Suffering is the great awakener and the only adequate response is to be glad to be awakened.

When we suffer, we seek remedies, we look for an escape from suffering. Krishnamurti says that our various escapes are completely ineffective, mere concepts which help us to forget ourselves as long as we are busy in their construction, but are unable to uncover the deep and permanent roots of sorrow. It is only when we do not turn our eyes away from suffering, when we open ourselves entirely to its cleansing rays, it can complete its task and disappear spontaneously, without leaving any residue.

In other words: out way to liberation from suffering lies through the suffering itself. "Suffering is but intense clarity of thoughts and feelings which makes you see things as they are", says Krishnamurti. He speaks from his own experience. When his beloved brother died, his suffering was immense, but by not escaping from his own experience into any form of consolation, he says it transformed itself suddenly into ecstasy. This experience pervades his entire teachings:

"As you would not like to change something very beautiful: the light of the setting sun, the shape of a tree in the field, so do not put obstacles in the way of suffering. Allow it to ripen, for with its flowering understanding comes. When you become aware of the wound of sorrow, without the reaction of acceptance, resignation or negation, without any artificial invitation, then suffering itself lights the flame of creative understanding"

This integral liberation through suffering is not the relief which psycho-analysis brings and which is a process in time, based on memory and aiming at adjustment within society. Krishnamurti speaks of integral liberation through the integral acceptance of what is.

(Translated from the French)

Chapter 30

Mind and Intelligence
by Maurice Frydman

Man must know the nature, structure and the use of the only instrument for living at his disposal, which is his mind. Otherwise he cannot be truly human and realise all his potentialities. Here the word 'mind' covers both superficial, the conscious and the deep, the unconscious, the former manifesting itself as our daily consciousness, the latter as the impulses, urges, tendencies and motivation. Consciousness is that portion of the mind which is kept in the focus of attention. Besides attention which is motivated and therefore limited there is also the power of awareness. Awareness of the mind makes possible consciousness, which contains sensations, perceptions, memories, feelings, desires, ideas etc. Awareness here is the very substratum of experience: it is what makes experience happen.

Every conscious being is potentially aware, for awareness is inherent in attention. The teachings of J. Krishnamurti contain an analysis of the mind extremely useful for the willing, deliberate and conscious growth of man. With man, he says, nature has completed her task. With the creation of a self-conscious being, capable of purposive thought and deliberate action she has reached a point beyond which she cannot and need not go. Man is the only living being who knows, whose further growth lies entirely in his own hands, who can either stagnate on the subhuman level of a clever tool-maker and word-spinner, or, deliberately and willingly, set himself to the discovery and development of his human stature, which is as much above and unlike the sub-human, as the self-centered, acquisitive and aggressive sub-human is above the instinctive and fundamentally passive animal.

The mind, as the instrument for biological survival, gave man the mastery of earth, yet man as a species is in danger of extinction for the very same reason which gave supremacy: cleverness in the service of self-centered and aggressive acquisitiveness. To get out of the impasse, man must begin to use his mind in a different way, not as an instrument for self protection, self-perpetuation and self-expansion.

While man has been eminently successful in the jungle, where personal survival is all that matters, as a social being he has largely been a failure. Even insects have reached a level of social integration far above and beyond what human society has achieved.

Of course, animal societies are based on instinct only; they are rigid and do not adapt themselves to changing circumstances. Human society must be able to reflect the infinite adaptability of the human physical and mental structure to the ever changing conditions of life. It is immaterial whether nature changes or society — man, to survive and grow as a social and spiritual entity must find a way of adapting himself.

Society, to become and remain truly human must be in a state of permanent revolution, of continuous re-evaluation, experimentation and re-organisation. It should become and remain a social laboratory where new forms of social life, new patterns of relationship between man and man, man and society, are evolved and tested with the touch-stone of happiness and creativity.

A truly human society will be integrated economically and politically and at the same time present a far greater variety of cultural patterns than we have at present, when culture follows largely the economics of production and distribution.

Krishnamurti maintains that a human society cannot come into being, remakes itself radically. The mind which is now being used in the service of ego-centered acquisitiveness becomes the builder of a social organism infinitely more rich, vital and enduring than any individual can dream of, and in which every individual is free to participate to the full extent of his capacities and yet without thereby lessening the opportunities of others.

However great may be man's personal capacities and achievements, man-in-society is infinitely more able, powerful and creative. Of all the living beings man alone is able to share experience consciously and deliberately; not only with his neighbours in space, but also in time — with the future generations. This capacity to share with the future is both the foundation of society and also the means for its growth and flowering.

Krishnamurti's teaching deals, among other things, with the emergence of the social mind, different from the personal, biological mind, to which society is only for the satisfaction of personal desires. The social mind sees in society more than a group of persons; it sees in it a living entity, organic, not merely organised, the highest expression and fulfilment of its members.

The difference between an organised and organic society lies in its moral standards; the morality of an organisation is cruder and lower than that of its members, while the morality of an organic unit is higher and nobler. In other words, the organic society elevates while an organisation lowers the moral tone.

According to Krishnamurti, the meaning of society is in helping man to reach the highest levels of growth. Man's fruition as a self-centered, and acquisitive sub-human has already been reached and the future holds for him nothing but the inevitable decay, suffering and death. The only hope for man's survival and further growth is in his clear awareness and correct evaluation of the human situation. Every collective problem, when examined closely, reveals itself as being both the sum total and the resultant of the many individual desires, fears, illusions and conflicts. Unless they are tackled on their own, personal level, the social problems cannot be dealt with adequately. As Krishnamurti puts it — the individual problem is the world problem. There is no radical solution to social chaos, unless the personal chaos in every man and woman is brought to an end.

This cannot happen through any political or social revolution, through formal rearrangements in the hierarchy of separation, oppression and exploitation. The individual will always shape society in his own image and all the revolts and revolutions cannot change the image. This image man alone can change — when he sees the need for change.

Man must become fully conscious or there is no salvation for him. He must be aware of himself as both the cause and the effect of chaos. Unless he sees himself as essentially the result of inner and outer confusion, of psychological and social disorder, of lack of clarity and purpose in his relationship to himself and others, he will remain both the creator and the creature of the world in which he lives.

The acceptance of one's own responsibility is the first step of liberation. Once man has realised that the cause of all the world's chaos lies in himself, he is already at the only starting point from which the right departure can be made. He will deliberately and resolutely set himself to examine the structure, functioning and motivation of his sub-human mind, not in order to improve, ennoble or enlighten it, but to understand it and thereby be free from it.

All Krishnamurti's teaching is centered on the transformation of the mind from the sub-human to the human, from self-concern, from senseless worry to quiet love. The means for this transformation lie in the very nature of man, in his capacity to perceive, to compare, to establish relationship, to trace effects to their causes and causes to their effects, to project himself into others and others into himself — in short — in his intelligence.

The awakening of intelligence is Krishnamurti's supreme task; not of the intellect which cares for results only and is indifferent to means, but of wisdom, which, confident that right means are all that matters, that the ends are in the means, is entirely centered in the present and free from all motivation.

Intelligence or wisdom is the fruit of self-knowledge, of knowing oneself integrally, minutely and correctly, without condemnation or justification, not as a preliminary to self-improvement, but as an expression of willingness to see things as they are.

Wisdom is in seeing things as they are and not in trying to make them better. A clear perception of their immediate and ultimate causes makes one free from these causes and leads to the spontaneous, although sometimes delayed extinction of their effects. While the intellect fights with symptoms and wears itself out in futile struggle, wisdom uncovers the causes and effortlessly watches their results to wither away, since the causes, like roots of plants, need the darkness of ignorance to spread.

In daily life intelligence manifests itself in constant awareness of every movement of every thought, feeling and action and in the uncovering of the unconscious motivations, the hidden urges, the unavowed desires and fears that crowd the unconscious mind.

The bringing of the unconscious into the conscious is the first fruit of intelligence. It marks the reaching of the human level, on which there is no conflict between the conscious and the unconscious. This integration of the entire mechanism of consciousness will open to awareness vistas of perception and experience, of affection and action beyond our boldest dreams.

J. Krishnamurti Ancient or Modern?
by B.N.

A student of J. Krishnamurti is prone to look for antecedents and discover to his great joy or dismay that what Krishnamurti says was already stated by every great teacher in human history. Man's essential freedom from time and necessity and his inalienable right and opportunity to actualise his immense potentialities — these truths were repeated again and again along humanity's long and weary road. The followers and disciples have kept the form and lost the spirit, but every time we make an attempt to go down to the original teaching, we find the same insistence on the significance of man and the immense vista of perception and action open to him merely for his willingness to reach out. Krishnamurti says nothing more because nothing more needs and can be said, "All the Buddhas speak the same Truth".

What is it then that makes each teacher unique? That they are unique there is no doubt and their uniqueness, petrified in their disciples, has been the cause of much violence and hatred. In what way is Krishnamurti unique, inimitable, incomparable?

The truth about man is simple and universal and does not change with time and place. But what does change is the human situation, the need of people at some crucial period of human history. The greatness and uniqueness of a teacher lies in his being supremely adequate to the epoch in which he lives; he fulfils an urgent need; he brings the remedy exactly in the form in which it is required.

We need not labour this point, even a cursory study of the life and work of ancient (and modern) teachers will show the completeness and depth of their response to the needs and problems of the society in which they lived.

Their society might have been big or small, localised or scattered; the greatness of the teacher is not in the number of his followers, but in the revolution in what they are and what they do. Through them his influence spreads in ever widening circles and although much of it is lost or thwarted, the mark he leaves is unmistakable and permanent.

Krishnamurti's claim to be a teacher in his own right lies in the supreme adequacy of his approach to the problems of modern society and in the efficiency of the remedy he offers. After all, the great religious traditions of mankind still exist, with their scriptures and faithful priests and temples. Yet they are incapable of lifting humanity from the present impasse. If they could, they would. But they cannot, because times have changed and they have not. This is the fate of every great movement. It becomes formulated, formalised, obsolete, inadequate, useless, a nuisance, a menace and finally an obstacle to survival. It may not be the fault of the original teaching, but all forms decay *inevitably*.

The supreme danger that faces humanity at present is not religion, ideology, or the 'ultimate weapon'. It is mind control, the development of powerful means of shaping and controlling the human psyche, both individual and collective. From speech to press, from press to radio, from radio to television, the power and reach of propaganda is increasing from day to day. Insidious ways of influencing and changing human thought and action through all forms of drugging, by chemical, through all the channels of the sense and the mind have become a sinister menace. Reshaping of human personality is growing from skill to art and from art to science. Not that our personalities need no reshaping, but they must grow towards creative freedom, not towards productive slavery, which they do when manipulated by any form of vested interests, political, economic or religious.

Man's greatest problem at the present moment is to resist this overwhelming pressure and develop the power and the art of exploring the endless horizons of one's own being. We need a race of men immune to authority both outer and inner, free from external and internal compulsions. Such people are the nightmare of a leader. To agree they must understand and to act they must love. They are loyal to the truth of every situation and will accept no substitute; unswayed by fear or desire, they know one master only: their own true heart. Their thoughts are clear and free from all confusion; their sole concern is with what calls for compassionate action. Unmoved by compulsion, gross or subtle, they are the seeds of humanity's brighter future, free from uniformity and fear. Independent in understanding, united in their feeling for each other, each unique in creative self-expression of his deepest being — such people only can create a happy world, not the shaped and guided products of a machine-made welfare state.

Krishnamurti is the seed of humanity liberated from its past, from the course of its animal and sub-human heritage. In a way every true teacher was such a seed. But Krishnamurti is supremely actual, his is the truth of the present moment. We need exactly what he brings — freedom from inner, unconscious slavery to the authority of the leader and the book, the party and the state, or authority of own's opinions and ideas. By stripping man of all that binds, he sets him free. The great surge of life that freedom gives strikes in us a source of causeless joy, the best sign that our soul is again our own.

Chapter   32

Truthfulness
by Maurice Frydman

Listening to Krishnamurti, just like reading him, is invariably an intense personal experience. He never addresses himself to masses; in a way he is not at all concerned with the masses. His work seems to be entirely with the individual, for, he says, when all goes well with man, society inevitably takes its proper shape.

The individual, his unique way of living his life and reacting to the life around him, cannot possibly be right unless he is in direct and constant touch with reality. Reality is not an experience to take place in the past or in the future; it is not on the line of time. It is in the way we experience, in the very manner of experiencing. It can, therefore, be had only in the present, for all experiencing is in the present. The moment of the 'now', is the only moment of time we know, but somehow we take it for granted and never investigate the immensities it contains. If we watch our minds we shall see that they oscillate all the time between memories and expectations, between what creates the past and what creates the future and never stay in the present. To live in the 'now' we must abandon the habit of uninterrupted thinking; thought must stop if we have to go beyond it. Reality is where thought does not reach; the verbal realm of thinking is the realm of illusory conventions.

To be without thought and yet conscious is a state which may be called awareness; it is a state free from emotions and mental connotations. While it is difficult to describe, it is easy to experience, for it is inherent in every conscious state. Every state of consciousness presupposes the content and also the awareness of the content. Out of habit we are mixing up the two. All that Krishnamurti is asking us to do is to be clear in our minds that the content is not all there is in consciousness, that apart from it there is the power to perceive; that while content changes all the time and is deeply coloured by the feelings and emotions it evokes, awareness makes consciousness possible without being in any way affected by what we are conscious of.

All that we have to do is to dissociate ourselves emotionally from the ever varying contents of our consciousness and to remain as a centre of pure awareness "without like and dislike, without identification, without choice". While this attitude of pure awareness is rather a state of relaxation, since effort and tension belong to the emotionally charged contents, it is not easy to remember to dissociate oneself from the content of one's consciousness for the habit of intense personal participation is too powerful. Yet there is no other way to reality; all inadvertence destroys it. We do not perceive the real because we are not alert enough; we cannot be sufficiently alert as long as we are utterly engrossed and concerned.

We cannot stop the flow of events, but we can cease being carried away by them; we can let them come and go, for to come and go is their very nature; but we can remain alert and fresh, unaffected by the past, unprepared for the future.

Every event, every fact that happens has energy and vitality; when we look at it in 'passive awareness' in 'affectionate detachment', in a strange and mysterious way, the energy and vitality of the event become our own and we are enriched by what happens. When we are not aware, when we do not pay attention to the present fact, we collapse into difference, stupor and death. If, on the other hand, we misjudge and misevaluate the event and relate it to that bundle of memories and expectations, hopes and fears which we call 'me', we live an illusory life, hanging between, and giving energy to the opposites of life and death, pleasure and pain, misunderstood as good and evil.

The first step towards the real lies through the full awareness of the unreal. Or, in other words, one can not know the true without knowing the false; that by which the false is known is also the means of knowing the true. Or, again in different words, the knowledge of the false is the first intimation of the real that we can have. For, after all knowledge is of the true or it cannot be properly called knowledge. The taking of the false to be true is a state of ignorance, not knowledge. Knowledge presupposes insight into reality and insight into the falseness of the false is obvious by insight into the reality of a situation. We can not be wrong in knowing that we are wrong; there is something unmistakable in the perception of a mistake. Therefore Krishnamurti is tireless in repeating that our perception of the real grows with our recognition of the false as false. As long as we take the false to be true, we are just stupid and reality is definitely not for the fool.

So this is our problem: how to put an end to our stupidity. We are stupid when we take the false for true, the unreal for the real. We do so because our minds are clothed with ideas and ideals, jealousies and ambitions, loves and hatreds. We meet life and face facts through a thick layer of personal, national and racial memories, we *are* all those memories and we act from them, not from the reality of a given situation. Every moment of life contains its own challenge and its own way of meeting it; but we are blinded by our memories and expectations and act as we feel and not as life demands. We fall out of tune with the situation, with the laws of our own being and suffer in consequence; and there can be no relief for us, except in seeing our mistakes and undoing them. All that is needed is a tendency towards impersonal awareness operating constantly and spontaneously. It is neither painful, nor does it demand much effort; it is, in a way, more natural to be aware than to be engrossed; but we get engrossed by habit and it is hard to break a habit of a lifetime which was never questioned before.

Influenced by the precept and example of others we have created a 'self', as 'me', a concept: 'I am so and so', the 'so-and-so' including all that is there in the unconscious. All the mistakes made, all the right responses missed, all the misunderstandings and misbehaviours of the past are contributing to the building of the 'I', which is the distilled essence of our stupidity, of all the failures of the past to meet life squarely and rightly.

Pleasure and pain are incidents in living but they cannot be the laws by which to live. Life contains both and goes beyond both like all opposites they contain and merge into each other. The man guided by the pleasure-pain reaction will run in circles and reach nothing in the end.

The question: what is there to reach in life? is not easy to answer for all our possible and imaginable answers are in terms of escape from pain and attainment of pleasure. We should look for the answer to our question in the state of being which lies beyond both; a state in which they may be present but do not matter, for they are shortcircuited in what may be called ecstasy, but which is really high intensity of thought and feeling and bold immediacy of action and response.

While one cannot possible 'train' oneself for and 'practise' living reality, one can see that one does not live it. The awareness of the falseness of our life is the only awareness we can have as long as our life remains false but since its falseness is due to lack of insight and understanding, in awareness it is bound to dissolve.

Krishnamurti puts great stress on the integrating and healing action of awareness; to him it is the golden key to the kingdom of happiness and freedom. But its doors are guarded by our sad and shameful past which we must in all humility accept before we can cross over. This means the end to all hypocrisy and arrogance, to deceit and make — belief, to vain assumptions and pretentions. To find truth man must be truthful both to himself and to others. The truth that can set us free is the truth of our present condition; if we open ourselves to it, it will lead us beyond our present state.

Krishnamurti and the Problem of Immortality

by S.D.

Krishnamurti defines the 'I' as the urge to continue, the longing for permanency. Does it mean, by contrast, that the man liberated from the 'I'-complex has no continuity?

It seems to me, that the liberated man is supremely permanent. But his permanency, like his creativeness, need not be thought and willed and sought. Spontaneity is his way of life. There is no constant effort, there is no groping towards anything. He is spontaneous from moment to moment. This inherent steadiness in being oneself always should not be mixed up with the continuity of the 'I', which is but a series of reactions to life's challenges essentially conditioned to the point of being entirely automatic. The 'I' always imitates. When it does not repeat one's yesterday's reactions, it tries to copy somebody else's. This chain of repetitions the 'I' takes for permanence. Therefore we must distinguish between the permanence of a centre of perception and the continuity of a centre of self-identification and imitation.

Outside circumstances influence the 'I' by their appeal to its desires and fears. The liberated man is beyond desires and fears, and therefore unassailable from outside. When confronted with lure or threat, he remains supremely sensitive and open and just allows the challenge to exhaust itself without reacting to it in any way. He is very steady in his not reacting, yet his no-reactions is not automatic, but the outcome of fine sensitivity and clear understanding. This permanence of freedom from reaction is not something laboriously conquered and maintained with effort, but just an attribute of himself in action. He need not visualise, shape and control it. It is his by virtue of his freedom from the causes of memory, laden desires and fears which constitutes the 'I'.

The absence of 'I' does not prevent him from being an individual in the fullest sense. An integrated man is a man of power, of immense internal resilience. His basic attitude to life is very clear and contains no internal contradictions. Without having a self he is always himself.

Soon after his great liberating experience, Krishnamurti said that he wants to do something in the world and he shall do it with unwavering concentration. The course his life has taken shows how truly he has kept his word. Yet he did not express himself quite correctly. He could have said: "I am the doing of something in the world".

I have just said that the liberated or integrated man is perma-nent in the sense of being consciously and willingly impermanent as far as his action and responses go. Effortless life implies the acceptance of every challenge and of the right response, as dictated by the challenge itself. He is what he is permanently, because the 'I', the centre of distortion and corruption, has ceased to operate. He makes no attempt to be true to himself; he is true to himself, he is real in all he thinks and feels and does.

The ordinary man is not true to himself, but to the idea he has of himself. This idea is imposed on him by his surroundings, which condition him to think of himself as this or that. His faithful adherence to this idea is made into supreme virtue and to him the entire problem of immortality hangs on the continuity of his idea of himself.

The liberated man has no idea of himself to which he must

conform. He simply is, and in this simplicity of being he attains a permanency both inevitable and spontaneous.

It is because it is not a permanency of possession and expression, but the total freedom from all dependence, that he does not crave continuity, for the uninterrupted succession of incidents. Being comfortable with changes he may not display the virtue of consistency because of his utter and effortless consistency with his own being. His actions and pursuits may appear discontinuous, but this is due to the deep permanency of his being really himself and responding correctly to the ever varying challenges of life.

It is the peculiarity of complete and perfect responses that they leave no residue of memory, no tendency to repeat, no compulsion to pursue. One may say that a perfect action dies integrally without in any way burdening the next moment.

Not only does each moment exhaust itself completely and suddenly without leaving behind a residue, but the next moment also is born afresh, untainted by the emotional or verbal remnants of the previous moment. In other words, there is, between two successive moments, an 'interval', a state of suspense, of no-thing-in-particular, free from all memory of the past and from anticipation of the future, from all thought, if by thought we mean the retentive and projective functions of the mind.

One could say that this state of 'interval' forms the background in the life of the liberated man, against which his actions succeed each other like lightnings against the night sky. They strike suddenly and unpredictably and disappear completely. Their variety and transitoriness is brought out in relief by the silent and permanent state of 'interval', a vital and intense potentiality of an infinite number and variety of actualities.

On the other hand, when consciousness is made dual by the 'I'-process, each action seeks to be continued by another action, seeks to repeat, improve and perfect itself in the next movement of life, like a man, who seeks in his progeny the fulfilments he did not find in his own existence. When the past action, because of its incompleteness, obsesses the present moment, the present action cannot be new, fresh, full of its own meaning. It becomes a mere extension, a repetition, a distorted or corrected copy of what had happened before.

But when life becomes a sequence of complete action being related by desire or fear to a previous action, then each experience is fresh and new, entirely unique not comparable with any other, something which never was and never will be the same. It knows no ancestry and no descendants, it owes no allegiance to a precedent or a principle. Each moment has its own being and is absolutely free, for it is not an element in a series of happenings, each determined by the past and determining the future. Time, which is the succession of causes and effects, has no power over an integrated man.

His life is a sky fill of lightnings, each lightning having its own strength and beauty, unprecedented, unimitable. Nothing continues, nothing discontinues, for his mind does not work in opposites and is free from the tyranny of time. His life corresponds to what Krishnamurti calls a state of being which is its own immortality.

C h a p t e r   34

Knowing Ourselves
by Charis Leybourne-White

To me it is transparently urgent for Man to understand more
deeply what Man is, and especially the human mind. We have
by now explored far, and with such unbelievable success, outside
of Man, into the Atom and now into Space. But we are all
witnesses of the psychological immaturity of the human beings
in whose hands these newly discovered secrets of Nature are
being used to threaten Man himself, the whole structure of our
life. We must also have felt the force of materialistic values, the
greed for possession of things, sweeping away our finer
sensitivities, and values for that which cannot be bought and
sold. How penetrating and mighty are the influences which play
upon us constantly. Yet in facing the outer world and its impacts,
if we are a little thoughtful, we realise, that influences from
outside, cannot affect us, without striking an answering chord
within us. It is to this answer that we have to listen, and hear
its echo from our own depths. Only then can the echo die away
and leave our minds clear and free, unshaken by whatsoever
outer storms may come. In the present World Crisis, it is
important that there should be some people who are thus free,
to remain unshaken and steady, to be lamps steadily glowing,
whatever darkness may be outside — darkness of Man's uncon-
sciousness, even if we avoid the grim darkness of another world

conflict. Most of us may have known that the Great Teachers of Mankind have always urged the importance of man's knowing himself, and have said that this self-knowing must fill the journey of our life. But until now, the challenge has gone unheeded, or largely unheeded, down the generations. It is significant that in this very age of such discoveries and such conflict and turmoil, precisely now there has arisen anew, and from several quarters, the stimulus to us to become widely and deeply aware of ourselves. What is unconscious in individuals becomes cumulatively the hidden and unknown in the mind and heart of humanity, and our individual lives and our collective societies are being battered and sundered by all this. We *must* awaken. But not only *must* we. It is not mere necessity. Indeed, it is surely the way to that which it is to be truly human. Herein lies the way to our greater happiness, creativity and freedom. Julian Huxley has even told us that in general terms the way of further evolution is towards extending awareness.

The mind, our mind, has great depths hidden under the surface mind of everyday rational action and thought and decision. Modern psychology has, in theory at least, made us aware of the unconscious mind. Therefore, any enquiry into the hidden background of our minds would need to be pushed very deeply. It would need to go deeply into what is special to ourselves, our own personal, but hidden, aspirations, ideals, hopes, fears etc. And the enquiry would also need to go deeply into what we have in us in common with our neighbours, and ultimately with men everywhere. (The collective unconscious, as the great Swiss Psychologist C.G. Jung has termed it.) In these hidden depths of our minds, some residue of past cultures there may be, but also we have to be ready to confront the marks within us of all the influences, of all the family and social prejudices, the community conventions and demands, and the imprint of age-old religious bigotries: The subtle, and yet powerful, impact of these is constantly moulding and defining our lives. We are under the sway of collective fears and superstitions, of collective hopes and unfulfilled, but long pursued, dreams. The scars of the whole of humanity are within us, expressing themselves as primordial fears and violent passions. There are remnants within us still of the primitive man who was our ancestor: From parents to children, generation by generation, all this is handed on, especially in the exposed, vulnerable years of infancy and early childhood. The heritage is planted within us, without our ever knowing it. The surface of our minds, all we usually know of ourselves, and what we usually think is the whole, may be correct, confirming, respectable. We may feel we are indeed 'cultured'. But that surface is only a veneer. Underneath it, lie emotions and cravings, and passions and fears which the conscious mind may shun to recognise most of the time, but which still boil and ferment under that deceptive surface. Human culture was becoming so refined, we thought, so enlightened. But obviously we deceived ourselves. During this very century there has been eruption after eruption of brutality and violence in massively destructive wars, in social revolutions, in racial hatred, in religious strife. Man's inhumanity to Man has been flagrant and wanton. And now, out of the scientific discovery of the means to split the atom, man has forthwith devised weapons of mass destructiveness and horror, beyond the device of any prior epoch. Yet all this is the complete opposite of the so-called 'culture' of our surface minds, individually and collectively. So how could Man act in all these ways with brutality and violence, unless the potentiality for such action lay within him, even if normally deeply suppressed from expression, even if hidden away from his own consciousness about himself? And how could communities and Nations be so, which is collectively Mankind, unless, for the most part, individuals were themselves in such a condition of conflict, violence, tension — and above all in such ignorance of their own depths and powers and passions? The deep and violent tensions are hidden even to ourselves in that mostly we live for a lifetime with ourselves without ever knowing ourselves.

Now those who undertake the voyage of self-discovery, who are therefore steadily uncovering all that had previously been hidden in themselves and so coming to a real self-knowing would come to discover a secret well of loneliness, most deeply within. They would discover a hidden fear at the heart's core, the fear of "me" alone, and separate from the whole movement of life. They would then obviously have to enquiry deeply into the very essence of this sense of intense loneliness, and this fear. Our minds revolve in endless self-centred thinking, around "me" and "my" gains and losses, "my" desires and despairs, "my" past and "my" future. And this very thinking around "myself", endlessly self-centred, brings always more unhappiness than happiness to us all. But is this the inevitable and final state of our minds? J. Krishnamurti, to me greatest of psychologists, and more than that also, emphasises that a total change in all this, in the whole manner of functioning of the mind is *necessary*, and is *possible*. That such a change is necessary, any thinking person contemplating our individual lives, and the world situation between man and man, will surely recognise. But to discover whether such a radical change is *possible* or not, demands from us the hard work of delving very deeply into our own minds. The mind must indeed know all the ways of itself, down to its most profound depths. But J. Krishnamurti also urges that the mind cannot fundamentally change itself from within itself, that is, by a perpetuation of its usual processes of analysing, evaluating, comparing, idealising, condemning and making effort. We all try to clarify the mind from within itself. But how could the mind with all its old movement, and with all its old burdens, bring a complete renewal to itself? *Obviously* it could not. We must come to a state of complete humility. We must come to the realisation that psychological thinking, however far pursued, cannot bring about a wholly new quality and functioning in the mind. The whole issue is very simple really. The mind, our mind, has only to see, be aware of itself totally, and in that awareness there must be no reaction of any kind, no analysis, no evaluation, no comparison, no argument. Simply an intense awareness of every movement of itself is needed. Then the mind would remain still, with the realisation that only *that* which comes through silence can resolve our problems, can free our minds totally from all the problems. What can happen then? The surface mind having thus become still, then the deeper mind can unburden more of itself to the surface and become known. There is progressively more conscious and less unconscious in the mind. In this way, the extent of the still layer of mind increases, becomes more extensive. Until at last the whole mind may be still, receptive, passive, listening and no longer the intensely active initiator. Then that moment might be reached when the mind abandoned its self-centred movement, its endless movement around the "me', and instead, waited totally upon the action of THAT SOMETHING from beyond itself. Then, and only then, could the mind be said to be an utterly new mind. It would be freed of its old involvement with the burden as well as the fascination of the past, and with the anxious concern for "me" and "my" affairs in the future. Freed of all this, the restlessness stilled, then our minds would become truly creative. At the same time, our hearts, freed at last of the mind's calculations, would be truly open to love. Then our whole beings would be truly open to the Highest, to the direct religious experience.

Uses of the Past
by B.N.

We need not condemn the past — it is enough not to look to it for inspiration and guidance.

What are then the legitimate uses of the past?

The past acts in two ways: the mechanical and the organic. The mechanical part operates when the past becomes the pattern for the present, when the future becomes a copy of the past on the excuse that a consistent plan of action is necessary, that a pre-established model is essential, that one should distrust the urge for integral freedom of action. But the urge is there — most real because our deepest vital instinct is towards total freedom.

The other way the past can act is organic. Whatever the metaphysics of the subject may be, the psychology of it does not demand that the present should necessarily be entirely the creation of the past. The present can have a creativity of its own, intrinsic and instantaneous. It can draw its energy from a source which may contain all the residues of the past and yet leave the present free to shape itself with immediate spontaneity. There is a vast difference between the compulsory past of dogma and tradition and the intimate, organic past which fertilizes our present without moulding it. The dead past preserves its dead while the living past nourishes life.

There exists a famous definition of culture as that which remains when all else is forgotten. In other words culture is of the unconscious, while civilization is of the conscious. The technology of a civilization must be recorded and remembered; it is always deliberate, never spontaneous; while culture must be an effortless expression of one's entire being, primarily of the unconscious; for without the free and total participation of the unconscious cultural behaviour is unthinkable. We can change our civilization overnight, even go back to the stone age or go forward to travelling in space and time at will and yet change little but our past determines our culture totally and inexorably.

Culture is the sum total of our valuations, of our emotional responses. It is the shape of our character of our mind.

It is the truly the underground shape, the one of which we are little aware and which manifests itself on the spur of the moment in action.

The tragedy of our age is that we are civilized without being cultured, that we have gone ahead intellectually and therefore technically and grievously lag behind emotionally and therefore socially. This gap between the intellectual and the emotional must be filled; our culture must catch up with our civilization. How to go about it? Here the right use of the past comes in: in the mirror we can re-live our past experiences as and when they come to the surface — we can welcome them and look at them with attention and dispassion and try to understand now what we have not understood in the past — without justification or condemnation.

Our unconscious contains enormous layers of undigested material — there is no end to it for it covers not only the short span of this life, but also the wide stretches of past lives, personal, ancestral and social. They are all there within our reach waiting for being taken in hand and understood and built into the structure of our character. The function of memory is to preserve what is yet to be made our own — we need no longer remember what has become a part of ourselves. We can be free from memory and its intrusions only when we have done it full justice — we can be free from the hold of the past only when we have met it in affectionate awareness in the present. There is such a thing as the forgiveness of sins, but it is we who have to forgive ourselves and this can be done only when we have understood our sins so fully, that we can sin no more. When innocence becomes our own being, the past comes to an end. Freedom of the past is in fulfilling it and it is fulfilled when understood. Awareness is the will to understand and therefore our golden key to freedom.

J. Krishnamurti and the Materialists
by Maurice Frydman

When J. Krishnamurti speaks of the necessity of going beyond intellect and realising pure intelligence as a state of "harmonious integration" of man's mental and emotional faculties, he does not speak in terms of matter and spirit, or body and mind as two or as one.

For understanding him it is not necessary to read into his words epistemological and ontological theories, dealing with the nature of and the ground for cognition.

It is perfectly immaterial to him whether the body creates the mind, or the mind creates the body, or the two are only two aspects of a mode of being which is neither, although not observable and describable except in terms of mind and body.

Let us assume that the so-called materialistic assertion that thought is a physiological process had been demonstrated in a laboratory by feeding some chemicals into one end of a man-made piece of machinery and getting a book on epistemology at the other end. Let it be proved to the hilt that brain secretes thought as liver secretes bile.

In no way does it change Krishnamurti's stand. To him the exploration of the mind is not important; he is only concerned with the use we make of it.

And for making the right use of the mind, whatever its physical or metaphysical foundations, we need not waste time on purely theoretical discussions.

We may substitute the word "brain" for the word "mind" without in any way changing or solving the problem that confronts us. Let sensation and perception, memory and thought, feeling and insight, intuition and inspiration, ecstasy and rapture, character and holiness, the sense of the true, the good, the beautiful, be all a matter of brain and never of structure and function.

Still it is supremely important to us, this structure and this function.

Have we reached the limit of cerebral organisation, or organic integration? Are we the most perfect feeling, thinking, acting, experiencing machines possible? Are we supremely adapted to the universe around us, to each other, to oneself, to life, in short?

The sorry mess we are making of this business of living, individually and collectively, calls for insight and action. Even if we have very good reason to think that man is a process totally describable in physical and chemical terms, still we have no basis, no need for refusing to listen to Krishnamurti, who is solely and supremely concerned with the use we make of our physical and mental endowment, whatever may be its ultimate nature, material, mental or neither.

The real problem is not in the nature of the mind, but in the strange assumption, taken for granted by so many materialists, that since the mind is a product of "material" phenomena, it should concern itself only with "material" pursuits.

Obviously the world "material" is used here in two different meanings. Man may be a "material" being, but he need not and should not be materialistic in the sense of giving undue importance to his physiological needs and to the enjoyments derived from their satisfaction.

Not that those needs are imaginary and the enjoyment is illegitimate. But the saying "not by bread alone...." is valid, whatever the theories of the body and the mind and of their relationship.

The argument that since mind is matter, man is just a blob of protoplasm of not much importance, is puerile in the extreme. It is supremely important to this blob what is the content of its proto-plasmic consciousness.

Obviously the word "material" is used here in two different senses not for the sake of a soul or a God, but for the width and the depth of living they make possible. After all, our main concern is with living a life and not with theories.

So, when Krishnamurti talks of going beyond intellect and living intelligently, fully, happily, the validity of what he says is not abolished by the argument, that the mind is a function of the brain. Let it be.

Still there is work to be done. The brain is pliable, mouldable, teachable. It can yield a variety and intensity of conscious states of which we may have only heard from a few exceptional individuals.

Krishnamurti may be one of them, and it would be utterly irrational to dismiss him on the ground that thought is a physiological secretion. Still it matters enormously what kind of thought we think.

When he talks of the utter stillness of the mind into which Reality can flow, there is no need of jumping at once into a discussion on the physical nature of the mind and the metaphysics of Reality. The mind may mean the brain and Reality may mean full and harmonious correspondence and co-ordination between consciousness and the world which it reflects.

Silent and choiceless awareness of all that is going on from moment to moment within and outside the "brain", or the "body" may be just training the "mind" to function in a new and rather unusual way. Still it is an interesting experiment, the results of which hardly depend on the religious or philosophical background of the experimenter.

Again and again Krishnamurti warns us: if you would discover, give up preconceived notions. To see things as they are, cease to look at them through the eyes of yesterday.

Deliberately and patiently erase the grooves of mental habits, of fixed ways of feeling and thinking, so that there will be no misalignment and misunderstanding between the subject and the object of your consciousness.

It is like creating a vacuum in a fluorescent tube. When a certain degree of vacuum is reached, the spark strikes and the tube begins to shine. Whatever the theory of it, the light is good.

Revolt and Revolution
by Maurice Frydman

A study of the social and political upheavals in history will show that after each revolt against oppression a reaction sets in and the revolt continues in a different from, manned by a different set of people, yet essentially the same. The reaction rarely takes the shape of a counter-revolution for the restoration of the old order; it more often shows itself in the corruption of the new, theoretically perfect institutions.

What is a revolution? In the accepted meaning of the word it is a total change, a turning upside down, a complete reversal, a fundamental reconstruction. What calls for a revolution? Obviously, only suffering calls for a change. Happy people do not need revolutions. They are quite willing to leave things as they are. It is the man who suffers that desires a change.

A revolt is blind, violent, temporary and superficial. The deep causes of evil are not affected. But a revolution is not worth the name if it does make a fundamental change in the existing situation. The situation is of suffering and the revolution lies in the removal of the causes of suffering.

There were many revolts against political and social, religious and economic institutions, but change in situations does not remove the evil heart that has created or corrupted them.

In revolt the tendency is to attack institution and those whose interests are vested in them. But institutions are not always the cause of evil, they are often only its symptoms. The outcome of a revolt may be a set of completely different institutions, but they will inevitably perpetuate the same evil as long as its real causes are not removed. On the other hand, the removal of the real causes will change the situation radically even if the outer forms had remained the same.

Can the man who is in trouble create a revolution? He can only revolt against his suffering. He has neither the will nor the clarity to discover and examine the causes of suffering, which cannot be removed unless they are uncovered and fully grasped in their interplay and ramifications. For the search for the causes of suffering is not an easy matter. It needs a clear and unbiased mind, a heart that makes no difference between friend and foe. And these exactly are the qualities which the man who suffers usually lacks.

When the victim of oppressions rises in revolt against the oppressor, he may succeed in liquidating a particular oppression or system of oppression and yet the oppression will remain because its real causes were not understood and its deep roots not uncovered. It is but an instance of a general law that the removal of the symptom does not affect its cause. A successful revolution will undo the causes while a revolt will at best remove the symptoms only to see them return in another and often an aggravated form. A revolt is always followed by a reaction, while a revolution is final.

Neither a revolt nor a revolution need be sweeping; sometimes they are associated with vast social, political and religious changes; more often they happen on a very small scale, in a narrow sector of human life. the scale does not matter to the people involved in the change. What matters is that revolt deals with symptoms, while a revolution attacks the true causes of suffering..

Nor is there such a thing as pure revolt or pure revolution. In practice there is an element of revolt in every revolution. To the extent to which root causes of suffering are discovered and done away with a revolution happens. As Krishnamurti would put it, there is a complete transformation. To the extent to which the symptoms are bound to set in.

Philanthropy in the ordinary sense of the world is not a revolution. It is merely a safety valve which postpones the explosion by letting off the steam. However sincerely it may be practised; it shows a complete disregard for the true causes of suffering. It is not a question of distributing surplus wealth. There should be no surplus wealth in the hands of a few individuals and no scope for becoming benefactors, for sharing or not sharing as fancy dictates. The real revolution demands the understanding of the causes of the urge to accumulate, to dominate, to exploit, to oppress and the setting oneself free from all such causes.

The oppressed cannot make a revolution. Whatever they do will be only a revolt, which will bring in reaction and create some other pattern of oppression. A new set of oppressors will replace the old. We can see it happen all over the world.

This does not mean that those who suffer should do nothing. As long as they suffer they will revolt. The oppressor, capitalistic or bureaucratic, may try to release the accumulated pressure by creating the illusion of 'democracy' which is merely a device for shifting the blame to the exploited, but as long as there is suffering, there will be revolts and fresh suffering and more revolts, in a vicious circle.

At present the conflict in the world has taken the shape of a struggle between the partisans of ownership of the means of production by the state and the partisans of ownership in the hands of financial and industrial corporations. Both these forms of ownership are only slightly different symptoms of the same causes. A revolt may change one form of ownership for the other, but a deep gulf will remain between the producer and the consumer and also between the producer and the means of production. Call it 'people's' democracy or 'dictatorship of the 'proletariat' or 'welfare state', wage slavery will remain a tool of oppression, a cause of degradation and misery.

The real causes of conflict lie much deeper. There are many levels of causation; there is the desire to dominate and the willingness to submit; behind the first there is the desire to expand, behind the second the desire to continue. Wherever we start in our search for the deeper causes of human suffering, we find ourselves invariably led to the conclusion that the root causes of the chaos in the world are psychological. The various social, political and religious institutions are not the causes but merely the symptoms of the confusion and chaos in the hearts of men.

Therefore a true revolution must be an inner one, a transformation in our ways of feeling and thinking. There must be a change in the approach, a reversal of values, a different attitude to the problems of human relationship, which is the foundation of social life. We are now far away from all insistence on merely changing institutions (not that institutions do not require change). With the change in the psychological approach they will change quietly and quickly, without causing suffering and disturbance.

The trouble with the ideologies is that they do not go deep enough. They invariably take the symptom for the cause and while they can supply the revolt with a doctrine, they cannot create a revolution, because they shirk from admitting that the causes of the chaos in the world are primarily psychological.

This point can not be stretched too much: all revolt against symptoms will leave the causes untouched; the causes cannot be done away with unless they are laid bare; they can not be discovered unless they are searched for carefully and patiently; this careful and patient search is not possible when the mind is made dull by suffering. It requires clarity, alertness, leisure and wide and deep sympathy.

The man who suffers is not in the right mood for a revolution. He is too much in a hurry; he will give ear to anybody who promises quick relief from the outer symptoms, the apparent causes of his agony. The political and other leaders take advantage of his impatience and use him for the organisation of a revolt which will put them into power without much benefit to their followers.

It is the oppressor himself who must revolt against his oppression. How can it happen? As a matter of fact it happens all the time. There are always in the world a few individuals who give up their privileged positions and attack the causes of oppression where they can reach them: in their own lives. They may be few and far between, but they are a very significant pointer in the right direction. When we examine the lives of the great revolutionaries, we find that invariably either they came from the privileged classes or they managed to secure for themselves all the leisure necessary for their broodings and ponderings.

A true revolution happens when the oppressor and the oppressed meet with the intention of putting an end to the oppression by discovering and eliminating its real, psychological causes. This meeting will be first an inner state — the oppressor realising within himself the oppressed and the oppressed discovering within himself the oppressor. The result of such inner meeting will be the inner freedom from the causes of oppression. Those who are inwardly free will be able to go deep into the causes and bring about the outer meeting between the oppressor and the oppressed, who will jointly put an end to oppression. Can such a revolution in approach happen on a mass scale? Yes and no. A psychological revolution is like a chain reaction: it starts with the very few and then spreads explosively to the many. A revolution always begins with those who, having understood the causes of suffering have ceased to perpetuate them in their own lives. As Krishnamurti puts it, freedom must begin with the individual. If the individual transforms himself, his life, then for him there is freedom; and because he is the result of a total process, when he liberates himself from nationalism, from greed, from exploitation, he has direct action upon the whole.

Self-concern can never lead to a revolution, only to revolt. He alone who is concerned with the sufferings of others will have the courage to go far enough and deep enough into the causes of suffering. Revolt flows from hatred, while revolution is the fruit of compassion.

Chapter 38

The Purpose of Living
by A.N.

Two types of criticism are levelled at Krishnamurti — one that he has nothing new to say, the other that what he teaches is so revolutionary that if it were carried into effect it would produce chaos and selfishness. Both these criticisms are due to a lack of understanding.

With regard to the first, as Krishnamurti has truly said, there is no new thing under the sun, but all things are new to the man who understands. When you arrive at a new understanding of life, its meaning and purpose, you look out upon a different world, but yourself. All things are made new to the man who is ever renewing himself.

That the teachings of Krishnamurti, if properly understood and carried into practice, would turn the world upside down is true because it necessitates a revolution in our whole thought and outlook upon life; but that revolution would lead to order and not to chaos, it would bring about a greater beauty in life instead of a greater ugliness. It is also true that the attempt to cling to the old and yet to understand the new is productive of chaos, both in the individual and in the world. It is impossible to turn both without and within, to live in freedom and in bondage, to walk to wards the south and towards the north at the same time. A choice has to be made, the change of direction must be radical. We cannot hold on to accepted traditions and beliefs and yet be free of them. Krishnamurti is like a giant wave which has swept away the foundations, on which our lives are built, and we have to find new foundations, new bricks, with which to build, anew. If we can understand him, we must examine what he says with unbiased mind and open heart, not fearing to face all that it may involve for us of change and even of heart-break.

"Truth is a pathless land", says Krishnamurti. Therefore no one can lay down for another the path by which he shall attain it. Neither can any man see for another his vision of perfection. Each must have his own vision and carve his own way to its attainment. At our present stage, we live by our experiences and the ideas of being beyond experience conveys to us the thought of negation, of cessation, of death. But while we are still held in the grip of experience, we cannot fully express the life within us. Our energy is spent in battling against the bars of our prison house. To be free, to be perfected, to be beyond the yoke of experience, must be to live at that high tension of perfect poise, of complete control, which Krishnamurti characterises as "true creation". Only as we are becoming truly creative are we truly living.

The expressions of life are the reflection of the life within. If the life within is not yet pure, strong and free, the expressions of that life will of necessity be weak, ugly, maimed and distorted. Each man must be his own saviour, as he alone can set free the life within himself and shape the expressions of that life to the vision which he alone can see. The vision, the goal of each man is unique, and so also must be the realisation of that vision. No man can purify the source of life for another, and therefore no man can radically change another or save another. We are naturally influenced more or less by our circumstances and environment, for as a great scientist puts it: "Living always implies a give-and-take between the creature and its surroundings, or, to put it more technically, between the organism and its environment. Indeed, we might call this the unending problem of life, — "to establish and keep up good relations between the living creature and its surroundings".

The purpose of living, according to Krishnamurti, is to become master of your environment. That is what perfection means; and when we have realised it, it is not that we may stagnate, but that for the first time we may make full use of all our faculties, of all our circumstances, of all the expressions of life which hitherto have been our masters. To be liberated within is to be liberated from all the compulsions of the without, and that is why perfection means liberation, means the fulfilment of life and nothing else.

"Then we have to get away from such catchwords as "love", "service", "brotherhood", "helping the world", which, like charity, cover a multitude of sins. Love may be the most beautiful thing in the world, but it can also be the most cruel and the most binding. Love of God has inspired much brutality as well as much kindness, in man. The inquisitors were doubtless inspired by love for the souls of men, but it did not prevent them from torturing their bodies. Most parents love their children but, in many cases, that very love stifles and crushes life in objects of their love. All human love is subject to jealousy which is ever "cruel as the grave".

"Service of the world" is often but another name for interference. We want to change the world according to our pattern, according to our conceptions of right and wrong.

Every religion is built on the conception of a Deity in some form or another, except possibly Buddhism. All religions teach men to worship, to pray, to believe according to a creed or a system of philosophy, to act according to a code of morality and ethics laid down by some divinely inspired guide. And now Krishnamurti tells us that religions are but the frozen thoughts of men and that, if we found truth, we would be free of all religions.

Religion has been responsible for much beauty in thought, in art; it has inspired many noble and heroic deeds. It has also been responsible for almost incredible cruelty, superstition and the enslavement of the human mind. The recording angel alone can decide on which side the scales are weighted.

If we begin with a new conception of life in which religion plays no part, it means a revolution of a very radical kind, it is going to be very difficult for a generation, brought up in religious faiths, to free themselves. That is why Krishnamurti is so anxious to establish schools where a new generation may be educated without any of the old beliefs, traditions and superstitions. It is a great experiment and one which should arouse the enthusiasm of all those who believe that the God in man is the only God he can ever really know.

Krishnamurti and Spiritual Heritage
by Rene Fouere

"As the animals in the circus are trained to act for the amuse-
ment of crowds, so the individual, through fear, looks for these
spiritual performers, the so called priests and swamis, the
dispensers of spurious spirituality and of all the inanities of
religion. Their main function is to entertain; they invent rituals,
disciplines and worship, which may look beautiful but soon
degenerate into superstition and knavery under the cloak of
service."

These words were said by Krishnamurti as early as in 1934 and
harsh as they are, they show the utterly uncompromising attitude
of the Indian sage.

Krishnamurti is a spiritual teacher who is violently against all
spiritual authority; a destroyer of idols. an enemy of churches;
loyal to Truth, he refuses to be loyal to anything else. Even in
India, the land of tradition where his high spiritual standing is
not denied, he makes nothing of all tradition. Therefore among
the great teachers of India his position is unique. Not only is his
way of expression free from all the traditional terminology of
the Indian philosophical genius, not only does he address the
modern man in a modern language, but he also is the only
Indian teacher who is completely free from all tradition, eastern
or western.

I am in full agreement with what Krishnamurti says about religions. I also consider all rituals and ceremonies to be dangerous distractions, taking man away from the only thing that matters. Maybe he is too sweeping in his condemnation of all men of religion; the intentions of many of them may be of the best; all generalizations tend to be false. I am sure that Krishnamurti would agree with me on this point. The controversy between Krishnamurti and the protagonists of orthodox religions is not for me to solve. All polemics tend to be sterile. Instead, I would rather find a point of view from which Krishnamurti's attitude can be at least explained, if not justified.

Krishnamurti himself denies being a speculative philosopher. His message is born out of a personal, everpresent experience. He does not separate his teaching from himself. He clearly says: In the light of what I live my words are true.

Krishnamurti is still alive and his teaching may undergo further developments. I must stress this point before I proceed with the examination of his thought. And also I must say a few words on the form of language used by him. It is simple language, direct, psychologically true, free from all allusion to mythology, I would add: free from all terminology for Krishnamurti is in the habit of charging plain and commonplace words with some unusual and unexpected meaning. In words which should to us be homely and familiar he opens vertiginous depths of import and significance. In that way he is a great philosopher, if by philosophy we mean the art of revealing the hidden and unknown side of things which appeared to us well known and familiar, of showing them from some unexpected and startling angle. The very clarity of Krishnamurti's expression contains often astonishing depths. However clear his words may seem to be, they bewilder, when we read them for the first time. Often it seems that he has compressed in a handful of apparently simple and inoffensive words all the secrets of the universe and the mystery of our own being. They yield meaning after meaning, like a reflection between two mirrors.

Krishnamurti is concerned only with the immediate transformation in his listeners and consistently refuses to build a doctrinal or philosophic system. Therefore we must not be astonished to see him taking up, from moment to moment, an entirely opposite standpoint. He cares little for intellectual constructions; he seeks only to uproot his listener, to dislodge them from the positions of certitude in which their hearts and minds have gone to sleep. Once he said; people need not be taught, they need to be woken up. This explains partly Krishnamurti's vehemence of expression which may appear contemptuous and even crude.

Because of all these tactical distortions it is not easy to penetrate to the very core of Krishnamurti's teaching. I shall try nevertheless, on my own responsibility; to make a short, maybe too short, summary of a teaching which, although repetitive, is extraordinarily vast and rich and full of unexpected and subtle implications. Yet I must stress again that what follows are merely my own explanations and interpretations.

At the very outset we are faced with the question: is it appropriate to talk of Krishnamurti's own teaching? He himself says that what he says is so universally valid, that it cannot be specifically his own.

Were we to disregard the peculiar conditions in which his spiritual awakening took place, we would see in it merely a mystery, one among many. But in his case the emergence into reality was preceded by a most violent revolt against all authority and all tradition. He realized, as he himself says, not through obedience and conformity but through revolt and refusal. Hence the liberating value he gives to doubt and denial of all accepted values. Some may think that Krishnamurti derives a kind of pleasure in accusing the professionals of religion of their mistakes and depravities. I do not believe this to be the exact picture. It does not tally with his extreme sensitivity, so abundantly revealed in his poems and writings and also in the personal and sincere kindness and affection with which he meets the very people whose doctrines, attitude and actions he attacks so violently in his lectures.

It is not a case of mere violent and destructive rebellion against all authority. What he wants is to make us examine the values authority seeks to impose on us and to take them up as our own only, if after due examination, we think them to be true and sane. But then those values are ours, we know every reason for accepting them and we do so on our own responsibility. We have, so to say, recreated them within ourselves; now they have sprouted from within us instead of remaining a strange growth grafted onto our living flesh. Krishnamurti does not automatically oppose any current opinion; doubt to him is a means for reaching a state of unshakeable certainty. Doubting merely for the sake of doubt has no meaning. Krishnamurti insists on the need for living in full responsibility for oneself, of being entirely and freely answerable for one's actions and of taking charge of, in all clarity, one's own destiny. Man's salvation thus becomes the fruit of his own courage. Any order, even if quite the right one, is dangerous and destructive when obeyed blindly, without realizing its meaning and seeing its necessity. Mere obedience creates the habit of irresponsible action, of lazy abdication of choice, of fatal passivity which makes us persist in a mistake when once, by chance, somebody has pushed us into it.

It is reported that a priest asked Krishnamurti: should I not leave the church? To this Krishnamurti answered: Why should you? The priest took it as an encouragement to continue in the church. He was wrong, of course Krishnamurti only invited him to be aware of the reasons for leaving the Church. His reply was perfectly consistent with his attitude.

To those who seek in authority a shelter against their own anxieties, Krishnamurti shows that such shelter just does not exist. Whatever may be our illusions, we ourselves are the ultimate and the only judge of our Being, truth and action. To a listener in New Zealand, who claimed the need of spiritual authority, Krishnamurti said: You think you need a priest to take you to truth. But, unless you know truth already, how can you be sure that you are guided well? And if you know it, why do you seek a guide? This kind of logical shortcut, a purely verbal trap, may seem to put an end to all trust in another, to all value given to his advice. Yet there is good sense in Krishnamurti's answer, for in the last analysis, when we accept authority, we ourselves have decided whose authority we are going to accept. Thus we become responsible for the authority we have imposed on ourselves and for all the certitudes we derive from it. This is a valid point which we are only too apt to forget.

The anarchists may accept Krishnamurti as their own because of his assaults on the very foundations of spiritual authority. This conclusion would have been too hasty. Unlike many others, he does not seek in his struggle against authority a way to raise his own status and increase his value as a person. He aims much higher. If I may say so, he seeks man's eternal salvation and not mere sterile rebellion against established power.

According to him, man's spiritual freedom must come from within, for each one objectively, is alone. No external authority must dominate his inner and perfect freedom. And if man has to liberate himself completely, to transform totally his life, he must accept responsibility for the full change of his actions and behaviour, take firm hold of himself by his own hand. As long as he has not done it, he does not really act. His actions are not his own, they are imposed on him from the outside. He lives in a sort of fascination: he ceases to be a person and only reacts automatically, like a machine.

But merely taking charge of one's life is not enough. One has to find the light that will show the lonely way. This living light will not be found unless one is willing and eager to think anew about all the elements of one's existence. Krishnamurti rejects all authority in order to give man a chance to do his own and deep thinking; he seeks to establish a sort of sanitary screen between the pure source of man;s spirit and the contamination by outer values. Then only thought can be like the lamp sheltered from all wind, which the Bhagavad Gita puts forth as an example of the effective mind.

The individualism of which Krishnamurti speaks is not in opposition to society. He does not want to break, nor even to loosen the bonds which link us to each other. But he wants the individual to be an island of deliberate and solitary enquiry and search raised above the stormy sea of opinions. As he puts it: the individual must be liberated from the false. His individualism is in the dissociation of the mind from every form of pressure.

I may add here that the freedom Krishnamurti speaks of has nothing in common with blindly yielding to impulse. It is the freedom of the man who refuses to imitate: who is himself creative; who threw off every superimposition and has discovered the pure note of his own being, his natural and original vocation, his own genius, his individual uniqueness which in no way can be equated with egotism.

Krishnamurti sees in liberation the freedom to create, and in all that tends to smother and to strangle the creator who dwells potentially in each of us Krishnamurti, naturally, sees an obstacle to spiritual unfolding. Therefore he is so much against all rituals and religious authority which always make man's thoughts and feelings entirely automatic, promoted by external stimuli. He is not so very much concerned with spiritual authority as such, as with the freeing from its grip the living man, the man responsible for himself and to himself, the man who alone can be truly liberated.

It can be seen that Krishnamurti's revolt against authority is neither temperamental nor personal, but has sound reasons and is inspired by real love of man. The outer expression of this revolt may appear rude to the point of shocking but, as Claude Bragdon puts it: Krishnamurti's teachings will exasperate us until we perceive that in his blows he aims only at our chains".

(Translate from the French)

Can Illumination be Transmitted?
by R.P.

One hears much talk these days about the possibility of obtaining
initiation into the life of enlightenment by a direct transmission,
silent or otherwise, from "advanced" individuals. Not a few are
considering a visit to Japan as a worthwhile spiritual investment, for — who knows? — maybe some Zen Master may give
to them that for which they have been searching all their lives.

Is not this way of thinking very similar to the prevalent outlook
on grace? A miraculous granting of spirituality by some external
entity — and whether that benign entity is a God or a Master
makes very little difference. The idea is basically to get something
for nothing, and as in worldly affairs so here also there is the
panting for "attainment" — as though it concerned the
procurement of some merchandise — when in actual fact it is
not even "something". Others are — a little less irrationally, but
still thoughtlessly — pinning their faiths on "do-it-yourself"
systems which are peddled by Masters and religious sects,
without ever looking into the whole problem whether any system
can ever do anything for them in the spiritual life.

Most of the so-called religious people are really trying to commit
mental suicide, by killing off the ego through constant violent
effort, by suppression, meditation, self-denial and various other

pious practices. But mental suicide is not death, it is only life at war within itself. Mental suicide is an acute state of conflict; and while pretending to immolate itself, the "I" is fighting for its survival as strongly as ever.

The fundamental question is can there be death without dying? And can there be dying when there is still burning desire, and whether that desire is for sexual or spiritual ecstasy is immaterial.

So long as there is a desire for experience, the experiencer is thriving. Now dying is the very opposite — that begins when experience is seen to be void. This Void is Death itself, and it is only Death that can make us die. Life can only die when it willingly and lovingly allows Death to pervade it, for by itself it is incapable of ending. For that life is continuity, and can continuity ever give rise to anything but continuity, can it ever break its own bond in time?

Continuity can never be broken on its own level; it can only cease to be when submerged in another dimension — and that dimension is the Timeless, manifesting itself on the level of continuity as Death.

Chapter   41

The Free Mind
by Robert Powell

Every experience leaves an imprint on the mind, whose strength
is according to the intensity of pain and pleasure involved. This
imprint, the residue of the past, become the seed around which
thought in the present crystallizes and grows. This means that
everything is immediately translated by the mind in terms of
pain or pleasure. *The mind does not know how to be neutral.* Even
an experience to which it is initially indifferent, like reading a
newspaper, eating and drinking certain types of food, having
one's meals at a certain restaurant, listening to the radio, watching
television, soon becomes either attractive or repulsive to an
obsessive extent (although we are no longer aware of these
things). Then, with repetition there is habit formation and
ultimately bondage, either positively or negatively. So we see
that the mind continually craves attachments, and if it drops
one habit it soon picks up another.

Even that mind which, through increasing awareness, has freed
itself to a limited extent is soon driven back by the Void to
attach itself on to something, like a leach nourishing itself on
the host. To understand this particular propensity of the mind,
let us look a little more closely into the whole background of
habit.

Everything in nature happens by association, although this manifests itself to the self-conscious individual — perceiving within the framework of space and time — as cause and effect. Association, on the physical level, means determinism, and determinism means absence of freedom; a law of nature is a case of specialization where only one sequence of events is valid out of an infinite number of possibilities. Just so is association limiting in the case of mind; when operating by means of Memory, association results in habit, which is the creation of psychological time, the very stuff of which Suffering is made.

Becoming aware of habit, the mind tries to overcome it, and in the very overcoming of one habit sets up another — the habit of repression. Thus, it must be clear that within the pattern of duality there is no release from habit, and that there can only be the cessation of it, when we go above and beyond the conflicts of duality. Only through understanding the whole mechanism of habit formation — and seeing it in actual operation, which requires great alertness and patience — can thought free itself from habit.

So we have seen that from pleasant and painful experience, the mind builds its house of thought; and the continuity of this edifice in time gives rise to the entity, the "thinker". Once, however, a man has learned to look inward, and begins to study his habitual mechanical reactions he is getting less and less fettered by his experience, and so no longer strengthens the house of thought, which is also his prison. Then ultimately, if he succeeds in completely isolating and identifying the individual elements of association that together constitute the prison, the latter collapses like a pack of cards. (It is very much like the illusion of animation in a motion picture, which is disrupted, as soon as — by lowering the film's running speed — its elements, the individual frames, become identifiable).

In that destruction man finds a new Freedom, which is not a freedom from painful experiences, but a release from the scar these experiences used to leave on the mind.

Krishnamurti and the Problem of Opposites
by Rene Fouere

Krishnamurti, in his teachings, lays bare the illusion of opposites. For instance, those who struggle against possessiveness and cultivate the virtue of non-possessiveness make of it a new acquisition and are caught in the net of illusion. Their pretended victories are merely unrecognized failures.

The opposites which are mutually exclusive on a certain level, become identical on a higher level, a level of vision both clearer and more subtle.

For Krishnamurti, like for Buddha, the only sin is ignorance, not-knowing. What liberates us with certainty and finality is not renunciation achieved with effort and inner contradiction, but the understanding fully of the condition in which we are. We shall play with a poisonous snake only so long as we do not realize that it is poisonous. But once we know its danger we have no desire to come near to it.

It is the man who is afraid that cultivates courage. He flees from fear into its opposite; at the root he is still afraid. But when he knows the source of his fear, it ceases on its own. Then he is neither brave nor coward. He just is. He comes to a state of being which is free of all opposites.

But then what is true virtue, according to Krishnamurti? He would reply, for instance, that to him "humility consists in not knowing that one is different from others". A reply disarming all criticism in its simplicity and depth. It means that virtue is not something positive but the 'being nothing', "Be as nothing", says Krishnamurti and life will be extraordinary beautiful and simple. But few can grasp the sublimity and greatness of this approach. It holds nothing for the shallow mind, for the man who at all costs wants to be something.

All our life is clogged with the fruitless resistance against opposites, with, what we call, the pursuit of the ideal. Its true motive is the desire to gain something of pleasure or to avoid some cause of pain.

Never do we do a thing for its own sake. We are always aiming through it at something else, at some future which always changes and always escapes us, leaving the present, which should have been full and vibrant with life, for the empty, false and sad, an endless expectation with some flashes in between.

We pass from the desire for a piece of clothing to the desire for a woman and then to the desire for God and we imagine that we have made great progress. In reality, our desire has merely changed its object and we are still caught in the circle of desire, which means of dissatisfaction and of pain.

In the same way does Krishnamurti examine the common notions of evolution and of the ideal goal. They are merely the movement of desire over the surface of things; such movement will never bring us to the sudden breaking up of the circle of desire which is the essence of liberation.

"To me," he says, "there is only one truth — the freedom from all hungering and thirsting. All else is mere illusion, infinite in its varieties, its vanities, its glories. The saint, the sinner, the slave, the victor, the man of virtue and the so-called spiritual man, are all equal in their illusion, all rooted in longing. Immense space and time may separate them from each other, but the saint who has gone so far beyond the sinner has merely moved from an inferior illusion to a superior".

(Translated from the French)

Chapter 43

Krishnamurti and Ritualism
by R.F.

You must live with earnestness, with attention, with ardour in every thought, feeling and action, supremely centered in the present moment, which is neither near nor far, but now, in the supreme harmony of understanding and love.

This defines Krishnamurti's attitude to rituals: he explodes them from within, for he makes every moment of life a sacrament.

To Krishnamurti liberation does not consist in doing something special, artificial or unusual, it is in the doing of the ordinary thing in an extraordinary way, with the same care and attention, which the ritualists give to their rites and ceremonies.

"Meet each instant of your life as if it were a crisis" says Krishnamurti.

The followers of organized religions, without caring much for the way they live their daily life, repeat diligently and punctiliously certain standard formulas and gestures which bestow on them, in their own opinion, some distinction, even excellence, supply them with a definition of themselves and a pride in their own status among their fellowmen.

Attention given to daily actions is never spectacular. There is no self-assertion in it; nobody is much noticed for living his life perfectly. A life well lived is very simple; however great its inner riches. It does not strike the eye.

Krishnamurti keeps on reminding us that fundamentally it is not what we do that matters but how we do it and why. By asking us to abandon invented rites, to go deep into the substance and the meaning of daily actions, he makes every moment and every movement, parts of an immense ritual of living, simpler, greater and more effective than all the rituals invented by man. The ritual of a life well lived is most significant for in it the individual and the social values are integrated. Man can live his life in full intensity as an individual and also with a meaningful purpose as a social being. The harmony of the individual and social purpose is the essence of morality.

No ceremonial, made up activities, can claim a similar value. Full attention given to every moment of life goes infinitely beyond what rituals can claim or prove.

Krishnamurti would have nothing to do with rituals for another reason. To him liberation is never a result, it can not be promoted or stimulated. Many hold on to rites and ceremonies for the sake of the pleasant emotional responses they provoke and which could also be secured by the use of some drug more or less common. Such people seek sensory and emotional satisfaction rather than liberation. They are like the worshippers who prefer God's favours to God Himself. Liberation can never fall into greedy hands. Those who seek its benefits will never get them. For, by seeking profits, they refuse the life which is free of all seeking. The seekers for spiritual riches are not better than the seekers for material goods, as St. John of the Cross has wisely pointed out.

At the root of all orthodox behaviour is education moulded by tradition. Not that tradition is completely useless. It is always a mixture of some precious truth with a lot of horrible errors. Tradition makes us heirs both to wisdom and to folly of the past. Sometimes it brings some light, but generally it is like an infection which each generation hands over to the next.

We must not forget that humanity is like a man who always learns and never dies. But when tradition takes the place of wisdom, man is lost. Therefore Krishnamurti says in one of his poems:

"I have burst the rock on which I grew".

Krishnamurti talks of the eternal, in which no personal delay can hide itself. "To know that the knowledge of truth is always in the present; that there is nothing higher than the reality which is in man and that his reality is beyond time and the divisions of time beyond unity and separation is the beginning of wisdom". Elsewhere he says: "There is no other God but man made perfect". We must not understand this statement as that the physical and the social man is God. For Krishnamurti God is not an external being to be met, but a state of consciousness to be realized. It would be futile to make prostrations before a God which is but a person magnified on a cosmic scale.

(Translated from the French)

Chapter 44

The New Man
by Sunya

"A completely new age is beginning with new tasks and new demands on the heart and on human dignity: A silent age which will never be proclaimed and allowed voice, but will grow more real every day without noticing it. That is why "Dr. Z" is the most important piece of work I have been able to do — and in my consciousness the humility of your expression and recognition will remain for ever, with ego-humble gratitude. And now the hard heart of the world is not my business, even the `problems' of sin and death, hellfire and brimstone, when before the eyes of all, I have grown one with you, in my boundless sorrow and my infinite joy, as the graft grown one with the tree?

(Boris Pasternak)

The new emerging types of humanity do naturally recognise one another. To mind-ridden, respectable egojis they may seem freaks or sports or queer mutations. They do not approve, or understand and their analyses come to grief, yet these integral intuitive or mystical fellow-pilgrims in consciousness are often likeable and lovable, happy and harmfree. Often they emanate an unassertive — and calmly radiating Grace, an effort free acceptance, a natural harmony, balance and integral strength. They respond rather than reply and answer — and are good listeners, but cannot otherwise be useful to egojis or played upon in Shakti business. They rarely assert, aggress or make demands, nor do they preach or predicate, crave or lust. They may not be intellectual, They may not 'know-how' or understand, but they inner stand. Inner and outer realms of consciousness are unified. Tools and bodies coexist harmoniously in healthy self-interplay and in joyous ease of inter-penetration: A joyous ease in a kind of fourth dimensional (Turiya) consciousness, integral awareness or agefree, timefree, effortfree, deathfree Adwaita experiencing.

There is an ego-free realm of conscious Self-Awareness in which it is not only possible but natural to be, wholly, one's integral Self-Nature, in self-controlled spontaniety; no effort and no conceit of agency or of lusty urges, no becoming or begoing in the ever-changing Self-interplay; no coming to grief or causing harm to others — when there are no 'others' — only one, non-dual Self. Egojis can try to know and be their Self, but, in mature awakening, effort will cease and egojis cease to exist (as a reality). The Self ever Is — in and beyond the duality and ego-consciousness of the Maya Lila, in and beyond: Mature integral awakening is all. Swadarshan is not a multi-dimensional vision of existence. It is a darshan in Being- Awareness, an intuitive, integral experiencing in Ananda-Awareness. A man who is not free idealises his bondage, but bondage, like egoji, is delusive. Each egoji his own prison makes. Be still to awaken and purely that which Is. Keep silent. If you cannot tell the truth of your experience (your vanishing in Adwaita experiencing), then simply live it. Live your Swadharma at joyous ease and Anandaful Grace. Only the Eternal is Real. Aware It and live it also in time and in ego-full. It means reawakening into the integral realm of Being consciousness. I AM alone, All-one, and in non-duality vanish all complimentary opposites, all Phariseehypocricy — and all pious ego-deception. "To live integral life is not as easy as crossing a field". Yet man is born to live. Why substitute this childish harlequinade of adolescent phantasies, these juvenile escapades into mere knowledge, powers, possessions and policies, when there is the comforting awareness of the inter-woveness of all human lives. All that lives is holy, wholly and integrally one. Religion means realignment, not as dogmas and doctrines, rituals or Churchanity, but as a living, vital factor in practical empirical Empathy. Wu!

Krishnamurti postulates the necessity and the urgency of an immediate 'revolution' or mutation of the individual 'mind' of man: The awakening and the mature use of the intuitive faculty in the light of integral wisdom — and in Karuna-rhythm. We are divorced from nature, from our true and natural health and harmony.

From babyhood we are conditioned physically, emotionally and psychically, into mental conformity and by imposition of false values and ego-identity. We are mentalised and mechanised into externalities and superficial activities, without intuitive and integral awareness and conscious touch with the Ground and Source of all. Thus our inner emptiness, which is not Sunyafulness, thus our outer fluttering in vital but dis-eased quest — and thus our neurosis,, psychosis, schizophrenia and powerful egomegalomania. Our sensitivity is highly specialised. Our attitude and approach to Things are partial, analytical and blinkered and our psychic disease needs a radical cure, a mutation into integrality, or a transcending of mind and ego and time-values. Only the Eternal is real — and how few are mature, sincere and ego-free to experience and live the integral Silence; the joyous ease of conscious, calm Self-Awareness in natural spirituality — and in Self-controlled spontaniety? Krishnamurti, one of the experienced, unitive and intuitive types, uses a psychological, or mental word-language, ego-symbols concepts and abstractions, in order to get across to egojis — and to awaken us into facing out ego-made confusion, conflicts and problems. He tries to awaken us into attention, into awareness of cause and cure, symptoms and source. He tries to awaken us into integral awareness, into conscious Prajnana-Light and Karuna-rhythm into integral Being-consciousness, into being healthy artists in Life. It is an attempt to awaken rather than to teach, and we must innerstand intuitively rather than try to understand the word-play mentally and literally. Wu!

Perhaps he tries too much in confusing mental terms and semantic word-symbol, yet awaring very well that words blur and prevent integral innerstanding, and that what he is, and is aware in, is richly more than what he says and explains. He uses mind and duality symbols to bring intellect to suicide, to integrality or to ego-transcendence. Intellect is not intelligence, knowledge is not inherent wisdom; ego-power corrupts and is not integral strength and inner Grace. Spiritual suffering is a contradiction in term-symbols. Only in conscious Self-Awareness or integral experiencing do we live the Eternal in time — and Be psychically whole and mindfree in all diseases, in all phenomenal Self-interplay. Ego-oblivion is Self-Awareness — in the divine Maya Lila Self-play Krishnamurti still speaks of "controlling the mind"-, as he speaks to and at diseased, cantankerous and bumptious egojis. But who is the controller; who has a mind, a spirit or a mortal ego soul to control, to possess, or to be controlled by? The I, Me and Mine are false ideas and idealised abstractions, and `control' is conceit of agency: cute, swell and proud ego-bumptiousness, delusive concepts, illusory bondage and false Self-i-dentity.

The intuitive and integral type of human Being which, Krishnamurti advocates, proclaims and tries to awaken, is manifesting more and more, quickly in our atomage, there have always been the relatively few individuals that mature among us — mystics, and mental egojis, seeming cranks, fools and lunatics, though often more or less harmfree, more or less amusing or pitiable. We seem to be aware, also in so-called high places and influential positions, the 'new' type of intuitively aware and integral Being-awareness. Some wear world-famous names, but we also meet them everywhere, in life and in literature. They have digested their experiences and have come through to the experiencing of Within and Beyond. Wu!

The Basic Truth
by Maurice Frydman

When we consider the many legends created round Krishnamurti from the early days of his ministry, the spare of explanations and interpretations submerging his first few timid words of self-found truth, the incense of adoration smothering the sensitive young seeker, whose courage was as great as it was painful, we wonder how much would have been left of him without the tape-recorder and the printing press.

We can imagine what must have happened at the time of some other great teacher, when the art of printing was unknown, when all depended on oral testimony and everybody was free to distort the truth by merely stating: 'thus have I heard'.

The truths which seem to us so natural and convincing, when we hear them spoken by Krishnamurti, were they never spoken before? There were others before him — as great in wisdom and compassion. There was a Christ, there was a Buddha. But there was no printing press to preserve and disseminate their words.

We cannot hold out against those who have betrayed the truth they have heard by wanting to teach it to others. They did not intend to turn false the words of wisdom. But how could they, imperfect as they were, transmit without corrupting the message of perfection? Even if true to the letter of what they heard, how could they transmit its spirit?

The perfect man was struggling against the stream of human suffering born from oppression and violence. But his own words were at once swept away by the torrent of evil and used for justifying tyranny and violence. When he was no more, his life and work were built into walls of darkness and oppression, which had imprisoned man for ever after. Nothing was left of the original teaching, except maybe a faint perfume of the flowers that have blossomed and withered long ago.

It would have been a most interesting task to try to find in the various religious scriptures the old authentic teachings. Some traces remain and it is because of them religions still attract men of integrity and goodwill. This is regrettable indeed, for the earnest spirits get trapped in the net of rituals and dogmas. For what is dogma if not the ritual of the mind? Religious institutions are never in tune with the essential truth. Every religion is full of contradictions which breed conflict and violence.

The first thing to remember is that every great teacher was a rebel and an iconoclast. Invariably he refused to abide blindly by the traditions and the dogmas of the past. And the greatest and the most pernicious of these traditions was the belief that truth can be had from another, that one can discover and experience for another.

The first act of every great teacher was to break the yoke of dependence and proclaim the simple truth, that man can build only on what he is and not on what he can be made into. All dependence on another is an obstacle and a hindrance to the experience of the real.

This inner freedom, this non-reliance, non-obedience. Where can it lead us? To such truths, obviously, which can neither be received nor learnt, which must be found deep within our hearts or not at all.

None can be free from another; none can be wise for another; none can be compassionate for another. One must find the inner core of one's being, abide in it and act from it; there is no substitute for independence.

Chapter 46

J. Krishnamurti – Master of Reality
by Henry Miller

(*Abstracted from the Chapter *Krishnamurti* of *The Books in My Life*. Reproduced with permission of Peter Owen Ltd.)

There is a name ...which stands out in contrast to all that is secret, suspect, confusing, bookish and enslaving: Krishnamurti. Here is one man of our time who may be said to be a master of reality. He stands alone. He has renounced more than any man I can think of, except the Christ. Fundamentally he is so simple to understand that it is easy to comprehend the confusion which his clear, direct words and deeds have entailed. Men are reluctant to accept what is easy to grasp. Out of a perversity deeper than all Satan's wiles, man refuses to acknowledge his own God-given rights: he demands deliverance or salvation by and through an intermediary; he seeks guides, counsellors, leaders, systems, rituals. He looks for solutions which are in his own breast. He puts learning above wisdom, power above the art of discrimination. But above all, he refuses to work for his own liberation, pretending that first "the world" must be liberated. Yet, as Krishnamurti has pointed out time and again, the world problem is bound up with the problem of the individual. Truth is ever present, Eternity is here and now. And salvation? What is it, O man, that you wish to save? Your petty ego? Your soul? Your identity? Lose it and you will find yourself. Do not worry about

God — God knows how to take care of Himself. Cultivate your doubts, embrace every kind of experience, keep on desiring, strive neither to forget nor to remember, but assimilate and integrate what you have experienced.

Roughly, this is Krishnamurti's way of speaking. It must be revolting at times to answer all the petty, stupid questions which people are forever putting to him. Emancipate yourself! he urges. No one else will, because no one else can. This voice from the wilderness is, of course, the voice of a leader. But Krishnamurti has renounced that role too.

It was Carlo Suares' book on Krishnamurti* which opened my eyes to this phenomenon in our midst. I first read it in Paris and since then have reread it several times. There is hardly another book I have read so intently, marked so copiously, unless it be The Absolute Collective. After years of struggle and search I found gold.

This book by Carlo Suares is invaluable. It is replete with Krishnamurti's own words culled from speeches and writings.

In pages 116 to 119 of Suares' book the reader may find for himself the text of which I herewith give the substance....

After a long discussion with a man in Bombay, the latter says to Krishnamurti: What you speak of could lead to the creation of supermen, men capable of governing themselves, of establishing order in themselves, men who would be their own masters absolute. But what about the man at the bottom of the ladder, who depends on external authority, who makes use of all kinds of crutches, who is obliged to submit to a moral code which may, in reality, not suit him?

Krishnamurti's answer: See what happens in the world. The strong, the violent, the powerful ones, the men who usurp and wield power over others, are at the top; at the bottom are the

---

* *Krishnamurti* : Editions Adyar, Paris, 1932. This work has now been replaced by another, entitled Krishnamurti et l'unite humaine (Krishnamurti & the Unity of Man).

weak and gentle ones, who struggle and flounder. By contrast think of the tree, whose strength and glory derives from its deep and hidden roots; in the case of the tree the top is crowned by delicate leaves, tender shoots, the most fragile branches. In human society, at least as it is constituted today, the strong and the powerful are supported by the weak. In Nature, on the other hand, it is the strong and the powerful who support the weak. As long as you persist in viewing each problem with a perverted, twisted mind you will accept the actual state of affairs. I look at the problem from another point of view . . .Because your convictions are not the result of your own understanding you repeat what is given by authorities; you amass citations, you pit one authority against another, the ancient against the new. To that I have nothing to say. But if you envisage life from a standpoint which is not deformed or mutilated by authority, not bolstered by others' knowledge, but from one which springs from your own sufferings, from your thought, your culture, your understanding, your love, then you will understand what I say — "car la meditation du coeur est l'entendement" . . .Personally, and I hope you will understand what I say now, I have no belief and I belong to no tradition. I have always had this attitude towards life. It being a fact that life varies from day to day, not only are beliefs and traditions useless to me, but, if I were to let myself be enchained by them, they would prevent me from understanding life . . .You may attain liberation, no matter where you are or what the circumstances surrounding you, but this means that you must have the strength of genius. For genius, is, after all, the ability to deliver oneself from the circumstances in which one is enmeshed, the ability to free oneself from the vicious circle . . .You may say to me — I have not that kind of strength. That is my point of view exactly. In order to discover your own strength, the power which is in you, you must be ready and willing to come to grips with every kind of experience. And that is just what you refuse to do!

This sort of language is naked, revelatory and inspiring. It pierces the clouds of philosophy which confound our thought and restores the springs of action. It levels the tottering superstructures of the verbal gymnasts and clears the ground of rubbish. Instead of an obstacle race or a rat trap, it makes of daily life a joyous pursuit. There is something about Krishnamurti's utterances which makes the reading of books seem utterly superfluous.

One of the salient differences between a man like Krishnamurti and artists in general lies in their respective attitudes towards their roles. Krishnamurti points out that there is a constant opposition between the creative genius of the artist and his ego.

The artist imagines, he says, that it is his ego which is great or sublime. This ego wishes to utilize for its own profit and aggrandizement the moment of inspiration wherein it was in touch with the eternal, a moment, precisely, in which the ego was absent, replaced by the residue of its own living experience. It is one's intuition, he maintains, which should be the sole guide. As for poets, musicians, all artists, indeed, they should develop anonymity, should become detached from their creations. But for most artists it is just the contrary — they want to see their signatures attached to their creations. In short, as long as the artist clings to individualism, he will never succeed in rendering his inspiration or his creative power permanent. The quality or condition of genius is but the first phase of deliverance.

What distinguishes Krishnamurti even from the great teachers of the past, the masters and the exemplars, is his absolute nakedness. The one role he permits himself to play is — himself, a human being. Clad only in the frailty of the flesh, he relies entirely upon the spirit which is one with the flesh. If he has a mission it is to strip men of their illusions and delusions, to knock away the false supports of ideals, beliefs, fetishes, every kind of crutch, and thus render back to man the full majesty, the full potency, of his humanity. He has often been referred to as "the World Teacher." If any man living merits the title, he does. But to me the important thing about Krishnamurti is that he imposes himself upon us not as a teacher, nor even as a Master, but as a *Man* — "Find out for yourself," he says, "What are the possessions and ideals that you do not desire. By knowing what you do not want, by elimination, you will unburden the mind, and only then will it understand the essential which is ever there."'

C h a p t e r   47

The Art of Spiritual Insight
by Aldous Huxley

(*Abstracted from two essays *Education of An Amphibian* and
Knowledge & Understanding, appearing in *Adonis and the Alphabet.*
Reproduced with permission of Mrs. Laura Huxley and Chatto
& Windus Ltd.)

The aim of the psychiatrist is to teach the (statistically) abnormal
to adjust themselves to the behaviour patterns of a society
composed of the (statistically) normal. The aim of the educator
in spiritual insight is to teach the (statistically) normal that they
are in fact insane, and should do something about it. The problem
is how to get out one's own light. Our business is to free ourselves
from eclipsing bad habits — bad habits not merely on the moral
level but also, and more fundamentally, on the cognitive,
intellectual and emotional levels. For it is these bad habits of
unrealistic thinking, inappropriate feeling and debauched
perception which incite the ego to behave as it does. We must,
in Krishnamurti's phrase, achieve "freedom from the known" —
freedom from the unanalyzed postulated in terms of which we
do our second-hand experiencing, freedom from our
conventional thoughts and sentiments, freedom from our ster-
eo-typed notions about inner and outer reality.

The end proposed is the rediscovery within ourselves of a virgin not-mind capable of non-verbally not-thinking a response to immediate experience. But the ends we actually achieve are always determined by the means we employ. Perfect freedom will not be achieved by means of systematic limitation. Virginity of mind will not be discovered in a context of predetermined beliefs and dogmas. The unitive not-thought which experiences life in its totality will never emerge from concentrated thinking, in terms of words or visual images, about some particular aspect of life, isolated from the rest.

For what is ordinarily called meditation is merely, in Krishnamurti's words, "the cultivation of resistance, of exclusive concentration on an idea of our choice". Yoga is the process of "building a wall of resistance" against every thought except that which you have chosen. But what makes you choose? "Obviously the choice is based on pleasure, reward or achievement; or it is merely a reaction to one's conditioning or tradition". Then why choose?

"Instead of creating resistance, why not go into each interest as it arises and not merely concentrate on one idea, one interest?" Constant and intense self-awareness, free from preconceptions, comparisons, condemnations — this will result in what Krishnamurti calls "clarity", what Eckhart calls "virginity", what the Zen masters describe as "no-mind". "This clarity is not to be organized, group thought is merely repetitive. . .Without understanding yourself, you have no basis for thought; without self-knowledge, what you say is not true." Truth repeated is no longer truth; it becomes truth again only when it has been realized by the speaker as an immediate experience.

Knowledge is acquired when we succeed in fitting a new experience into the system of concepts based upon our old experiences. Understanding comes when we liberate ourselves from the old and so make possible a direct, unmediated contact with the new, the mystery, moment by moment, of our existence.

The new is the given on every level of experience — given perceptions, given emotions and thoughts, given states of unstructured awareness, given relationships with things and persons. The old is our home-made system of ideas and word patterns. It is the stock of finished articles fabricated out of the given mystery by memory and analytical reasoning, by habit and the automatic associations of accepted notions. Knowledge is primarily a knowledge of these finished articles. Understanding is primarily direct awareness of the raw material.

Understanding is not inherited, nor can it be laboriously acquired. It is something which, when circumstances are favourable, comes to us, so to say, of its own accord. Understanding comes when we are totally aware — aware to the limits of our mental and physical potentialities. This, of course, is a very ancient doctrine. "Know thyself" is a piece of advice which is as old as civilization, and probably a great deal older. To follow that advice, a man must do more than indulge in introspection. If I know myself, I must know my environment; for as a body, I am apart of the environment, a natural object among other objects, and, as a mind, I consist to a great extent of my immediate reactions to the environment and of my secondary reactions to those primary reactions. In practice what does total awareness reveal? It reveals, first of all, the limitations of the things which each of us calls "I", and the enormity, the utter absurdity of its pretensions. "I am the master of my fate." poor Henley wrote at the end of a celebrated morsel of rhetoric, "I am the captain of my soul." Nothing could be further from the truth. My fate cannot be mastered, it can only be collaborated with and thereby, to some extent, directed. Nor am I the captain of my soul; I am only its noisiest passenger — a passenger who is not sufficiently important to sit at the captain's table and does not know, even by report, what the soul-ship looks like, how it works or where it is going. Total awareness starts, in a word, with the realization of my ignorance and my importance.

Total awareness, then, reveals the following facts: That I am profoundly ignorant, that I am impotent to the point of helplessness and that the most valuable elements in my personality are unknown quantities existing "out there," as mental objects more or less completely independent of my control. This discovery may seem at first rather humiliating and even depressing. But if I whole-heartedly accept them, the facts become a source of peace, a reason for serenity and cheerfulness. I am ignorant and impotent and yet, somehow or other, here I am, unhappy, no doubt, profoundly dissatisfied, but alive and kicking. In spite of everything, I survive, I get by, sometimes I even get on. From these two sets of facts, my survival on the one hand and my ignorance and impotence on the other — I can only infer that the not-I, which looks after my body and gives me my best ideas, must be amazingly intelligent, knowledgeable and strong. As a selfcentered ego, I do my best to interfere with the beneficient workings of this not-I. But in spite of my likes and dislikes, in spite of my malice, my infatuations, my gnawing anxieties, in spite of all my over-valuations, of words in spite of my self-stultifying insistence on living, not in present reality, but in memory and anticipation, this not-I, with whom I am associated, sustains me, preserves me, gives me a long succession of second chances. We know very little and can achieve very little; but we are at liberty, if we so choose, to cooperate with a greater power and a completer knowledge, an unknown quantity at once immanent and transcendent, at once physical and mental, at once subjective and objective. If we co-operate, we shall be all right, even if the worst should happen. If we refuse to co-operate, we shall be all wrong even in the most propitious of circumstances.

These conclusions are only the first-fruits of total awareness. Yet richer harvests are to follow. In my ignorance I am sure that I am eternally, I. This conviction is rooted in emotionally charged memory. Only when, in the words of St. John of the Cross, the memory has been emptied can I escape from the sense of my watertight separateness and so prepare myself for the understanding, moment by moment, of reality on all its levels. But the memory cannot be emptied by an act of will, or by systematic discipline or by concentration — even by concentration on the ideas of emptiness. It can be emptied only by total awareness. Thus, if I am aware of my distractions —

which are mostly emotionally charged memories or phantasies based upon such memories — the mental whirlgig will automatically come to a stop and the memory will be emptied, at least for a moment or two. Again, if I become totally aware of my resentment, my uncharitableness, these feelings will be replaced, during the time of my awareness by a more realistic reaction to the events taking place around me. My awareness, of course, must be uncontaminated by approval or condemnation. Value judgements are conditioned, verbalized reactions to primary reactions. Total awareness is a primary, choiceless, impartial response to the present situation as a whole. There are in it no limiting conditioned reactions to the primary reaction, to the pure cognitive apprehension of the situation. If memories of verbal formulas of praise or blame should make their appearance in consciousness, they are to be examined impartially as any other present datum is examined. Professional moralists have confidence in the surface will, believe in punishments and rewards and are adrenalin addicts who like nothing better than a good orgy of righteous indignation. The masters of the spiritual life have little faith in the surface will or the utility, for their particular purposes, of rewards or punishment, and do not indulge in righteous indignation. Experience has taught them that the highest good can never, in the very nature of things, be achieved by moralizing. "Judge not that ye be not judged" is their watchword and total awareness is their method.

Chapter   48

Has Krishnamurti Failed?
by Luis S.R. Vas

Forty odd active years as a travelling non-guru is a long time;
time enough perhaps to assess the impact of the man of the
people he has reached. On the face of it J. Krishnamurti's
influence has been large from the start and has been widening
ever since. Krishnamurti Foundations have sprung everywhere
and carry his message, such as it is, to many more than could
otherwise reach him. Taped lectures are played throughout the
world for those interested. His books are now available in
paperback and are in great demand.

Yet such superficial indications of popularity are deceptive. How
deep is Krishnamurti's impact on his listeners? To judge from
his listeners' questions to him after his usual talks, we find that
the bulk of his audience go home more confused than they were
when they started out.

Did Krishnamurti spurn the organisation that built him up as a
World Teacher, only to end up leaving a cluster of organisations
— the Krishnamurti Foundations — more widely flung than the
Order of the Star? No doubt, the new organisations avowedly
propagate new religion, worship no Messiah and accept no converts. Still, isn't the picture of a rapt audience, seated before a
tape-recorder as it plays back a Krishnamurti lecture, sus-

piciously like a religious service of the electronic age, or of the Brave New World?

Jacob Needleman echoes this fear in a brilliant analysis of Krishnamurti in "The New Religions". "With unequalled clarity and coherence [Krishnamurti] tells us that our lives are merely a reflection of our inner condition. He invites us, in a way that absolutely no one else does, to follow him in the effort of instantaneous self-observation, and to verify for ourselves that it is the endlessly busy, interpreting mind which generates our life and its disorder. But what are we to do when we return home and discover not that we cannot make this effort in his absence — which would at least be truth — but that we are sure we are able to do it any time we wish (though not right now)? I wonder if we shall not simply end by *believing in self-observation.*"

The danger seems real enough. Has then Krishnamurti failed? The question raises semantic problems. How is one to judge "success" and "failure" in Krishnamurti's case? If he were a preacher, he could be judged by the number of converts. But he isn't, despite the impassioned zeal with which he has been lecturing for so many decades. He has said so many times that agreeing or disagreeing with him is irrelevant. But understanding him is of the essence. So, do we judge him by the number of people who understand him? Assuming that we do, we are confronted with more problems: How do I know that someone has comprehended Krishnamurti? Is there an objective test? More important: how do I know that even I understand what Krishnamurti is saying? Is there at least a *subjective* test?

One suddenly realises then that it is not a matter of judging Krishnamurti. For Krishnamurti never pretended to *make* you understand him. He merely hopes to provoke you into understanding yourself, into seeing through yourself. So there is no question of judging yourself either. Why this hankering after the certainty that I have got Krishnamurti right? So that I may cling to it? Judging, assessing Krishnamurti would imply that something could be wrong with him. Judging myself would imply that something could be wrong with me. In judging the world I worry whether something may not be wrong with it. It does not occur to me that the fault may lie, not so much with either, but in our relationship with each other.

As a conditioned human being I have become the unwilling recipient of my cultural assumptions. The East has tried to make me look inward, to withdraw from the worldly illusions. The West has fostered an analytical preoccupation with everything around me, all nicely calculated to make me forget myself. The Eastern attitude has resulted in purposeless meditation; a sterile, paralysing vicious circle. The West has fostered mindless activism — a sure road to frustration. Beyond both lies the interplay between the inner and the outer: the one in direct touch with the other, free of analysis and judgement. It is "the spontaneous activity of the total integrated personality". Spontaneous activity is not automatic, thoughtless activity dictated by outside demands.Physical activity is only a small incidental part of it. It is the play of one's perception that synchronises one's emotional awareness, intellectual analyses and sensory activity in one `will'. Then you don't feel one way. The integration is not the result of enforced discipline but the consequence of a man having become `transparent to himself'. The `why' of his activities becomes visible. Though he may seem to act as before his reasons for doing things are different: he sleeps when tired, not to escape from wakefulness. He eats when hungry, not for emotional fulfilment. It is a heightened sensitivity altogether. It has been compared to an artist's vision even if he lacks the talent of the latter to crystallise it into a specific art form. It is not a mere heightened awareness of sights and sounds. It is a receptiveness to people's emotions, views, actions and a certain empathy for them. It is as if "I were he", while at the same time "leaving me intact as my being me, *feeling within me* how he feels".

The functions of the organism and personality are hindered by cultural and social conditioning. When this conditioning is seen for what it is, namely a needless 'cover' to discipline you, it can be peeled off the way a banana skin is discarded. When you have discarded it you have nothing to cling to, you *need* nothing to cling to. You are a psychic vacuum. One writer has described it as disembodied laughter and it is an apt metaphor. That is what it feels like — disembodied laughter. "Then a great tranquility steals over you. It trickles like water through the cells of your mind washing them clean. You think of nothing, nothing at all, but are with a crystalline awareness . . ."

But what is it? "I do not know and I believe I cannot know. . .I can only say that the space within the heart seems to be some core of consciousness which had been overlaid by all the necessities of living, and it may be the core that sustains us against all the changes and chances we must suffer from the day of our birth" . . .

To some temperaments the whole thing will sound like so much high-falutin mystical nonsense. Patently bogus. Of what use is this mumbo-jumbo anyway? will ask the activist. And this is the most common charge brought against Krishnamurti — that his philosophy is not sufficiently positive. His reply: "You don't need to search for the positive, don't force it. It is always there, though hidden beneath a huge pile of old experiences. Eliminate all of them and truth or what you call the positive will be there. It comes up automatically. You cannot help it".

Can this awareness be transmitted? John Needleman writes "something in (Krishnamurti's)_ speech, his presence, his line of thought, call it what one will *helps* the act of self-observation. Not so much that it compels me or causes me, but that something comes to my mind and in the moment I choose to try. That is really all one could say; one cannot, and perhaps one need not be sure if it is Krishnamurti's language, the silent presence of so many others also in my situation, or something else. . . . Then, in this sense, one obviously cannot deny that he is a *teacher*, a channel of help for the self-initiated effort of self-observation . . .Can this help, whatever it is, be increased, extended or depended upon? An approach like Krishnamurti's may thus open an entirely new idea of what it means for people to be organised for the sake of psychological freedom. For it may well be that all organisation that we know of is useless and even an obstacle, if the aim is this freedom.

A p p e n d i x   A

The Dissolution of the Order of the Star
by J. Krishnamurti

We are going to discuss this morning the dissolution of the Order of the Star. Many people will be delighted, and others will be rather sad. It is a question neither for rejoicing nor for sadness, because it is inevitable, as I am going to explain.

You may remember the story of how the devil and a friend of his were walking down the street, when they saw ahead of them a man stoop down and pick up some thing from the ground, look at it, and put it away in his pocket. This friend said to the devil, "What did that man pick up?" "He picked up a piece of Truth," said the devil. "That is a very bad business for you, then" said his friend. "Oh not at all, the devil replied, "I am going to help him organize it."

I maintain that Truth is a pathless land, and you cannot approach it by any path whatsoever, by any religion, by any sect. That is my point of view, and I adhere to that absolutely and unconditionally. Truth, being limitless, unconditioned, unapproachable by any path whatsoever, cannot be organised; nor should any organisation be formed to lead or to coerce people along any particular path. If you first understand that, then you will see how impossible it is to organise a belief. A belief is purely an individual matter, and you cannot and must not organise it. If you do, it becomes dead, crystallised; it becomes a creed, a sect, a religion, to be imposed on others. This is what every one throughout the world is attempting to do: Truth is narrowed down and made a plaything for those who are weak, for those who are only momentarily discontented. Truth cannot be brought down, rather the individual must make the effort to ascend to it. You cannot bring the mountain-top to the valley. If you wish to attain the mountain-top you must pass through the valley, climb the steeps, unafraid of the dangerous precipices. You must climb towards the Truth, it cannot be "stepped down" or organised for you. Interest in ideas is mainly sustained by organisations, but organisations only awaken interest from without. Interest, which is not born out of love, of Truth for its own sake, but aroused by an organisation, is of no value. The organisation becomes a framework into which its members can conveniently fit. They no longer strive after Truth or the mountain-top, but rather carve for themselves a convenient niche in which they put themselves, or let the organisation place them, and consider that the organisation will thereby lead them to Truth.

So that is the first reason, from my point of view, why the Order of the Star should be dissolved. In spite of his, you will probably form other Orders, you will continue to belong to other organisations searching for Truth. I do not want to belong to any organisation of a spiritual kind, please understand this. I would make use of an organisation which would take me to London, for example; this is quite a different kind of organisation, merely mechanical, like the post or the telegraph. I would use a motor car or a steamship to travel, these are only physical mechanisms which have nothing whatever to do with spirituality. Again, I maintain that no organisation can lead man to spirituality.

If an organisation be created for this purpose, it becomes a crutch, a weakness, a bondage, and must cripple the individual, and prevent him from growing, from establishing his uniqueness, which lies in the discovery for himself of that absolute, unconditioned Truth. So that is another reason why I have decided, as I happen to be the Head of the Order, to dissolve it. No one has persuaded me to this decision.

This is no magnificent deed, because I do not want followers, and I mean this. The moment you follow someone you cease to follow Truth. I am not concerned whether you pay attention to what I say or not. I want to do a certain thing in the world and I am going to do it with unwavering concentration. I am concerning myself with only one essential thing; to set man free. I desire to free him from all cages, from all fears, and not to found religions, new sects, nor to establish new theories and new philosophies. Then you will naturally ask me why I go the world over, continually speaking. I will tell you for what reason I do this; not because I desire a following, not because I desire a special group of special disciples. (How men love to be different from their fellow-men however ridiculous, absurd and trivial their distinctions may be! I do not want to encourage that absurdity.) I have no disciples, no apostles, either on earth or in the realm of spirituality.

Nor is it the lure of money, nor the desire to live a comfortable life, which attracts me. If I wanted to lead a comfortable life I would not come to a Camp or live in a damp country! I am speaking frankly because I want this settled once and for all. I do not want these childish discussions year after year.

One newspaper reporter, who interviewed me, considered it a magnificent act to dissolve an organisation in which there were thousands and thousands of members. To him it was a great act because, he said: "What will you do afterwards, who will any longer listen to you." If there are only five people who will listen, who will live, who have their faces turned towards eternity,it will be sufficient. Of what use is it to have thousands who do not understand, who are fully embalmed in prejudice, who do not want the new, but would rather translate the new to suit their own sterile, stagnate selves? If I speak strongly, please do not misunderstand me, it is not through lack of compassion. If you go to a surgeon for an operation, is it not kindness on his part to operate even if he causes you pain? So, in like manner, if I speak straight, it is not through lack of real affection — on the contrary.

As I have said, I have only one purpose: to make man free, to urge him towards freedom, to help him to break away from all limitations, for that alone will give him eternal happiness, will give him the unconditioned realisation of the self.

Because I am free, unconditioned, whole — not the part, not the relative, but the whole Truth that is eternal — I desire those, who seek to understand me, to be free; not to follow me, not to make out of me a cage which will become a religion, a sect. Rather should they be free from all fears — from the fear of religion, from the fear of salvation, from the fear of spirituality, from the fear of love, from the fear of death, from the fear of life itself. As an artist paints a picture because he takes delight in that painting, because it is his self-expression, his glory, his well-being, so I do this and not because I want any thing from anyone.

You are accustomed to authority, or to the atmosphere of authority, which you think will lead you to spirituality. You think and hope that another can, by his extraordinary powers — a miracle — transport you to this realm of eternal freedom which is Happiness. Your whole outlook on life is based on that authority.

You have listened to me for three years now, without any change taking place except in the few. Now analyse what I am saying, be critical so that you may understand thoroughly fundamentally. When you look for an authority to lead you to spirituality, you are bound automatically to build an organisation around that authority. By the very creation of that organisation, which, you think, will help this authority to lead you to spirituality, you are held in a cage.

If I talk frankly, please remember that I do so, not out of harshness, not out of cruelty, not out of the enthusiasm of my purpose, but because I want you to understand what I am saying. That is the reason why you are here, and it would be a waste of time if I did not explain clearly, decisively, my point of view.

For eighteen years you have been preparing for this event, for the coming of the World-Teacher. For eighteen years you have organised, you have looked for someone who would give a new delight to your hearts and minds, who would transform your whole life, who would give you a new delight to your hearts and minds, who would transform your whole life, who would give you a new understanding; for someone who would raise you to a new plane of life, who would give you a new encouragement, who would set you free — and now look what is happening! Consider, reason with yourselves, and discover in what way that belief has made you different — not with the superficial difference of the wearing of a badge, which is trivial and absurd. In what manner has such a belief swept away all the unessential things of life? That is the only way to judge: in what way are you freer, greater, more dangerous to every Society which is based on the false and the unessential? In what way have the members of this organisation of the Star become different?

As I said you have been preparing for eighteen years for me. I do not care if you believe that I am the World-Teacher or not. That is of very little pertinence. Since you belong to the organisation of the Order of the Star, you have given your sympathy, your energy, acknowledging that Krishnamurti is the World-Teacher — partially or wholly: wholly for those who are really seeking, only partially for those who are satisfied with their own half-truths.

You have been preparing for eighteen years, and look how many difficulties there are in the way of your understanding, how many complications, how many trivial things. Your prejudices, your fears, your authorities, your churches new and old — all these, I maintain, are a barrier to understanding. I cannot make myself clearer than this. I do not want you to agree with me, I do not want you to follow me, I want you to understand what I am saying.

This understanding is necessary because your belief has not transformed you but only complicated you, and because you are willing to face things as they are. You want to have your own gods — new gods instead of the old, new religions instead of the old, new forms instead of the old — all equally valueless, all barriers, all limitations, all crutches. Instead of old spiritual distinctions you have new spiritual distinctions, instead of old worships you have new worships. You are all depending for your spirituality on someone else, for your happiness on someone else, and although you have been preparing for me for eighteen years, when I say all these things are unnecessary, when I say that you must put them all away and look within yourselves for the enlightenment, for the glory, for the purification, and for the incorruptibility of the self, not one of you is willing to do it. There may be a few, but very, very few.

So why have an organisation?

Why have false, hypocritical people following me, the embodiment or Truth? Please remember that I am not saying something harsh or unkind, but we have reached a situation when you must face things as they are. I said last year that I would not compromise. Very few listened to me then. This year I have made it absolutely clear. I do not know how many thousands throughout the world — members of the Order — have been preparing for me for eighteen years, and yet now they are not willing to listen unconditionally, wholly, to what I say.

So why have an organisation?

As I said before, my purpose is to make men unconditionally free, for I maintain that the only spirituality is the incorruptibility of the self which is eternal, is the harmony between reason and love. This is the absolute, unconditioned Truth which is Life itself. I want therefore to set man free, rejoicing as the bird in the clear sky, unburdened, independent, ecstatic in that freedom. And I, for whom you have been preparing for eighteen years, now say that you must be free of all these things, free from your complications, your entanglements. For this you need not have an organisation based on spiritual belief. Why have an organisation for five or ten people in the world who understand, who are struggling, who have put aside all trivial things? And for the weak people, there can be no organisation to help them to find the Truth, because Truth is in everyone; it is not far, it is not near; it is eternally there.

Organisations cannot make you free. No man from outside can make you free; nor can organised worship, nor the immolation of yourselves for a cause, make you free; nor can forming yourselves into an organisation, nor throwing yourselves into work make you free. You use a typewriter to write letters, but you do not put it on an altar and worship it. But that is what you are doing when organisations become your chief concern. "How many members are there in it?" That is the first question I am asked by all newspaper reporters. "How many followers have you? By their number we shall judge whether what you say is true or false." I do not know how many there are. I am not concerned with that. As I said, if there were even one man who had been set free, that were enough.

Again, you have the idea that only certain people hold the key to the Kingdom of Happiness. No one holds it. No one has the authority to hold that key. That key is your own self, and in the development and the purification and in the incorruptibility of that self alone is the Kingdom of Eternity.

So you will see how absurd is the whole structure that you have built, looking for external help, depending on others for your comfort, for your happiness, for your strength. These can only be found within yourselves.

So why have an organisation?

But those who really desire to understand, who are looking to find that which is eternal, without beginning and without an end, will walk together with a greater intensity, will be a danger to everything that is unessential, to unrealities, to shadows. And they will concentrate, they will become the flame, because they understand. Such a body we must create, and that is my purpose. Because of that true friendship. Because of that true friendship — which you do not seem to know — there will be real cooperation on the part of each one. And this is not because of immolation for a cause, but because you really understand, and hence are capable of living in the eternal. This is a greater thing than all pleasure, than all sacrifice.

So these are some of the reasons why, after careful consideration for two years, I have made this decision. It is not from a momentary impulse. I have not been persuaded to it by anyone — I am not persuaded in such things. For two years I have been thinking about this, slowly, carefully, patiently, and I have now decided to disband the Order, as I happen to be its head. You can form other organisations and expect someone else. With that I am not concerned, not with creating new cages, new decorations for those cages. My only concern is to set man absolutely, unconditionally free.

A p p e n d i x   B

What is the Religious Mind?
by J. Krishnamurti

I would like, if I may, to talk about what is the religious mind. But before I go into that I would like to point out, and I think it is relevant, that there must be the denial of thought. We never deny. We are all 'yes-sayers'. We accept according to our tendencies, idiosyncrasies; and when we do deny, that denial is a reaction and, therefore, not a denial at all. I would like to talk a little bit about it for it is important to understand that in order to pursue and find out for oneself what is the religious mind. We never deny and if you have observed yourself sufficiently, carefully and seriously, we have always accepted, found an easy path, the easiest solution. We have accepted tradition, the various cultural, economic, social influences. We have never stood against them, or if we have stood, we have stood against them by force, not willingly, not comprehendingly; and so our denial is always tinged with fear. It has always come about through a form of acceptance in which there is a hope. It is never a denial of not knowing what is going to come; it is a denial with an acceptance of a regulated orderly future.

Please do listen to what I am saying, because when we talk about religious minds we are going to deny the whole structure of religion as it is, totally, because it is utterly false, it has no meaning whatsoever. And to understand what we are going to say a little later you must, if I may point out, comprehend deeply this act of denial. You can be forced to deny; circumstances force you or compel you to say 'no' — circumstances, lack of money, environmental influences, some trouble or the other, can force you to say 'no'; but to say 'no' with clarity, without any motive, without wanting a further reward or fearing punishment, but deliberately to say 'no' to something to which you have given your thought completely, uncompromisingly, to say 'no' when you have thought out the problem completely, seriously, I mean, to go into the problem to the very end, not romantically, not emotionally, not according to your particular idiosyncrasy or vanity or pleasure or desire, but to go to the very end of the thing, putting aside your personal fancy, myth, likes and dislikes. To go to the very end of a thought, an idea, a feeling, a subject, is to be serious.

I would like to go into this question of religion because I feel that if we could have a very clear, strong religious mind, we would solve our problems because religion is something that includes everything; it is not exclusive. A religious mind has no nationality. It is not provincial; it does not belong to any particular organized group. It is not the result of ten thousand years of propaganda, or two thousand years of propaganda. It has no dogma, no belief. It is a mind that moves from fact to fact. It is a mind that understands the total quality of thought, not only the obvious superficial thought, the educated thought, but also the uneducated thought, the deep down unconscious thought motives. The totality of this enquiry and the realization of that enquiry and the denial of that enquiry which it sees, feels, and the totality of that enquiry which it sees, feels, and the totality of that denial bring about that quality of mind which is new, which is religious, which is revolutionary. But for most of us religion is not only the word, the symbol, but it is the result of our conditioning. You are a Hindu or a Muslim or a Christian, or what you will, because you have been told from your childhood that you are a Hindu, with all the beliefs, dogmas, traditions, and you have accepted it. As the communist accepts in his youth that there is no God, you accept that there is God.

There is not much difference between you and the person who denies God; both are the result of a conditioned mind.

Please, I am not attacking you. therefore, there is no need to defend; you do not have to resist. We are dealing with facts and it would be utterly stupid to resist a fact. It has no meaning. When the house is burning, when the world is in such chaos, even if you deliberately set about to make the world more chaotic than it is, you could not succeed, in spite of the politicians. And it needs a very sharp, clear, decisive, sane mind to resolve the chaotic problems, and I do not think such a mind can come about except through a religious perception. And if you will follow not the word, not the speaker, agreeing or disagreeing with the speaker, but if you follow the operations of your own mind, if you watch your own conditioning, not because I tell you but because it is a fact, when you look at the fact, when you become aware of that fact, then we can proceed to find out how to dissolve that fact that conditioning. But, first, one must be aware of the fact that the mind is conditioned, that your mind when it says it is a Hindu, is conditioned; it is shaped by the past, by the centuries of culture; it is the result of a historical process and a mythical process and the religions that you have are the result of other people's experiences. It is not your own direct experience. It is what you have been told either in the book or by some teacher or by some philosopher; it is not something which you perceive. When the mind is completely unconditioned then only can you experience or discover if there is something real or not. But before you uncondition your mind, to say that you are religious, that you are a Hindu, a Muslim, a Buddhist or a Christian has no meaning whatsoever. That is pure romanticism which is exploited by the priest, by the organized group politically, religiously, because they have their vested interest in it. These are all facts, whether you like them or not. I am merely describing the fact. And these divisions into religious groups, believing this and that, believing this dogma and denying that dogma, going from prison to prison, from temple to temple, doing endless *puja* — all that is not a religious mind at all, it is merely a traditional mind bound by fear. And surely a mind that is afraid can never find out if there is, or if there is not, something beyond the word, beyond the measure of the mind.

So, do please listen not only to what I am saying but also to the operations of your own mind. I use that word 'listen' in a special significance. Listening is an art, because we never do listen. We listen half-heartedly with our thoughts elsewhere. We listen with condemnation or a comparison. We listen with likes and dislikes. We listen either to agree or to disagree. We listen by comparing what we hear with what we already know. So, there is always distraction; there is never an act of listening. And it would be worthwhile if I may point out to you that you could listen without any of these distractions of thought, so that the very act of listening is the breaking down of that condition, because when I use the word 'religion' all kinds of images come to your minds, all kinds of symbols; to a Christian his own symbols, dogmas and beliefs; to the Hindu, to the Muslim, to all the people who call themselves religious. They have a peculiar approach, an idiosyncratic approach, a traditional approach so that they could never think clearly about the matter. They are first Hindus or Muslims and then they begin to seek. So, to find out if there is, or if there is not, something which is beyond the thought, which is not measurable by the mind, the mind must be first free. Surely that is logic.

You see, another peculiarity with religious people is that they are totally illogical. Psychologically, they have no sanity. They accept without enquiry and their enquiry is motivated by fear, by the desire for security which pervades their thought; they become romantic; because it pleases them, they become devotional. It gives them a sense of joy, happiness. But that is not a religious mind at all. It is a fanciful mind; it has no reality. So, if you observe your own mind you will see how cluttered up and burdened it is with beliefs. And you say that belief is necessary. We use it as a hypothesis, which is sheer nonsense. When a man is enquiring, he does not start out with a hypothesis. He has a free mind. He is not attached to any dogma and he is not bound by any fear. He starts out denying all that and then begins to seek. But you never do deny for various reasons, because it would not be respectable. In a very respectable society, which is a rotten society, you never deny because you might lose your job or position. You never deny because of your family. You have to marry your daughter, your son, to do this and that and, therefore, you are bound, consciously or unconsciously, through fear to the dogma, to the tradition in which you have been brought up. Again, this is a fact; this is not my fancy. This is a psychological everyday fact. And so a mind which is bound to belief, to a dogma however ancient, or however modern like that of a communist, such a mind is incapable of bringing about an orderly world, a sane world. Such a mind is incapable of being free from sorrow, from conflicts. Surely, it is only the mind that is free from conflict, free from problems, free from sorrow that can find out, and you must find out because that is the only way out of this misery, this confusion that we have created in this world, not by joining innumerable groups or going back to the old tradition which is dead, or following a new leader.

I do not know if you have observed that when you follow somebody, you have destroyed your own thoughts, you have lost your own independence, you have lost your freedom not only politically but much more psychologically, not only outwardly but much more inwardly. So, where there is a following and where there is a leader in matters that are really spiritual, really psychological, there is bound to be confusion because in that there is a contradiction between what your own deep down urges, compulsions are, and the imposition placed upon them by the leader, by what you think you should do. So, there is a contradiction psychologically and that contradiction leads to conflict and where there is a conflict there is effort and where there is effort there is distortion. So, a religious mind has no conflict. The religious mind does not follow anyone. It has no authority because authority implies imitation; authority implies conformity; and there is conformity because you want success, you want to achieve; and, therefore, there is fear. Without dissolving fear completely, how can you proceed to enquire, how can you proceed to find out? These are no rhetorical questions. If I am frightened, I am bound to seek comfort, shelter, security in whatever comes along because fear dictates, not sanity, not clarity. So, fear dictates conformity — that I must imitate, follow somebody in the hope that I shall find comfort. So, the religious mind has no authority of any kind, and that is very difficult for people to accept because we have been bred in authority — the Gita, the Upanishads, the Bible, the Koran. . .They have taken the place of our own thinking, of our own suffering. . .

And where religious matters are concerned we become totally irrational, insane, and all these build the walls of our conditioning. Again, this is a fact, a psychological, undeniable fact. You are going to the temple; you are reading the Gita and muttering a lot of words which have lost their meaning. That is not a religious mind at all. Such reading, such repetition, makes the mind dull, insensitive. Therefore there is a contradiction between real living and what you think is real living. There is no living a religious life. So, you have divorced life from religion, ethics from religion and a mind that lives in this duality, in this contradiction, in this cleavage, such a mind is creating the world at the present time. It is bringing into the world more and more chaos. Where there is confusion, where there is misery, people turn to authority, to tyranny, not only politically but also religiously. Gurus, teachers, ideas, beliefs, dogmas multiply and flourish because we have never looked into ourselves deeply to find out for ourselves what is true.

So, the beginning of self-knowledge is the beginning of the religious mind; not the knowledge of the Supreme Self; that is sheer nonsense because how can a petty mind, a narrow mind, an inelastic mind, a mind that is begotten through fear, through compulsion through imitation, through fear, through compulsion, through authority, how can that petty, shallow mind try to find out what is the Supreme mind? It is an escape; it is pure, unadulterated romanticism. The fact is, you have to understand yourself first. How can a thought which is the result of fear enquire? How can a thought which is the result of contradiction, of sorrow, of pain, of ambition, of envy, how can that thought search out the unsearchable? Obviously it cannot, but that is what we are doing all the time. So, the beginning of understanding yourself as you are is the beginning of wisdom and is also the beginning of meditation. To see without distortion the fact of what you are, not what you think you should be, is the beginning of wisdom. When you think that you are the Supreme Self, when you think that — as most of you do — there is a spiritual entity which is in you, it is the result of your past conditioning. You have to be aware of that fact and not accept that you are the Supreme Self. what has meaning and significance is the fact of what you are; what you are everyday, not what you should be. Again, the idea, the ideation, the ideal, is a mythology; it has no significance. The fact has significance; the fact that you are envious has significance, not that you should be in a state of non-envy.

... The scientist is concerned with the fact. He is investigating matter, investigating life in his laboratory. He is investigating it under the microscope. He has no fear; he moves from fact to fact and he builds up knowledge, and that knowledge helps him to investigate further only along a particular narrow, restricted line which is science. But we are concerned with the totality of life, not with science only; not only with brick-building but with anger, with ambition, with quarrels, what you are, how limited our minds are, the totality of life.

Science does not include the totality of life but a religious mind does. When the economists or the sociologists try to solve human problems, they are dealing with them only partially and therefore bringing about more chaos, more misery. But the religious mind is not concerned with the partial; it is concerned with the total entity of man. That is, outward movement of life is the same as the inward movement. The outward movement is life the ebb, the tide that goes out and then comes in. If the two are divorced, if the two are separated, the outer and the inner, then you have conflict, you have misery and the so-called religious people have divided this life into the outer and the inner. They do not regard it as one unitary process. They avoid the outer by retreating to a monastery or putting on a *sanyasi's* robe. They deny the outer world but they do not deny the world of tradition, of their knowledge, of their conditioning. So they separate the two and therefore there is a contradiction.

The religious mind does not separate the two. It is one unitary movement of the tide that goes out and comes in. Do please listen to all this, neither accepting nor denying. Because I am not attacking you, you don't have to take refuge or resist; nor am I doing propaganda. I am just pointing out. If you can, you can accept it; you can see it or reject it, but first intellectually or verbally look at it. You may not want to go the whole way completely, totally, to the very end. But at least you can look at it verbally, intellectually and find out. And out of that intellectual comprehension, you will perhaps see the whole significance. So, knowing yourself is the beginning of meditation. Knowing psychologically as you are is the beginning of the religious mind. But you cannot know yourself if you deny what you see, if you try to interpret what you see. Please follow this. If you deny psychologically what you see in yourself, or if you want to change it into something else, then you are not understanding the fact of what is. If you are vain and if you try to change it and cultivate humility, then there is a contradiction. If you are vain and if you try to cultivate the ideal of humility, then there is a contradiction between the two and that contradiction dulls the mind. It brings about a conflict. But the fact is that you are vain; to look at that fact, you have to see that fact completely and not introduce a contradictory idea. You cannot see that you are vain if you say, 'I must not be vain'. Obviously that is a fallacy because to see something you must give your attention totally to it, and when you say that you must not be vain, your mind has gone away from that fact, and going away from that fact creates a problem. The fact never creates a problem. It is only the avoidance of the fact, running away from the fact, trying to change the fact, trying to conform or approximate to the ideal, that creates a problem never the fact of what is. So, when you observe yourself very clearly be aware of every thought, of every feeling; then you will come upon something which is: that there is a thinker and the thought, that there is an experiencer, an observer, and the experience, the observed. This is a fact, is it not? It is a fact that there is a senser, an entity which judges, evaluates, which thinks, which observes and the thing which is observed. Please search your own minds; you are not to listen to my words. Words have no meaning. Watch your mind in operation as I am talking. Then you will go away from here with a clarity, with a mind that is clear, sharp and sane.

So, there is a thinker and the thought. There is a division between the thinker and the thought, the thinker trying to dominate the thought, trying to change thought, trying to modify thought, trying to control, trying to force it, trying to imitate, and so on. This division between the thinker and the thought creates conflict, because the thinker is always the senser, the entity that judges the thought and evaluates; and that entity is the conditioned entity.

Thought is merely the reaction of conditioning, of memory; and the thinker arises as a reaction to thought. You understand. That is a very simple thing to find out for yourself. Thought is the reaction of memory. I ask you something and you respond according to your memory. The interval between the question and the answer is time and during that time you think it out and then you reply. If you are familiar with the answer, your answer is immediate, and if the question is very complicated, you need longer time, a lag, a greater distance between the answer and the question. During that lag your memory is responding, is reacting and then you answer. So, thought, is the response of memory, of association with the past. So, there is the thinker and the thought and the thinker is conditioned and his thought also becomes conditioned. And when there is a gap between the thinker and the thought there is endless conflict and misery. Now, is it possible to remove this contradiction, this conflict, which means there remains no thinker as the central entity which is acting, but only thinking? This is a very complex question and you are going to answer it in a minute. But you have to find out for yourself the whole implication of this problem.

We can go into details but this is not the time for that. But one can see the implication that where there is a division between the thinker and the thought there must be contradiction. And contradiction implies conflict, and conflict dulls the mind, makes the mind stupid, insensitive. Conflict of any kind, whether it is a conflict between your wife and yourself, between you and the society, between you and your boss, between you and anybody, every kind of conflict dulls the mind; if you want to understand the central conflict, you must enquire into this question — not to accept it — that there is a thinker first and thought afterwards. If you say that, you again resort to your tradition, to your conditioning. So, you have to find out through your thought how your memory responds, and as long as that memory which is conditioned by every influence, is there, there must be conflict and misery. If you go very deeply into it you will find out for yourself that action based on an idea — which is thought — breeds discord because you are approximating action to an idea. Therefore, you are not acting but approximating that action so that it should be according to the idea. You will find, if you ponder deeply for yourself, that action is not an idea. There is action without motive, and it is only the religious mind that has gone very deeply into itself, that has enquired profoundly within itself, that can act without an idea, without motive, because it has no centre, no entity as the thinker who is directing action. It is no chaotic action. So, self-knowledge or learning about oneself every day brings about psychologically, inwardly a new mind because you have denied the old mind. Through self-knowledge you have denied it, you have denied your conditioning totally, and that can be denied totally only when the mind is aware of its own operations, how it works, what it thinks, what it says, what are its motives.

There is another factor involved in this. We think this is a gradual process, that it will take time to free the mind from conditioning. We think that it will take many days or many years, that the mind is conditioned and to uncondition it will take time. Which means what? That we will do it gradually, day after day. What does that imply? Surely, it implies acquiring. A mind that is learning is never acquiring, but the mind that houses knowledge in order to arrive, in order to succeed, in order to achieve a sense of liberation, such a mind must have time. So, the mind says, I must have time to free myself from my conditioning, which means it is going to acquire knowledge, not learn, and when the knowledge expands it will become freer and freer — which is utterly false. So, through time, through the multiplication of many tomorrows, there is no liberation. There is freedom only in the denial of the thing which is seen immediately. You react immediately when you see a poisonous snake. There is no thought; there is immediate action. That action is the result of fear and of the knowledge that you acquired about the snake. That involves time. So, there is that quality of seeing through knowledge which demands time and a quality of seeing something which does not demand time.

I am talking of the mind that sees without time, that sees without thought, because the mind is the result of many yesterdays. The mind is the result of time. Again, this is a fact. We are dealing not with supposition, a theory. Your mind is the result of many yesterdays; your mind is the result of the past, and without being free of the past totally, it is not possible to have a new religious mind. Now, to see that past totally, completely, to see it immediately, is to break down the past immediately. But you cannot break it down immediately if your mind is in the grip of knowledge which will say: I will gradually accumulate and I will eventually break it. It must see the conditioning immediately. If you see the absurdity, the poison of nationalism, if you see it, if it is immediately comprehended — and you can apply your mind and if you give your attention to it completely, you can see the poisonous nature of nationalism — the moment you see it, it is gone....

Attention is the total denial of the past, the total denial of this division between the thinker and the thought. So, a religious mind is a mind that has no belief, that has no dogma, that has no fear, that has absolutely no authority of any kind, because it is a light to itself; and such a mind, being free, can go near; which is the freedom in yourself, in the understanding of yourself; then you can go very far. Then you will find out for yourself that extraordinary stillness of the mind. It is not an idea but an actual fact. A mind that is completely still, without any distraction, it is only the still mind, not the romantic mind, a mind that is not begotten through conflict, through contradiction, through misery, it is only such a mind that is completely quiet and therefore completely alive, totally sensitive. It is only such a mind that can perceive that which is immeasurable.

Courtesy Publications Division
Government of India

A p p e n d i x   C

Aphorisms
by J. Krishnamurti

(Krishnamurti's talks and writing have been attacked, not without reason, for being disorganised. The reader will have grasped by now the reason behind this lack of planning. To counter the obvious drawbacks inherent in these communications, we have found it expedient to compile a list of aphorisms which may do for some readers what his books and talks may not have achieved. Inevitably they are listed here regardless of their original context. Needless to say therefore that they are not intended to be read consecutively. The reader should, moreover, be warned against taking them at their face value, lest he read into them his own private meanings, which would defeat their purpose completely. In fact he should read them only after a thorough acquaintance with Krishnamurti's thought. Then alone can he hope to be receptive to the insights contained in these aphorisms and which he may have missed elsewhere — EDITOR.)

...

We have so many problems of our own that we have no time for those of others. To make another listen you have to pay either in coin, in prayer or in belief. The professional will listen, it is his job, but in that there is no lasting release. We want to unburden ourselves freely, spontaneously, without any regrets. The purification of confession does not depend on the one who listens, but on him who desires to open his heart. To open one's heart is important and it will find someone, a beggar perhaps, to whom it can pour itself out. Introspective talk can never open the heart; it is enclosing, depressing and utterly useless. To be open is to listen not only to yourselves but to every influence, to every movement about you. It may or may not be possible to do something tangibly about what you hear, but the very fact of being open brings about its own action. Such hearing purifies your heart cleansing it....

...

To be vulnerable is to live. To withdraw is to die.

...

We have to live in this world — that is the only inevitable thing in life.

...

Beware of the man who offers you a reward in this world or the next.

...

There are laws in some countries, I believe, which prohibit anyone from following you in the street and if someone does he can be arrested and put into prison. So, spiritually, I wish there were a police system which would put people into a spiritual prison for following others. In fact it does happen automatically.

...

Self-satisfaction, self-contentment, lack of determined effort and above all lack of ecstasy in any pursuit, is the essence of mediocrity.

...

What matters is to observe your own mind without judgement

— just to look at it, to watch it, to be conscious of the fact that your mind is a slave, and no more; because that very perception releases energy, and it is this energy that is going to destroy the slavishness of the mind.

...

The state of the mind that questions is much more important than the question itself. Any question may be asked by a slavish mind, and the answer it receives will still be within the limitations of its own slavery ....

...

Character is not a matter of being obstinate in one's knowledge or strong in one's experience. There is character only when the mind, being fully aware of its accumulated experience, is free of that background and is therefore capable of clarity. Only a mind that is clear has character.

...

....influence is often very subtle. In advertising they have tried subliminal propaganda — rapidly flashing an idea on the cinema or television screen, so rapidly that that the viewer is unaware of it; yet it is absorbed by the unconscious....To be aware of all these influences is not easy. But once you begin consciously, deliberately, incessantly to ask the right question, which is to uncover in yourself these various influences, then the mind becomes extraordinarily alert....

...

....to restrain oneself from violence by practising non-violence, is no change at all, though in this country (India) it is glibly talked about every day. Nonviolence with a motive is still violence.

...

....fulfilment is really the demand of a mind which is craving for power.

...

Clarity, at whatever level is completely necessary. If you are not clear about the way to your home, you get confused. If you are not very clear about your feelings, there is self-contradiction. If you do not clearly understand the ways of your own thinking, such lack of clarity leads to illusion.

...

Cultivated virtue is a horror, because the moment you cultivate a virtue it ceases to be a virtue. Virtue is spontaneous and timeless, it is ever active in the present.

...

Freedom from the desire for an answer is essential to the understanding of a problem.

...

When our hearts are empty, we collect things.

...

A consistent thinker is a thoughtless person, because he confirms to a pattern; he repeats phrases and thinks in a groove.

...

A cup is useful only when it is empty; and a mind that is filled with beliefs, with dogmas with assertions, with quotations is really an uncreative mind; it is merely a repetitive mind.

...

The craving for experience is the beginning of illusion.

...

Men of good will should have no formulas.

...

To seek fulfilment is to invite frustration.

...

To look to the future, to strain after an ideal, indicated sluggishness of the mind and a desire to avoid the present.

...

Wisdom and truth come to a man who truly says, "I am ignorant, I do not know."

...

Speculation and imagination are the enemies of attention.

...

Addiction to knowledge is like any other addiction; it offers an escape from the fear of emptiness, of loneliness, of frustration the fear of being nothing.

...

Knowledge prevents listening.

...

You can't go very far if you don't begin very near.

...

Relationship surely is the mirror in which you discover yourself.

...

To die rich is to have lived in vain.

...

When we hear a truth and do not act upon it, it becomes a poison within ourselves, and that poison spreads, bringing psychological disturbances, imbalance and ill health.

JAICO PUBLISHING HOUSE
Elevate Your Life. Transform Your World.

Established in 1946, Jaico Publishing House is the publisher of stellar authors such as Sri Sri Paramahansa Yogananda, Osho, Robin Sharma, Deepak Chopra, Stephen Hawking, Eknath Easwaran, Sarvapalli Radhakrishnan, Nirad Chaudhuri, Khushwant Singh, Mulk Raj Anand, John Maxwell, Ken Blanchard and Brian Tracy. Our list which has crossed a landmark 2000 titles, is amongst the most diverse in the country, with books in religion, spirituality, mind/body/spirit, self-help, business, cookery, humour, career, games, biographies, fiction, and science.

Jaico has expanded its horizons to become a leading publisher of educational and professional books in management and engineering. Our college-level textbooks and reference titles are used by students countrywide. The success of our academic and professional titles is largely due to the efforts of our Educational and Corporate Sales Divisions.

The late Mr. Jaman Shah established Jaico as a book distribution company. Sensing that independence was around the corner, he aptly named his company Jaico ("Jai" means victory in Hindi). In order to tap the significant demand for affordable books in a developing nation, Mr. Shah initiated Jaico's own publications. Jaico was India's first publisher of paperback books in the English language.

In addition to being a publisher and distributor of its own titles, Jaico is a major distributor of books of leading international publishers such as McGraw Hill, Pearson, Cengage Learning, John Wiley and Elsevier Science. With its headquarters in Mumbai, Jaico has other sales offices in Ahmedabad, Bangalore, Bhopal, Chennai, Delhi, Hyderabad and Kolkata. Our sales team of over 40 executives, direct mail order division, and website ensure that our books effectively reach all urban and rural parts of the country.

SINCE 1946